MANAVA DHARMA SASTRA

MANAVA DHARMA SASTRA,

OR

THE INSTITUTES OF MANU

ACCORDING TO THE

GLOSS OF KULLUKA,

COMPRISING THE

INDIAN SYSTEM OF DUTIES, RELIGIOUS AND CIVIL.

TRANSLATED BY

WILLIAM JONES,

EDITED BY

GRAVES CHAMNEY HAUGHTON

GYAN

Published by

Gyan Publishing House
5, Ansari Road
Daryaganj, New Delhi-110002
Phone: 011-47034999, 9811692060
E-mail: books@gyanbooks.com

Distribution Network
gyanbooks.com
India, USA, Canada, UK, Australia

ISBN: 978-93-6280-283-5 (PB)
First Published, 1863

2nd Impression 2024

Printed at: Gyan Press, Delhi.

MANAVA DHARMA SASTRA
Translator: WILLIAM JONES, Editor: GRAVES CHAMNEY HAUGHTON

MANAVA DHARMA SASTRA,

OR

THE INSTITUTES OF MANU

ACCORDING TO THE

GLOSS OF KULLUKA,

COMPRISING THE

INDIAN SYSTEM OF DUTIES,

RELIGIOUS AND CIVIL.

Verbally translated from the original,

WITH A PREFACE

BY

SIR WILLIAM JONES,

AND

COLLATED WITH THE SANSKRIT TEXT,

BY

GRAVES CHAMNEY HAUGHTON, ESQ., M.A. F.R.S. &c. &c.

PROFESSOR OF HINDU LITERATURE IN THE EAST INDIA COLLEGE.

THIRD EDITION

EDITED BY

THE REVD. P. PERCIVAL.

PROFESSOR OF VERNACULAR LITERATURE PRESIDENCY COLLEGE, MADRAS.

MADRAS:

J. HIGGINBOTHAM, MOUNT ROAD.

Law Bookseller and Publisher;

1863.

INTRODUCTION.

The Professor of Hindu Literature in the East India College, Graves Chamney Haughton, M. A., F. R. S., in the year One Thousand Eight Hundred and Twenty-five, published the original Sanskrit text of Mánava Dharma Sástra, or the Institutes of Manu. His beautiful Edition was, by permission, dedicated to the reigning Sovereign of the time. The views which the learned Professor of Haileybury entertained of this ancient record are clearly set forth in his dedication, as may be gathered from the following extract :—

"A course of events, unparalleled in the history of mankind, has placed among the subjects of the British Empire, a people renowned from the remotest antiquity, for wisdom, civilization and steadfast adherence to their peculiar religious opinions."

"The Institutes of Manu are not only revered by this unvarying race of men, as they were by their primeval forefathers, but have moreover contributed to preserve, in pristine force, opinions, usages and maxims, which by a law, which reverses in the moral, what is observed in the material world, have only grown the stronger by the use of ages."

Although the Editor had to perform the task he took in hand under great disadvantages,—having no native Pundits to consult on the countless nice points of criticism with which he had to deal,—his talent and his rare acquirements enabled him to complete it with great and acknowledged success. His Edition of the original text,—the result of a careful comparison of nine manuscripts, obtained from various parts of India, with a printed copy executed by Babu Rám, a learned Pundit of Calcutta,—was enriched by critical and explanatory notes. By the unanimous voice of competent judges, Haughton's Edition of the text of Manu has ever been considered as, "one of the most beautiful monuments of true philological research combined with sound criticism that Hindu Literature has to boast of."

More than thirty years before the Edition abovementioned issued from the press, Sir William Jones, justly celebrated for his profound and varied acquirements in different departments of learning, and, more particularly by reason of his great attainments in Oriental Literature, had directed his attention to the Code of Manu. He regarded it as one of the most important records of Hindu antiquity, and therefore resolved, if possible, to prepare an English version for the information of his countrymen. In the attempt to gain an adequate acquaintance with the ancient and sacred Shaster, he had to encounter obstacles almost insuperable. Bigotry and superstition alike opposed him, notwithstanding his high official position. At Benares, the Chief Native Magistrate was unsuccessful in his attempts to procure a Persian translation of the work, the Pundits being unanimous in their refusal to render assistance. The Pundit, with whom Sir William read Sanskrit, reluctantly consented to lend his aid, but only on certain days, when planetary influences were favorable. As preparations for the publication of an English version advanced, the Pundit became alarmed at the prospect of Sir William's success, and apprehending serious consequences to himself, he earnestly requested that his name might in no way appear in connection with the attempt to make known to foreigners the sacred Institutes of the revered Hindu legislator. Eventually a wealthy Hindu at Gaya, caused a version to be made, which assisted Sir William in his design, and enabled him, at an enormous expense of time and labor, to give the result of his endeavours to the European world in an English version. The translation appeared in the year 1792.

Knowing that the Code was revered by the Hindus as a divine revelation, and universally accepted by them as an unerring guide and directory in all things civil and religious, and consequently the basis on which National Institutions rested, the Government of India ordered an Edition of Sir William's translation to be printed in Calcutta, in a form convenient for reference: it came out of the press in the year 1794.

A new Edition of the version, carefully collated with the original text, was brought out by Professor Haughton in the year 1825.* It was printed uniformly with his Edition of the Sanskrit text. The English translation having become exceedingly scarce and dear, it being almost impossible to procure a copy either in London or Calcutta, the publisher determined to bring out a new impression in a cheap and convenient form. There is reason to believe that this new Edition of the Code will be heartily welcomed by all who have a just appreciation of its importance, and especially by those who are brought into contact with Her Majesty's Hindu subjects.

When the Institutes were first made known to Europe, they were carefully studied by oriental scholars and by antiquaries; not perhaps so much on account of their

---

* The King conferred the honor of knighthood on Mr. Haughton in the year 1833.

intrinsic value: they were rather appreciated as a literary curiosity, and particularly on account of their antiquity. For practical purposes they were studied only by those whose duties and occupations connected them with India. At that time the extent of British territory was very limited, and the number of public servants but few. And, except as they were represented by the three worthies who were banished from Calcutta to the Danish Settlement of Serampore, and the successors of Ziegenbalg, tolerated likewise by the Danes, on the Coast of Coromandel, teachers of Christian Theology and Western Science had no existence. How wonderfully has the scene changed. The Empire of Britain has, during the short time that has elapsed, been extended to the natural boundaries of the country. Public Servants have been greatly multiplied, and Christian Missionaries, and secular teachers, have been increased a hundred fold. Of late, European capital and enterprize have begun to send forth their Agents to develope the resources, and to share the wealth of the country. Under these altered circumstances a new impression of the Code of Manu must be regarded, not merely as opportune, but as a necessity. To public servants, to those who are engaged in the study and practice of the law, and to Christian teachers, a knowledge of the Institutes must be regarded as indispensable.

To public servants, who have to do with the Natives of the country, and to those who are engaged in our Courts of Justice, it must be considered of vital importance to have a correct idea of the principles held sacred by the people whose welfare they are bound to promote. It must not be overlooked that, in all arguments upon the topics of Indian politics, or of judicial amelioration, or of religious instruction, the Legislature of Great Britain has bound itself to act in accordance with those principles which the Hindus firmly believe to have been promulgated originally by the Supreme Being, and which are embodied in the Institutes. However the general public, at Home and in India, may affect to ignore the religious opinions of Her Majesty's Hindu subjects, as of trifling concernment, the servants of the State cannot, thereby, claim exemption from their study and consideration.

The scholar will study the Code of Manu because its vast antiquity,—in which it is inferior only to the Vedas,—commends it to him as a literary curiosity; or considering it as a picture of the domestic manners, the politics and the law of a remote age, he may hope to deduce therefrom valuable knowledge more or less of historic value; or he may pore over the singular views that are therein propounded respecting the visible world, and its invisible author, the origin and destiny of the soul, the views given of rewards of punishments, and the doctrine of the metempsychosis. And seeing that the views on these subjects are not those of a people who, like the Chaldees and Egyptians, have perished, but of millions of living beings, our fellow subjects, he cannot fail to cherish an intense interest in the opinions that regulate their conduct in this life, and their belief regarding a future state of being.

It has been frequently said by those who are best acquainted with the Hindus, that every custom prevalent amongst them is based on religion. This is certain. Religion,—the observance of rites and ceremonies, and of moral and social duties,—is, according to the teachings of the Shasters the final cause of the production of the visible universe. For the various regulations of society and intercourse, marriage and inheritance, birth-rites and funeral pyres, all spring from, and are perpetuated as equally of religious import-ance. To be convinced of the truth of this, we need only read through the Institutes.

If these things are so, it follows that Christian Mission-aries, and indeed all who have to do with the culture of the native mind, whether in matters religious or secular, should acquaint themselves with the sources whence instruction on these points is obtained by the Hindu. However true it may be, that some of the usages it prescribes have be-come obsolete, because intended, as some aver, for past and more perfect ages of human existence; and though it may be true, that few are found, especially in Districts in which Sanskrit is little known, that can quote at once an appro-priate sloke from the Code in support of their belief or practice, the whole body of Hindus are nevertheless moulded by their great legislator. Those who know them best, and the religious system they venerate, are com-pelled to believe that the Hindu of to-day is the same he was in the days of his great legislator. It cannot then be doubted, that those who seek to supersede an anterior system of religion by another, should, as far as practicable, make themselves acquainted with the religious theories of those whom they wish to bring "to the knowledge of the truth." The Christian teacher can no otherwise aim effectually at the opposite party than by knowing exactly the position he occupies, and its defensible strength. Such being the case, Christian teachers should make the Insti-tutes a text book for the study of the system they wish to replace by the introduction of the religion of the Bible. Though Hinduism is found to exist under varied modifica-tions in different sections of the Hindu population, it is essentially one in its source, and that source will be found to be the Code of Manu. The work is short,—a mere tract,—and its chief dogmas and precepts, especially those which form the greatest obstacles to the spread of Christianity, may be easily mastered.

Besides the classes already referred to in these practical remarks, there is another, and a rapidly increasing class, that will, it may be imagined, hail, with great pleasure, the appearance of the sacred ordinances of Hinduism in a new and cheap form. I allude to those who are instructed in the English language. The majority of these, having to devote so large a proportion of their youth to English, and the subjects taught through its medium, can scarcely hope to read the Code of Manu except in a Version. To them this translation must appear of surpassing value. Aided by Sir William Jones' English, the Anglo-Hindu scholar may make himself as perfectly acquainted with the teachings of Manu as if he read them in the Sanskrit, where they are found in their original classic beauty.

In this brief introduction to the present Edition of the Institutes, it is not designed to do more than direct attention to their practical bearing. Their intrinsic quality will be differently estimated by scholars of equal talent and erudition. Some, who have doubtless striven to do justice to the Code, have designated it as, "in some parts, the most worthless, in others, the most precious monument of all Hindu antiquity." The author, but dimly seen amid the mist of a remote antiquity, whoever he was,—whether the son or the grandson of Brahma,—was no doubt profoundly versed in the Vedas: that it contains the principal doctrines and precepts of those early records, is one of its chief excellencies. Apart from all other considerations, "as a picture of ancient manners, in a somewhat advanced state of society, and as a combination of religious precepts and human laws which to a certain extent supply the materials for History," this wonderful book, when rightly studied, will be found replete with valuable knowledge. There is nevertheless much that must prove highly offensive to a refined taste, much needless detail in things exceptionable ; there is much also that is high, noble and benevolent.

As indicated in the title page, this Edition is a re-print of Professor Haughton's. The only change introduced, relates to the transliterated words, which have been altered so as to bring them into harmony with the scheme approved by oriental scholars of the present time.

PRESIDENCY COLLEGE,
MADRAS,
August 27th, 1863.

P. PERCIVAL.

ADVERTISEMENT.

HAVING been for some time engaged in preparing the Institutes of Manu for publication in the Sanskrit language, it appeared to me, that as Sir WILLIAM JONES's translation had been long out of print, a new edition would not only be acceptable to the public at large, but more especially to those engaged in the study of the Sanskrit language, as the great difficulty of the original text made some help of the kind indispensable. In consequence the version of the learned translator has been carefully revised and compared; and as variations, though of trifling importance, have been discovered, they have been carefully recorded at the end of the work. The discrepancies in question may have arisen from some variety in the readings of the manuscripts consulted by Sir WILLIAM JONES. It appeared, however, advisable to take some notice of those which seemed of most importance to the Sanskrit student. The learned translator intended, as he has stated in his Preface, to mark by *Italic* letters all that he had borrowed from the Commentators on Manu, and to print the text of his author in *Roman* letters; an arrangement that was intended to afford the reader a precise idea of the original work. It will easily be understood by persons accustomed to the preparation of works for the press, that a rule like this would be occasionally forgotten. And indeed it has sometimes, though rarely, occurred, that passages have been printed in Italic that should have been put in Roman letters. Every attention has therefore been paid to fulfil the translator's intentions, and the reader may be certain that this singularly interesting record of antiquity is now submitted to him with an exactness and fidelity not attained in the former editions. But it is fair to state, that the first and twelfth books are those which are least literal: this is more particularly the case with the latter. The peculiarity of the doctrines contained in these books will account for the fact, and at the same time explain the difficulty the learned translator laboured under in conveying ideas so novel in their nature to the English reader. When, however, the probable antiquity of the original work, and the occasional obscurity of some of its texts, are considered, it must be conceded, that the translator has been generally happy in his interpretation. The great celebrity which has attended the work since its first appearance in England, encourages a hope that its republication will meet the approbation of those, who, though unacquainted with Oriental literature, take an interest in whatever regards the history of the human mind, and the progress of civilization, to which European nations are under so many obligations.

G. C. HAUGHTON.

East-India College, Herts,
6th Jan. 1825.

PREFACE

BY

SIR WILLIAM JONES.

It is a maxim in the science of legislation and government, that *Laws are of no avail without manners*, or, to explain the sentence more fully, that the best intended legislative provisions would have no beneficial effect even at first, and none at all in a short course of time, unless they were congenial to the disposition and habits, to the religious prejudices, and approved immemorial usages of the people for whom they were enacted; especially if that people universally and sincerely believed, that all their ancient usages and established rules of conduct had the sanction of an actual revelation from heaven; the legislature of *Britain* having shown, in compliance with this maxim, an intention to leave the natives of these *Indian* provinces in possession of their own Laws, at least on the titles of *contracts* and *inheritances*, we may humbly presume, that all future provisions, for the administration of justice and government in *India*, will be conformable, as far as the natives are affected by them, to the manners and opinions of the natives themselves; an object, which cannot possibly be attained, until those manners and opinions can be fully and accurately known. These considerations, and a few others more immediately within my province, were my principal motives for wishing to know, and have induced me at length to publish, that system of duties, religious and civil, and of law in all its branches, which the *Hindus* firmly believe to have been promulged in the beginning of time by MANU, son or grandson of BRAHMA', or, in plain language, the first of created beings, and not the oldest only, but the holiest, of legislators; a system so comprehensive and so minutely exact, that it may be considered as the *Institutes* of *Hindu* Law, preparatory to the copious *Digest*, which has lately been compiled by *Pandits* of eminent learning, and introductory perhaps to a *Code*, which may supply the many natural defects in the old jurisprudence of this country, and, without any deviation from its principles, accommodate it justly to the improvements of a commercial age.

We are lost in an inextricable labyrinth of imaginary astronomical cycles, *Yugas*, *Maháyugas*, *Calpas*, and *Manwantarás*, in attempting to calculate the time, when the first MANU, according to the *Bráhmans*, governed this world, and became the progenitor of mankind, who from him are called *Mánaváh*; nor can we, so clouded are the old history and chronology of *India* with fables and allegories, ascertain the precise age, when the work, now presented to the Public, was actually composed; but we are in possession of some evidence, partly extrinsic and partly internal, that it is really one of the oldest compositions existing. From a text of PARA'SARA, discovered by MR. DAVIS, it appears, that the vernal equinox had gone back from the *tenth* degree of *Bráhmani* to the *first* of *Aswini*, or *twenty three degrees and twenty minutes*, between the days of that *Indian* philosopher, and the year of your Lord 499, when it coincided with the origin of the *Hindu* ecliptic; so that PARA'SARA probably flourished near the close of the *twelfth* century before CHRIST: now PARA'SARA was the grandson of another sage, named VA'SISHTHA, who is often mentioned in the laws of MANU, and once as contemporary with the divine BHRIGU himself; but the character of BHRIGU, and the whole dramatical arrangement of the book before us, are clearly fictitious and ornamental, with a design, too common among ancient lawgivers, of stamping authority on the work by the introduction of supernatural personages, though VA'SISHTHA may have lived many generations before the actual writer of it; who names him, indeed, in one or two places, as a philosopher in an earlier period. The style, however, and metre of this work (which there is not the smallest reason to think affectedly obsolete) are widely different from the language and metrical rules of KA'LIDA'S, who unquestionably wrote before the beginning of our era; and the dialect of MANU is even observed, in many passages, to resemble that of the *Veda*, particularly in a departure from the more modern grammatical forms; whence it must at first view seem very probable, that the laws, now brought to light, were considerably older than those of SOLON or even of LYCURGUS, although the promulgation of them, before they were reduced to writing, might have been co-eval with the first monarchies established in *Egypt* or *Asia*: but, having had the singular good fortune to procure ancient copies of eleven *Upanishads*, with a very perspicuous comment, I am enabled to fix with more exactness the probable age of the work before us, and even to limit its highest possible age, by a mode of reasoning, which may be thought new, but will be found, I persuade myself, satisfactory; if the public shall on this occasion give me credit for a few very curious facts, which, though capable of strict proof, can at present be only asserted. The *Sanskrit* of the three first *Vedas* (I need not here speak of the fourth), that of the *Mánava Dharma Sástra*, and that of the *Puránas*, differ from each other in pretty exact proportion to the *Latin* of NUMA, from whose laws entire sentences are preserved, that of APPIUS, which we see in the fragments of the Twelve Tables, and that of CICERO, or of LUCRETIUS, where he has not affected an obsolete style; if the several changes, therefore, of *San-*

skrit and *Latin* took place, as we may fairly assume, in times very nearly proportional, the *Vedas* must have been written about 300 years before these Institutes, and about 600 before the *Purânas* and *Itihâsas*, which, I am fully convinced, were not the production of VYA'SA; so that, if the son of PARA'SARA committed the traditional *Vedas* to writing in the *Sanskrit* of his father's time, the original of this book must have received its present form about 880 years before CHRIST's birth. If the texts, indeed, which VYA'SA collected, had been actually *written*, in a much older dialect, by the sages preceding him, we must inquire into the greatest possible age of the *Vedas* themselves: now one of the longest and finest *Upanishads* in the second *Veda* contains three lists, in a regular series upwards, of at most *forty-two* pupils and preceptors, who successively received and transmitted (probably by oral tradition) the doctrines contained in that *Upanishad*; and as the old *Indian* priests were students at *fifteen*, and instructors at *twenty-five*, we cannot allow more than *ten* years, on an average, for each interval between the respective traditions; whence, as there are *forty* such intervals, in two of the lists, between VYA'SA, who arranged the whole work, and AYA'SA, who is extolled at the beginning of it, and just as many, in the third list, between the compiler and YA'JNYAWALKYA, who makes the principal figure in it, we find the highest age of the *Yajur Veda* to be 1580 years before the birth of our Saviour, (which would make it older than the five books of MOSES) and that of our *Indian* law tract about 1280 years before the same epoch. The former date, however, seems the more probable of the two, because the *Hindu* sages are said to have delivered their knowledge orally, and the very word *Sruta*, which we often see used for the *Veda* itself, means *what was heard*; not to insist, that KULLU'KA expressly declares the sense of the *Veda* to be conveyed in the *language* of VYA'SA. Whether MANU or MANUS in the nominative and MENO'S in an oblique case, was the same personage with MINOS, let others determine ; but he must indubitably have been far older than the work, which contains his laws, and, though perhaps he was never in *Crete*, yet some of his institutions may well have been adopted in that island, whence LYCURGUS, a century or two afterwards, may have imported them to *Sparta*.

There is certainly a strong resemblance, though obscured and faded by time, between our MANU with his divine Bull, whom he names as DHARMA himself, or the genius of abstract justice, and the MNEUES of *Egypt* with his companion or symbol, *Apis* ; and, though we should be constantly on our guard against the delusion of etymological conjecture, yet we cannot but admit that MINOS and MNEUES, or *Mneuis*, have only *Greek* terminations, but that the crude noun is compsed of the same radical letters both in *Greek* and in *Sanskrit*. 'That APIS and MNEUIS, ' says the Analyst of ancient Mythology, 'were both representations of some per-'sonage, appears from the testimony of LYCOPHRON and 'his scholiast ; and that personage was the same, who 'in *Crete* was styled MINOS, and who was also repre-'sented under the emblem of the *Minotaur* : DIODORUS, 'who confines him to *Egypt*, speaks of him by the 'title of the bull *Mneuis*, as the first lawgiver, and says, "That he lived after the age of the gods and heroes, "when a change was made in the manner of life among "men ; that he was a man of a most exalted soul, and "a great promoter of civil society, which he benefited "by his laws ; and those laws were unwritten, and re-"ceived by him from the chief *Egyptian* deity HERMES, "who conferred them on the world as a gift of the "highest importance." He was the same, adds my 'learned friend, with MENES, whom the *Egyptains* re-'presented as their first king and principal benefactor, 'who first sacrificed to the gods, and brought about a 'great change in diet.' If MINOS, the son of JUPITER, whom the *Cretans*, from national vanity, might have made a native of their own island, was really the same person with MANU, the son of BRAHMA', we have the good fortune to restore, by means of *Indian* literature, the most celebrated system of heathen jurisprudence, and this work might have been entitled *The Laws of* MINOS; but the paradox is too singular to be confidently asserted, and the geographical part of the book, with most of the allusions to natural history, must indubitably have been written after the *Hindu* race had settled to the south of *Himálaya*. We cannot but remark that the word MANU has no relation whatever to the *Moon*; and that it was the *seventh*, not the *first*, or that name, whom the *Bráhmans* believe to have been preserved in an ark from the general deluge: him they call the *Child of the Sun*, to distinguish him from our legislator; but they assign to his brother YAMA *the office* (which the *Greeks* were pleased to confer on MINOS) *of Judge in the shades below.*

The name of MANU is clearly derived (like *menees*, *mens*, and *mind*) from the root *men* to *understand*; and it signifies, as all the *Pandits* agree, *intelligent*, particularly in the doctrines of the *Veda*, which the composer of our *Dharma Śástra* must have studied very diligently; since great numbers of its texts, changed only in a few syllables for the sake of the measure, are interspersed through the work and cited at length in the commentaries: the Public may, therefore, assure themselves, that they now possess a considerable part of the *Hindu* scripture, without the dulness of its profane ritual or much of its mystical jargon. DA'RA SHUCU'H was persuaded, and not without sound reason, that the first MANU of the *Bráhmans* could be no other person than the progenitor of mankind, to whom *Jews*, *Christians*, and *Musalmàns* unite in giving the name of ADAM; but, whoever he might have been, he is highly honoured by name in the *Veda* itself, where it is declared, that 'whatever MANU pronounced, was a medicine for the soul;' and the sage VRIHASPATI, now supposed to preside over the planet *Jupiter*, says in his own law 'tract, that 'MANU held the first rank among 'legislators, because he had expressed in his code the 'whole sense of the *Veda*; that no code was approved, 'which contradicted MANU; that other *Śástras*, and 'treatises on grammar or logic, retained splendour so 'long only, as MANU, who taught the way to just 'wealth, to virtue, and to final happiness, was not seen 'in competition with them;' VYA'SA too, the son of PARA'SARA before mentioned, has decided, that the *Veda* 'with its *Angas*, or the six compositions deduced from 'it, the revealed system of medicine, the *Purànas*, or 'sacred histories, and the code of MANU, were four works 'of supreme authority, which ought never to be 'shaken by arguments merely human.'

It is the general opinion of *Pandits*, that BRAHMA' taught his laws to MANU in a *hundred thousand verses* which MANU explained to the primitive world in the very words of the book now translated, where he names himself, after the manner of ancient sages, in the third person; but, in a short preface to the law tract of NA'RAD, it is asserted, that 'MANU, having written the 'laws of BRAHMA' in a hundred thousand *slókas* or cou-'plets, arranged under *twenty-four* heads in a *thousand* 'chapters, delivered the work to NA'RAD, the sage 'among gods, who abridged it, for the use of mankind, 'in *twelve thousand* verses, and gave them to a son of 'BHRIGU, named SUMATI, who, for greater ease to the 'human race, reduced them to *four thousand*; that mor-'tals read only the second abridgement by SUMATI, 'while the gods of the lower heaven, and the band of 'celestial musicians, are engaged in studying the primary code, beginning with the fifth verse, a little 'varied, of the work now extant on earth; but that 'nothing remains of NA'RAD's abridgement, except an 'elegant epitome of the *ninth* original title *on the administration of justice*.' Now, since these institutes consist only of *two thousand six hundred* and *eighty-five* verses, they cannot be the whole work ascribed to SUMATI, which is probably distinguished by the name of the *Vridd'ha*, or ancient, *Mánava*, and cannot be found entire; though several passages from it, which have been preserved by tradition, are occasionally cited in the new digest.

A number of glosses or comments on MANU were composed by the *Munis*, or old philosophers, whose treatises, together with that before us, constitute the *Dharma Sástra*, in a collective sense, or *Body of Law*; among the more modern commentaries, that called *Medhátit'hi*, that by GO'VINDARA'JA, and that by DHARANI'-DHARA, were once in the greatest repute; but the first was reckoned prolix and unequal; the second, concise but obscure; and the third, often erroneous. At length appeard KULLU'KA BHATTA; who, after a painful course of study and the collation of numerous manuscripts, produced a work, of which it may, perhaps, be said very truly, that it is the shortest, yet the most luminous, the least ostentatious, yet the most learned, the deepest, yet the most agreeable, commentary ever composed on any author ancient or modern, *European* or *Asiatic*. The *Pandits* care so little for genuine chronology, that none of them can tell me the age of KULLU'KA, whom they always name with applause; but he informs us himself, that he was a *Bráhman* of the *Várêndra* tribe, whose family had been long settled in *Gaur* or *Bengal*, but that he had chosen his residence among the learned on the banks of the holy river at

Kási. His text and interpretation I have almost implicitly followed, though I had myself collated many copies of Manu, and among them a manuscript of a very ancient date: his gloss is here printed in *Italics*; and any reader, who may choose to pass it over as if unprinted, will have in *Roman* letters an exact version of the original, and may form some idea of its character and structure, as well as of the *Sanskrit* idiom, which must necessarily be preserved in a verbal translation; and a translation, not scrupulously verbal, whould have been highly improper in a work on so delicate and momentous a subject as private and criminal jurisprudence.

Should a series of *Bráhmans* omit, for three generations, the reading of Manu, their sacerdotal class, as all the *Pandits* assure me, would in strictness be forfeited; but they must explain it only to their pupils of the three highest classes; and the *Bráhman*, who read it with me, requested most earnestly, that his name might be concealed; nor would he have read it for any consideration on a forbidden day of the moon, or without the ceremonies prescribed in the second and fourth chapters for a lecture on the *Veda:* so great, indeed, is the idea of sanctity annexed to this book, that, when the chief native magistrate at *Benares* endeavoured, at my request, to procure a *Persian* translation of it, before I had a hope of being at any time able to understand the original, the *Pandits* of his court unanimously and positively refused to assist in the work; nor should I have procured it at all, if a wealthy *Hindu* at *Gayá* had not caused the version to be made by some of his dependants, at the desire of my friend Mr. Law. The *Persian* translation of Manu, like all others from the *Sanskrit* into that language, is a rude intermixture of the text, loosely rendered, with some old or new comment, and often with the crude notions of the translator;

and, though it expresses the general sense of the original, yet it swarms with errors, imputable partly to haste, and partly to ignorance: thus where MANU says, *that emissaries are the eyes of a prince*, the *Persian* phrase makes him ascribe *four eyes* to the person of a king; for the word *chár*, which means *an emissary in Sanskrit*, signifies *four* in the popular dialect.

The work, now presented to the *European* world, contains abundance of curious matter extremely interesting both to speculative lawyers and antiquaries, with many beauties, which need not be pointed out, and with many blemishes, which cannot be justified or palliated. It is a system of despotism and priestcraft, both indeed limited by law, but artfully conspiring to give mutual support, though with mutual checks; it is filled with strange conceits in metaphysics and natural philosophy, with idle superstitions, and with a scheme of theology most obscurely figurative, and consequently liable to dangerous misconception; it abounds with minute and childish formalities, with ceremonies generally absurd and often ridiculous; the punishments are partial and fanciful; for some crimes, dreadfully cruel, for others reprehensibly slight; and the very morals, though rigid enough on the whole, are in one or two instances (as in the case of light oaths and of pious perjury) unaccountably relaxed: nevertheless, a spirit of sublime devotion, of benevolence to mankind, and of amiable tenderness to all sentient creatures, pervades the whole work; the style of it has a certain austere majesty, that sounds like the language of legislation and extorts a respectful awe; the sentiments of independence on all beings but GOD, and the harsh admonitions even to kings, are truly noble; and the many panegyrics on the *Gáyatrí*, the *Mother*, as it is called, of the *Veda*, prove the author to have *adored* (not the visible material *sun*, but) *that divine and incomparably greater light*, to use the words of the most venerable text in the *Indian* scripture, *which illumines all, delights all, from which all proceed, to which all must return, and which alone can irradiate* (not our visual organs merely, but our souls and) *our intellects*. Whatever opinion in short may be formed of MANU and his laws, in a country happily enlightened by sound philosophy and the only true revelation, it must be remembered, that those laws are actually revered, as the word of the Most High, by nations of great importance to the political and commercial interests of *Europe*, and particularly by many millions of *Hindu* subjects, whose well directed industry would add largely to the wealth of *Britain*, and who ask no more in return than protection for their persons and places of abode, justice in their temporal concerns, indulgence to the prejudices of their old religion, and the benefit of those laws, which they have been taught to believe sacred, and which alone they can possibly comprehend.

W. JONES.

CONTENTS.

THE

LAWS OF MANU,

SON OF BRAHMA'.

CHAP. I.

On the Creation; with a Summary of the Contents.

1. MANU *sat* reclined, with his attention fixed on one object, *the Supreme* GOD; *when* the divine Sages approached *him, and*, after mutual salutations in due form, delivered the following address:

2. 'Deign, sovereign ruler, to apprize us of the sa-'cred laws in their order, as they must be followed by 'all the *four* classes, and by each of them, in their se-'veral degrees, together with the duties of every mixed 'class;

3. 'For thou, Lord, *and thou* only *among mortals*, 'knowest the true sense, the first principle, *and* the 'prescribed ceremonies, of this universal, supernatural '*Veda*, unlimited in extent and unequalled in author-'ity.'

4. HE, whose powers were measureless, being thus requested by the great Sages, whose thoughts were profound, saluted them all with reverence, and gave them a comprehensive answer, *saying:* 'Be it heard!

5. 'This *universe* existed only *in the first divine idea* 'yet *unexpanded, as if involved* in darkness, impercep-'tible, undefinable, undiscoverable by reason, *and* un-'discovered *by revelation,* as if it were wholly immers-'ed in sleep:

6. 'Then the *sole* self-existing power, himself undis-'cerned, but making this world discernible, with five 'elements and other principles *of nature,* appeared with 'undiminished glory, *expanding his idea, or* dispelling 'the gloom.

7. 'HE, whom the mind alone can perceive, whose 'essence eludes the external organs, who has no visible 'parts, who exists from eternity, even HE, the soul of 'all beings, whom no being can comprehend, shone 'forth in person.

8. 'HE, having willed to produce various beings from 'his own divine substance, first with a thought created 'the waters, and placed in them a productive seed:

9. 'The *seed* became an egg bright as gold, blazing 'like the luminary with a thousand beams; and in that 'egg, he was born himself, *in the form of* BRAHMA', the 'great forefather of all spirits.

10. 'The waters are called *nárá,* because they were 'the production of NARA, *or the spirit of* GOD; and 'since they were his first *ayana,* or *place of motion,* 'he thence is named NA'RA'YANA, or *moving on the* '*waters.*

11. 'From THAT WHICH IS, the first cause, not the 'object of sense, existing *every where in substance,* not 'existing *to our perception,* without beginning or end,

'was produced the divine male, famed in all worlds 'under the appellation of BRAHMÁ'.

12. 'In that egg the great power sat inactive a whole 'year *of the Creator*, at the close of which, by his 'thought alone, he caused the egg to divide itself;

13. 'And from its two divisions he framed the heaven '*above* and the earth *beneath:* in the midst *he placed* 'the subtile ether, the eight regions, and the permanent 'receptacle of waters.

14. 'From the supreme soul he drew forth Mind, 'existing substantially though unperceived by sense, im'material; and *before* mind *or the reasoning power, he* '*produced* consciousness, the internal monitor, the 'ruler;

15. 'And, *before them both,* he produced the great '*principle of* the soul, *or first expansion of the divine* '*idea;* and all vital forms endued with the three quali'ties of *goodness, passion,* and *darkness;* and the *five* 'perceptions of sense and the five organs of sensation.

16. '*Thus,* having at once pervaded, with emanations 'from the Supreme Spirit, the minutest portions of six 'principles immensely operative, *consciousness and the* '*five perceptions,* He framed all creatures;

17. 'And since the minutest particles of visible na'ture have a dependence on those *six* emanations from 'GOD, the wise have accordingly given the name of '*s'aríra or depending on six, that is, the ten organs on* '*consciousness, and the five elements on as many percep*'*tions,* to His *image or* appearance in visible nature:

18. 'Thence proceed the great elements, endued with 'peculiar powers, and Mind with operations infinitely 'subtile, the unperishable cause of all apparent forms.

19. 'This *universe,* therefore, is compacted from the 'minute portions of those seven divine and active prin-

'ciples, *the great Soul, or first emanation, consciousness,* 'and *five perceptions* ; *a* mutable *universe* from immu-'table *ideas.*

20. 'Among them each succeeding element acquires 'the quality of the preceding ; and, in as many degrees 'as each of them is advanced, with so many properties 'is it said to be endued.

21. 'He too first assigned to all creatures distinct 'names, distinct acts, and distinct occupations ; as they 'had been revealed in the pre-existing *Veda.*

22. 'He, the supreme Ruler, created an assemblage 'of inferior Deities, with divine attributes and pure 'souls ; and a number of Genii exquisitely delicate ; 'and he *prescribed* the sacrifice ordained from the be-'ginning.

23. 'From fire, from air, and from the sun he milked 'out *as it were*, the three primordial *Vedas*, named *Ṛig* '*Yajur* and *Sáma*, for the due performance of the sa-'crifice.

24. 'He gave being to time and the divisions of time, 'to the stars also, and to the planets, to rivers, oceans, 'and mountains, to level plains, and uneven valleys.

25. 'To devotion, speech, complacency, desire, and 'wrath, and to the creation, *which shall presently be* '*mentioned;* for He willed the existence of all those 'created things.

26. 'For the sake of distinguishing actions, He 'made a total difference between right and wrong, and 'inured these sentient creatures to pleasure and pain, '*cold and heat*, and other opposite pairs.

27. 'With very minute transformable portions, call-'ed *mátrás*, of the five elements, all this *perceptible* '*world* was composed in fit order ;

28. 'And in whatever occupation the supreme Lord 'first employed any vital soul, to that occupation the 'same soul attaches itself spontaneously, when it re-'ceives a new body again and again.

29. 'Whatever quality, noxious or innocent, harsh 'or mild, unjust or just, false or true, He conferred on 'any being at its creation, the same quality enters it *of 'course on its future births;*

30. 'As the *six* seasons of the year attain respective-'ly their peculiar marks in due time and of their own 'accord, even so the several acts of each embodied spi-'rit *attend it naturally.*

31. 'That the human race might be multiplied, He 'caused the *Bráhman*, the *Kshatriya*, the *Vaisya*, and 'the *Súdra* (so named from the *scripture, protection, 'wealth,* and *labour*) to proceed from his mouth, his 'arm, his thigh, and his foot.

32. 'Having divided his own substance, the mighty 'Power became half male, half female, *or nature active 'and passive;* and from that female he produced 'VIRA'J:

33. 'Know Me, O most excellent of *Bráhmans*, to 'be that person, whom the male *power* VIRA'J, having 'performed austere devotion, produced by himself; 'Me, the *secondary* framer of all this *visible world.*

34. 'It was I, who, desirous of giving birth to a race 'of men, performed very difficult religious duties, and 'first produced ten Lords of created beings, eminent in 'holiness.

35. 'MARI'CHI, ATRI, ANGIRAS, PULASTYA, PULAHA, 'KRATU, PRACHE'TAS, or DAKSHA, VASISHTHA, BHRIGU, 'and NA'RADA:

36. 'They, abundant in glory, produced seven other

'*Manus*, together with deities, and the mansions of 'deities, and *Mahárshis*, or great Sages, unlimited in 'power.

37. 'Benevolent genii, and fierce giants, blood-thirsty 'savages, heavenly quiristers, nymphs and demons, huge 'serpents and snakes of smaller size, birds of mighty 'wing, and separate companies of *Pitris*, or progenitors 'of mankind;

38. 'Lightnings and thunder-bolts, clouds and co-'loured bows of *Indra*, falling meteors, earth-rending 'vapours, comets, and luminaries of various degrees;

39. 'Horse-faced sylvans, apes, fish, and a variety 'of birds, tame cattle, deer, men, and ravenous beasts 'with two rows of teeth;

40. 'Small and large reptiles, moths, lice, fleas, and 'common flies, with every biting gnat, and immovable 'substances of distinct sorts.

41. 'Thus was this whole assemblage of stationary 'and movable bodies framed by those high-minded 'beings, through the force of their own devotion, and 'at my command, with separate actions allotted to each.

42. 'Whatever act is ordained for each of those 'creatures here below, *that* I will now declare to you, 'together with their order in respect to birth.

43. 'Cattle and deer, and wild beasts with two rows 'of teeth, giants, and blood-thirsty savages, and the 'race of men, are born from a secundine;

44. 'Birds are hatched from eggs, *so are* snakes, 'crocodiles, fish *without shells*, and tortoises, with other 'animal kinds, terrestrial, *as chamelions*, and aquatic, '*as shell-fish*:

45. 'From hot moisture are born biting gnats, lice,

'fleas, and common flies; these, and whatever is of 'the same class, are produced by heat.

46. 'All vegetables, propagated by seed or by slips, 'grow from shoots: some herbs, abounding in flowers 'and fruits, perish when the fruit is mature;

47. 'Other plants, called lords of the forest, have no 'flowers, but produce fruit; and, whether they have 'flowers also, or fruit only, *large woody plants* of both 'sorts are named trees.

'48. 'There are shrubs with many stalks from the 'root upwards, and reeds with single roots but united 'stems, all of different kinds, and grasses, and *vines* '*or* climbers, and creepers, which spring from a seed or 'from a slip.

49. 'These *animals and vegetables*, encircled with 'multiform darkness, by reason of past actions, have in-'ternal conscience, and are sensible of pleasure and pain.

50. All transmigrations, recorded *in sacred books*, 'from the state of BRAHMA', to that of plants, happen 'continually in this tremendous world of beings; a 'world *always* tending to decay.

51. 'HE, whose powers are incomprehensible, hav-'ing thus created both me and this universe, was 'again absorbed in the supreme Spirit, changing *the* 'time *of energy* for *the* time *of repose.*

52. 'When that Power awakes, *(for, though slumber* '*be not predicable of the sole eternal Mind, infinitely* '*wise and infinitely benevolent, yet it is predicated of* 'BRAHMA', *figuratively, as a general property of life,)* 'then has this world its full expansion; but, when he 'slumbers with a tranquil spirit, then the whole system 'fades away.

53. 'For, while he reposes, *as it were*, in calm sleep,

'embodied spirits, endued with principles of action, 'depart from their several acts, and the mind itself be- 'comes inert;

54. 'And when they once are absorbed in that su- 'preme essence, then the divine soul of all beings 'withdraws his energy, and placidly slumbers;

55. 'Then too this vital soul *of created bodies,* with 'all the organs of sense and of action, remains long 'immersed *in the first idea or* in darkness, and per- 'forms not its natural functions, but migrates from its 'corporeal frame:

56. 'When, being *again* composed of minute ele- 'mentary principles, it enters at once into vegetable 'or animal seed, it then assumes a *new* form.

57. 'Thus that immutable Power, by waking and re- 'posing alternately, revivifies and destroys in eternal 'succession, this whole assemblage of locomotive and 'immovable creatures.

58. 'He, having enacted this code of laws, himself 'taught it fully to me in the beginning: afterwards I 'taught Marí'chi and the *nine* other holy sages.

59. 'This *my son* Bhrigu will repeat the divine code 'to you without omission; for that sage learned from 'me to recite the whole of it.'

60. Bhrigu, great and wise, having thus been appointed by Manu to promulge his laws, address- ed all the *Rishis* with an affectionate mind saying: 'Hear!

61. 'From this Manu named Swa'yambhuva, or '*Sprung from the self-existing,* came six descendants, 'other Manus, *or perfectly understanding the scripture,* 'each giving birth to a race of his own, all exalted in 'dignity, eminent in power;

62. 'SWA'RO'CHISHA, UTTAMA, TA'MASA, RAIVATA like 'wise and KHA'KSHUSHA, beaming with glory, and VAI 'VASWATA, child of the sun.

63. 'The seven MANUS, (or *those first created, who* '*are to be followed by seven more*) of whom SWA'YAM-'BHUVA is the chief, have produced and supported this 'world of moving and stationary beings, each in his 'own *antara*, or *the period of his reign*.

64. 'Eighteen *nimêshas*, or *twinklings of an eye*, are 'one *kásht'há*; thirty *kásht'hás*, one *kalá*; thirty *kalás*, 'one *muhúrta*: and just so many *muhúrtas* let man-'kind consider as the duration of their day and night.

65. 'The sun causes the distribution of day and 'night, both divine and human; night being *intended* 'for the repose of *various* beings, and day for their ex-'ertion.

66. 'A month *of mortals* is a day and a night of 'the *Pitris* or *patriarchs inhabiting the moon*; and the 'division *of a month* being into equal halves, the half 'beginning from the full moon is their day for actions; 'and that beginning from the new moon is their night 'for slumber.

67. 'A year *of mortals* is a day and a night of the 'gods, or *regents of the universe seated round the north* '*pole*; and again their division is this, their day is the 'northern, and their night the southern course of the 'sun.

68. 'Learn now the duration of a day and a night 'of BRAHMA', and of the several ages which shall be 'mentioned in order succinctly.

69. 'Sages have given the name of *Krita* to an age 'containing four thousand years of the gods; the 'twilight preceding it consists of as many hundreds, 'and the twilight following it, of the same number:

70. 'In the other three *ages*, with their twilights 'preceding and following, are thousands and hundreds 'diminished by one.

71. 'The divine years, in the four *human* ages just 'enumerated, being added together, their sum, *or* 'twelve thousand, is called the age of the gods:

72. 'And, by reckoning a thousand such divine ages, 'a day of Brahma' may be known: his night also has 'an equal duration:

73. 'Those persons best know the divisions of the 'days and nights, who understand that the day of 'Brahma', which endures to the end of a thousand such 'ages, gives rise to virtuous exertions; and that his 'night endures as long as his day.

74. 'At the close of his night, having long reposed, 'he awakes, and awaking, exerts intellect, *or reproduces the great principle of animation*, whose property 'it is to exist unperceived by sense:

75. 'Intellect, called into action by his will to create 'worlds, performs *again* the work of creation; and 'thence *first* emerges the subtil ether, to which philosophers ascribe the quality of conveying sound;

76. 'From ether, effecting a transmutation in form, 'springs the pure and potent air, a vehicle of all scent; 'and air is held endued with the quality of touch:

77. 'Then from air, operating a change, rises light *or* '*fire*, making objects visible, dispelling gloom, spreading 'bright rays; and it is declared to have the quality of 'figure;

78. 'But from light, a change being effected, comes 'water with the quality of taste; and from water *is* '*deposited* earth with the quality of smell: such were 'they created in the beginning.

79. 'The before-mentioned age of the gods, or 'twelve thousand *of their* years, being multiplied by 'seventy-one, *constitutes what* is here named a *Manwantara, or the reign of a* MANU.

80. 'There are numberless *Manwantaras*; creations 'also and destructions of worlds, innumerable: the 'Being supremely exalted performs all this, *with as much ease* as if in sport; again and again, *for the sake of conferring happiness.*

81. 'In the *Krita* age *the Genius of* truth and right, '*in the form of a Bull,* stands firm on his four feet; 'nor does any advantage accrue to men from iniquity;

82. 'But in the following ages, by reason of unjust 'gains, he is deprived successively of one foot; and 'even just emoluments, through the prevalence of 'theft, falsehood, and fraud, are *gradually* diminished 'by a fourth part.

83. 'Men, free from disease, attain all sorts of 'prosperity, and live four hundred years in the *Krita* 'age; but, in the *Tretà* and the succeeding ages, their 'life is lessened gradually by one quarter.

84. 'The life of mortals, which is mentioned in the '*Veda,* the rewards of good works, and the powers 'of embodied spirits, are fruits proportioned among 'men to the order of the *four* ages.

85. 'Some duties are performed by *good* men in the '*Krita* age; others, in the *Tretà*; some, in the *Dwápara*; others, in the *Kali*; in proportion as those 'ages decrease in length.

86. 'In the *Krita* the prevailing virtue is declared 'to be in devotion; in the *Tretà,* divine knowledge; in 'the *Dwápara,* holy sages call sacrifice the duty 'chiefly performed; in the *Kali,* liberality alone.

87. 'For the sake of preserving this universe, the 'Being, supremely glorious, allotted separate duties to 'those who sprang respectively from his mouth, his 'arm, his thigh, and his foot.

88. 'To *Bráhmans* he has assigned the duties of reading the *Veda*, of teaching it, of sacrificing, of assisting others to sacrifice, of giving alms, *if they be 'rich*, and, *if indigent*, of receiving gifts:

89. 'To defend the people, to give alms, to sacrifice, to read the *Veda*, to shun the allurements of 'sensual gratification, are, in a few words, the duties of 'a *Kshatriya:*

90. 'To keep herds of cattle, to bestow largesses, to 'sacrifice, to read the scripture, to carry on trade, to 'lend at interest, and to cultivate land are *prescribed 'or permitted* to a *Vaisya:*

91. 'One principal duty the supreme Ruler assigns 'to a *Súdra;* namely, to serve the before-mentioned 'classes, without depreciating their worth.

92. 'Man is declared purer above the navel; but 'the self-creating Power declared the purest part of 'him to be his mouth.

93. 'Since the *Bráhman* sprang from the most excellent part, since he was the first born, and since he 'possesses the *Veda*, he is by right the chief of this 'whole creation.

94. 'Him, the Being, who exists of himself, produced in the beginning from his own mouth, that, 'having performed holy rites, he might present clarified 'butter to the gods, and cakes of rice to the progenitors of mankind, for the preservation of this world:

95. 'What created being then can surpass Him, with 'whose mouth the gods of the firmament continually

'feast on clarified butter, and the manes of ancestors, 'on hallowed cakes?

96. 'Of created things, the most excellent are those 'which are animated; of the animated, those which 'subsist by intelligence; of the intelligent, mankind; 'and of men, the sacerdotal class;

97. 'Of priests, those eminent in learning; of the 'learned, those who know their duty; of those who 'know it, such as perform it virtuously; and of the 'virtuous, those who seek beatitude from a perfect ac-'quaintance with scriptural doctrine.

98. 'The very birth of *Bráhmans* is a constant in-'carnation of DHARMA, *God of Justice*; for the *Bráh-'man* is born to promote justice, and to procure ulti-'mate happiness.

99. 'When a *Bráhman* springs to light, he is born 'above the world, the chief of all creatures, assigned to 'guard the treasury of duties, religious and civil.

100. 'Whatever exists in the universe, is all in effect, '*though not in form*, the wealth of the *Bráhman*; since 'the *Bráhman* is entitled to it all by his primogeniture 'and eminence of birth:

101. 'The *Bráhman* eats but his own food; wears 'but his own apparel: and bestows but his own in 'alms: through the benevolence of the *Bráhman*, in-'deed, other mortals enjoy life.

102. 'To declare the sacerdotal duties, and those of 'the other classes in due order, the sage MANU, sprung 'from the self-existing, promulged this code of laws:

103. 'A code which must be studied with extreme 'care by every learned *Bráhman*, and fully explained 'to his disciples, but *must be taught* by no other man '*of an inferior class*.

104. 'The *Bráhman* who studies this book, having 'performed sacred rites, is perpetually free from of-'fence in thought, in word, and in deed;

105. 'He confers purity on his living family, on 'his ancestors, and on his descendants, as far as the 'seventh person; and He alone deserves to possess 'this whole earth.

106. 'This most excellent code produces every thing 'auspicious; this code increases understanding; this 'code procures fame and long life; this code leads 'to supreme bliss.

107. 'In this *book* appears the system of law in 'its full extent, with the good and bad properties 'of human actions, and the immemorial customs of 'the four classes.

108. 'Immemorial custom is transcendent law, ap-'proved in the sacred scripture, and in the codes 'of divine legislators: let every man, therefore, of 'the three principal classes, who has a due reverence 'for the *supreme* spirit *which dwells in him,* diligently 'and constantly observe immemorial custom.

109. 'A man of the priestly, military, or commer-'cial class, who deviates from immemorial usage, 'tastes not the fruit of the *Veda:* but, by an exact 'observance of it, he gathers that fruit in perfection.

110. 'Thus have holy sages, well knowing that law 'is grounded on immemorial custom, embraced, as 'the root of all piety, good usages long established.

111. 'THE creation of this universe, the forms of 'institution and education, with the observances and 'behaviour of a student in theology; the best rules 'for the ceremony on his return from the mansion of 'his preceptor;

112. 'The law of marriage in general, and of nuptials in different forms; the regulations for the great 'sacraments, and the manner, primevally settled, of 'performing obsequies;

113. 'The modes of gaining subsistence, and the 'rules to be observed by the master of a family; the 'allowance and prohibition of diet, with the purification of men and utensils;

114. 'Laws concerning women, the devotion of hermits, and of anchorets wholly intent on final beatitude, the whole duty of a king, and the judicial 'decision of controversies.

115. 'With the law of evidence and examination; 'laws concerning husband and wife, canons of inheritance; the prohibition of gaming, and the punishments of criminals;

116. 'Rules ordained for the mercantile and servile 'classes, with the origin of those that are mixed; the 'duties and rights of all the classes in time of distress 'for subsistence; and the penances for expiating sins;

117. 'The several transmigrations in this universe, 'caused by offences of three kinds, with the ultimate 'bliss attending good actions, on the full trial of vice 'and virtue;

118. 'All these titles of law, promulgated by MANU, 'and *occasionally* the customs of different countries, 'different tribes, and different families, with rules concerning heretics and companies of traders, are discussed in this code.

119. 'Even as MANU, at my request, formerly revealed this divine *S'ástra*, hear it now from me without any diminution or addition.

CHAP. II.

On Education; or on the Sacerdotal Class, and the First Order.

1. 'Know that system of duties, which is revered 'by such as are learned in the *Vedas*, and impressed, '*as the means of attaining beatitude*, on the hearts of 'the just, who are ever exempt from hatred and inordi-'nate affection.

2. 'Self-love is no laudable motive, yet an exemp-'tion from self-love is not *to be found* in this world: 'on self-love is grounded the study of scripture, and the 'practice of actions recommended in it.

3. 'Eager desire *to act* has its root in expectation of 'some advantage; and with such expectation are sacri-'fices performed; the rules of religious austerity and 'abstinence from sins are all known to arise from hope 'of remuneration.

4. 'Not a single act here below appears ever to be 'done by a man free from self-love; whatever he per-'forms, it is wrought from his desire of a reward.

5. 'He, indeed, who should persist in *discharging* 'these duties without any view to their fruit, would 'attain *hereafter* the state of the immortals, and even 'in this life, would enjoy all the virtuous gratifications, 'that his family could suggest.

6. 'The roots of law are the whole *Veda*, the or-'dinances and moral practices of such as perfectly un-'derstand it, the immemorial customs of good men, 'and, *in cases quite indifferent*, self-satisfaction.

7. 'Whatever law has been ordained for any person 'by MANU, that law is fully declared in the *Veda*: for 'HE was perfect in divine knowledge:

8. 'A man of true learning, who has viewed this 'complete system with the eye of sacred wisdom, can-'not fail to perform all those duties, which are ordained 'on the authority of the *Veda*.

9. 'No doubt, that man who shall follow the rules 'prescribed in the *Sruti* and in the *Smriti*, will acquire 'fame in this life, and, in the next, inexpressible hap-'piness:

10. 'By *Sruti*, or *what was heard from above*, is meant 'the *Veda*; and by *Smriti*, or *what was remembered* '*from the beginning*, the body of law: those two must 'not be oppugned by heterodox arguments; since from 'those two, proceeds the whole system of duties.

11. 'Whatever man of the three highest classes, 'having addicted himself to heretical books, shall treat 'with contempt those two roots of law, he must be 'driven, as an Atheist and a scorner of revelation, from 'the company of the virtuous.

12. 'The scripture, the codes of law, approved usage, 'and, *in all indifferent cases*, self-satisfaction, the wise 'have openly declared to be the quadruple description 'of the juridical system.

13. 'A knowledge of right is a sufficient incentive 'for men unattached to wealth or to sensuality; and to 'those who seek a knowledge of right, the supreme au-'thority is divine revelation;

14. 'But, when there are two sacred texts, *apparent-'ly inconsistent*, both are held to be law; for both are 'pronounced by the wise to be valid and reconcilable;

15. 'Thus in the *Veda* are these texts: "let the sa-

'" crifice be when the sun has arisen," and "before it '" has risen," and, "when neither sun nor stars can be '" seen :" the sacrifice, therefore, may be performed at ' any or all of those times.

16. ' He, whose life is regulated by holy texts, from ' his conception even to his funeral pile, has a decided ' right to study this code ; but no other man whatsoever.

17. ' BETWEEN the two divine rivers *Saraswati* and ' *Drishadwati* lies the tract of land, which the sages ' have named *Brahmávrita, because it was* frequented ' by gods :

18. ' The custom preserved by immemorial tradition ' in that country, among the four *pure* classes, and ' among those which are mixed, is called approved ' usage.

19. ' *Kurukshetra, Matsya, Panchála*, or *Kányakub-* ' *ja*, and *Súrasena*, or *Mat'hurà*, form the region called ' *Brahmarshi*, distinguished from *Brahmávrita :*

20. ' From a *Bráhman* who was born in that coun- ' try, let all men on earth learn their several usages.

21. ' That country which lies between *Himawat* and ' *Vindhya*, to the east of *Vinasana*, and to the west of ' *Prayága*, is celebrated by the title of *Madhyadesa*, or ' *the central region.*

22. ' As far as the eastern, and as far as the western ' oceans, between the two mountains just mentioned, ' lies the tract which the wise have named *Aryávrita*, ' or *inhabited by respectable men.*

23. ' That land, on which the black antelope natu- ' rally grazes, is held fit for the performance of sacri- ' fices ; but the land of *Mlech'has* or *those who speak* ' *barbarously*, differs widely from it.

24. ' Let the three first classes invariably dwell in

'those before-mentioned countries; but a *Súdra,* distressed for subsistence, may sojourn wherever he chooses.

25. 'Thus has the origin of law been succinctly declared to you, together with the formation of this *universe:* now learn the laws of the several classes.

26. 'WITH auspicious acts prescribed by the *Veda,* must ceremonies on conception, and so forth, be duly performed, which purify the bodies of the three classes in this life, and *qualify them* for the next.

27. 'By oblations to fire during the mother's pregnancy, by holy rites on the birth of the child, by the tonsure of his head with a lock of hair left on it, by the ligation of the sacrificial cord, are the seminal and uterine taints of the three classes wholly removed:

28. 'By studying the *Veda,* by religious observances, by oblations to fire, by the ceremony of *Traividya,* by offering to the gods and manes, by the procreation of children, by the five great sacraments, and by solemn sacrifices, this human body is rendered fit for a divine state.

29. 'Before the section of the navel string a ceremony is ordained on the birth of a male: he must be made, while sacred texts are pronounced, to taste a little honey and clarified butter from a golden spoon.

30. 'Let the father *perform, or, if absent,* cause to be performed, on the tenth or twelfth day *after the birth,* the ceremony of giving a name; or on some fortunate day of the moon, at a lucky hour, and under the influence of a star with good qualities.

31. 'The first part of a *Bráhman's* compound name should indicate holiness; of a *Kshatriya's,* power; of a *Vaisya's,* wealth; and of a *Súdra's,* contempt.

32. ‘Let the second part of the priest's name imply prosperity; of the soldier's, preservation; of the merchant's, nourishment; of the servant's, humble attendance.

33. ‘The names of women should be agreeable, soft, clear, captivating the fancy, auspicious, ending in long vowels, resembling words of benediction.

34. ‘In the fourth month the child should be carried out of the house *to see the sun:* in the sixth month, he should be fed with rice; or that *may be done,* which, by the custom of the family, is thought most propitious.

35. ‘By the command of the *Veda,* the ceremony of tonsure should be legally performed by the three *first* classes in the first or third year *after birth.*

36. ‘In the eighth year from the conception of a *Bráhman,* in the eleventh from that of a *Kshatriya,* and in the twelfth from that of a *Vaisya,* let the father invest the child with the mark of his class:

37. ‘Should a *Bráhman,* or *his father for him,* be desirous of his advancement in sacred knowledge; a *Kshatriya,* of extending his power; *or* a *Vaisya,* of engaging in mercantile business; the investiture may be made in the fifth, sixth, or eighth years respectively.

38. ‘The ceremony of investiture hallowed by the *gáyatrí* must not be delayed, in the case of a priest, beyond the sixteenth year; nor in that of a soldier, beyond the twenty-second; nor in that of a merchant, beyond the twenty-fourth.

39. ‘After that, *all youths* of these three classes, who have not been invested at the proper time, become *vrátyas,* or outcasts, degraded from the *gáyatrí,* and contemned by the virtuous.

40. 'With such impure men, let no *Bráhman*, even 'in distress for subsistence, ever form a connexion in 'law, either by the study of the *Veda*, or by affinity.

41. 'Let students in theology wear *for their mantles*, 'the hides of black antelopes, of common deer, or of 'goats, with *lower vests of* woven *sana*, of *kshumá*, and 'of wool, in the direct order of their classes.

42. 'The girdle of a priest must be made of *munja*, 'in a triple cord, smooth and soft; that of a warrior 'must be a bowstring of *múrvá*; that of a merchant, 'a triple thread of *sana*.

43. If the *munja* be not procurable, their zones must 'be formed *respectively* of the grasses *kusa, asmántaka*, '*valvaja*, in triple strings, with one, three, or five knots, '*according to the family custom*.

44. 'The sacrificial thread of a *Bráhman* must be 'made of cotton, so as to be put on over his head, in 'three strings; that of a *Kshatriya*, of *sana* thread 'only; that of a *Vaisya*, of woollen thread.

45. 'A priest ought by law to carry a staff of *Vilva* 'or *Palása*; a soldier, of *Vata* or *Chadira*; a merchant 'of *Vénu* or *Udumbara*:

46. 'The staff of a priest must be of such a length 'as to reach his hair; that of a soldier, to reach his 'forehead; and that of a merchant, to reach his nose.

47. 'Let all the staves be straight, without fracture, 'of a handsome appearance, not likely to terrify men, 'with their bark perfect, unhurt by fire.

48. 'Having taken a legal staff to his liking, and 'standing opposite to the sun, let the student thrice 'walk round the fire from left to right, and perform, 'according to law, the ceremony of asking food:

49. 'The most excellent of the three classes, being

'girt with the sacrificial thread, must ask food with 'the respectful word *bhavati*, at the beginning of the 'phrase; those of the 2nd class, with that word in the 'middle; and those of the third, with that word at the 'end.

50. 'Let him first beg food of his mother, or of his 'sister, or of his mother's whole sister; then of some 'other female who will not disgrace him.

51. 'Having collected as much of the desired food 'as he has occasion for, and having presented it with-'out guile to his preceptor, let him eat some of it, 'being duly purified, with his face to the east:

52. 'If he seek long life, he should eat with his face 'to the east; if exalted fame, to the south: if pros-'perity, to the west; if truth *and its reward*, to the 'north.

53. 'Let the student, having performed his ablution, 'always eat his food without distraction of mind; and, 'having eaten, let him *thrice* wash his mouth com-'pletely, sprinkling with water the *six* hollow parts of 'his head, *or his eyes, ears, and nostrils.*

54. 'Let him honour all his food, and eat it with-'out contempt; when he sees it, let him rejoice and be 'calm, and pray that he may always obtain it.

55. 'Food, eaten constantly with respect, gives 'muscular force and generative power; but, eaten irre-'verently, destroys them both.

56. 'He must beware of giving any man what he 'leaves; and of eating any thing between *morning and* '*evening:* he must also beware of eating too much, and 'of going anywhither with a remnant of his food un-'swallowed.

57. 'Excessive eating is prejudicial to health, to

'fame, and to *future bliss in* Heaven; it is injurious to 'virtue, and odious among men: he must, for these 'reasons, by all means avoid it.

58. 'Let a *Bráhman* at all times perform the ablu-'tion with the pure part of his hand denominated from 'the *Veda*, or with the part sacred to the Lord of crea-'tures, or with that dedicated to the gods; but never 'with the part named from the *Pitris*:

59. 'The pure part under the root of the thumb is 'called *Bráhma*, that at the root of the little finger, '*Káya*; that at the tips of the fingers, *Daiva*; and the 'part between the thumb and index *Pitrya*.

60. 'Let him first sip water thrice; then twice wipe 'his mouth; and lastly touch with water the *six before 'mentioned* cavities, his breast, and his head.

61. 'He who knows the law and seeks purity will 'ever perform his ablution with the pure part of his 'hand, and with water neither hot nor frothy, standing 'in a lonely place, and turning to the east or the north.

62. 'A *Bráhman* is purified by water that reaches 'his bosom; a *Kshatriya*, by water descending to his 'throat; a *Vaisya*, by water barely taken into his 'mouth; a *Súdra*, by water touched with the extremity '*of his lips*.

63. 'A youth of the three highest classes is named '*upavíti*, when his right hand is extended *for the cord 'to pass over his head and be fixed on his left shoulder*; 'when his left hand is extended, *that the thread may be 'placed on his right shoulder*, he is called *práchináviti*; 'and *niviti*, when it is fastened on his neck.

64. 'His girdle, his leathern mantle, his staff, his 'sacrificial cord, and his ewer, he must throw into the 'water, when they are worn out or broken, and receive 'others hallowed by mystical texts.

65. 'The ceremony of *késánta*, or *cutting off the hair*, 'is ordained for a priest in the sixteenth year from con- 'ception ; for a soldier, in the twenty-second ; for a 'merchant, two years later than that.

66. 'The same ceremonies, *except that of the sacrifi- 'cial thread*, must be duly performed for women at the 'same age and in the same order, that the body may be 'made perfect ; but without any text from the *Veda :*

67. 'The nuptial ceremony is considered as the com- 'plete institution of women, ordained for them in the '*Veda*, together with reverence to their husbands, dwell- 'ing first in their father's family, the business of the 'house, and attention to sacred fire.

68. 'Such is the revealed law of institution for the 'twice born ; an institution in which their second birth 'clearly consists, and which causes their advancement 'in holiness : now learn to what duties they must after- 'wards apply themselves.

69. 'The venerable preceptor, having girt his pupil 'with the thread, must first instruct him in purifica- 'tion, in good customs, in the management of the con- 'secrated fire, and in the holy rites of morning, noon, 'and evening.

70. 'When the student is going to read the *Veda*, 'he must perform an ablution, as the law ordains, 'with his face to the north, and, having paid scriptural 'homage, he must receive instruction, wearing a clean 'vest, his members being duly composed :

71. 'At the beginning and end of the lecture, he 'must always clasp both the feet of his preceptor ; and 'he must read with both his hands closed : (this is 'called scriptural homage.)

72. 'With crossed hands let him clasp the feet of his

'tutor, touching the left foot with his left, and the 'right, with his right hand.

73. 'When he is prepared for the lecture, the pre'ceptor, constantly attentive, must say: "hoa! read;" 'and at the close of the lesson he must say: "take 'rest."

74. 'A *Bráhman*, beginning and ending a lecture on 'the *Veda*, must always pronounce to himself the syl'lable *óm*; for, unless the syllable *óm* precede, his learn'ing will slip away from him; and, unless it follow, 'nothing will be long retained.

75. 'If he have sitten on culms of *kúsa* with their 'points toward the east, and be purified by *rubbing* that 'holy grass on both his hands, and be further prepared 'by three suppressions of breath *each equal in time to* '*five short vowels*, he then may fitly pronounce *óm*.

76. 'BRAHMA' milked out, *as it were*, from the three '*Vedas*, the letter A, the letter U, and the letter M, '*which form by their coalition the triliteral monosyllable*, 'together with three mysterious words, *bhur*, *bhuvah*, '*swer*, or *earth*, *sky*, *heaven*:

77. 'From the three *Vedas*, also, the Lord of crea'tures, incomprehensibly exalted, successively milked 'out the three measures of that ineffable text, begin'ning with the word *tad*, and entitled *sávitrì* or *gáyatrì*.

78. 'A priest who shall know the *Veda*, and shall 'pronounce to himself, both morning and evening, that 'syllable, and that holy text preceded by the three 'words, shall attain the sanctity which the *Veda* con'fers;

79. 'And a twice-born man, who shall a thousand 'times repeat those three (or *óm*, the *vyáhritis*, and the '*gáyatrì*,) apart *from the multitude*, shall be released

'in a month even from a great offence, as a snake from 'his slough.

80. 'The priest, the soldier, and the merchant, who 'shall neglect this mysterious text, and fail to perform 'in due season his peculiar acts of piety, shall meet 'with contempt among the virtuous.

81. 'The three great immutable words, preceded by 'the triliteral syllable, and *followed by the gáyatrì* which 'consists of three measures, must be considered as the 'mouth, or *principal part* of the *Veda:*

82. 'Whoever shall repeat, day by day, for three 'years, without negligence, that sacred text, shall *here-'after* approach the divine essence, move as freely as 'air, and assume an ethereal form.

83. 'The triliteral monosyllable is *an emblem of* the 'Supreme, the suppressions of breath *with a mind fixed 'on* God are the highest devotion; but nothing is more 'exalted than the *gáyatrì: a declaration of* truth is more 'excellent than silence.

84. 'All rites ordained in the *Veda,* oblations to fire, 'and solemn sacrifices pass away; but that which passes 'not away, is declared to be the syllable *óm,* thence 'called *akshara:* since it is a *symbol of* God, the Lord 'of created beings.

85. 'The act of repeating his Holy Name is ten times 'better than the appointed sacrifice; an hundred times 'better when it is heard by no man; and a thousand 'times better when it is purely mental:

86. 'The four domestic sacraments which are ac-'companied with the appointed sacrifice, are not equal, 'though all be united, to a sixteenth part of the sacri-'fice performed by a repetition of the *gáyatrì:*

87. 'By the sole repetition of the *gáyatrì,* a priest

'may indubitably attain beatitude, let him perform, or 'not perform, any other religious act; if he be *Maitra*, 'or a *friend to all creatures*, he is *justly* named *Bráhmana*, or *united to the Great One*.

88. 'In restraining the organs which run wild among 'ravishing sensualities, a wise man will apply diligent 'care, like a charioteer in managing restive horses.

89. 'Those eleven organs, to which the first sages 'gave name, I will comprehensively enumerate as the 'law considers them in due order.

90. 'The nose is the fifth after the ears, the skin, the 'eyes, and the tongue; and the organs of speech are 'reckoned the tenth, after those of excretion and gene'ration, and the hands and feet:

91. 'Five of them, the ear and the rest in succes'sion, learned men have called organs of sense; and 'the others, organs of action:

92. 'The heart must be considered as the eleventh; 'which, by its natural property, comprises both sense 'and action; and which being subdued, the two other 'sets, with five in each, are also controlled.

93. 'A man, by the attachment of his organs to 'sensual pleasure, incurs certain guilt; but, having 'wholly subdued them, he thence attains heavenly bliss.

94. 'Desire is never satisfied with the enjoyment of 'desired objects; as the fire is not appeased with clari'fied butter; it only blazes more vehemently.

95. 'Whatever man may obtain all those gratifica'tions, or whatever man may resign them completely, 'the resignation of all pleasures is far better than the 'attainment of them.

96. 'The organs being strongly attached to sensual

'delights cannot so effectually be restrained by avoid-'ing incentives to pleasure, as by a constant pursuit of 'divine knowledge.

97. 'To a man contaminated by sensuality neither 'the *Vedas,* nor liberality, nor sacrifices, nor strict 'observances, nor pious austerities, ever procure fe-'licity.

98. 'He must be considered as really triumphant 'over his organs, who, on hearing and touching, on 'seeing and tasting and smelling, *what may please or* '*offend the senses,* neither greatly rejoices nor greatly 'repines:

99. 'But, when one among all his organs fails, by 'that single failure his knowledge of GOD passes away, 'as water flows through one hole in a leathern bottle.

100 'Having kept all his members *of sense and action* 'under control, and obtained also command over his 'heart, he will enjoy every advantage, even though he 'reduce not his body by religious austerities.

101. 'At the morning twilight, let him stand repeat-'ing the *gáyatrì* until he see the sun; and at evening 'twilight, let him repeat it sitting, until the stars dis-'tinctly appear;

' 102. 'He who stands repeating it at the morning 'twilight, removes *all unknown* nocturnal sin; and he 'who repeats it sitting at evening twilight, disperses 'the taint, that has *unknowingly* been contracted in the 'day.

103. 'But he who stands not repeating it in the 'morning, and sits not repeating it in the evening, 'must be precluded like a *Súdra,* from every sacred 'observance of the twice-born classes.

104. 'Near pure water, with his organs holden under

'control, *and* retiring from circumspection to some 'unfrequented place, let him pronounce the *gáyatrì*, 'performing daily ceremonies.

105. 'In reading the *Vedangas* or *grammar, prosody, 'mathematics, and so forth*, or even such parts of the '*Veda* as ought constantly to be read, there is no pro-'hibition on particular days; nor in pronouncing the 'texts appointed for oblations to fire:

106. 'Of that, which must constantly be read, and is 'therefore called *Brahmasatra*, there can be no such 'prohibition; and the oblation to fire according to the '*Veda*, produces good fruit, though accompanied with 'the text *vashat*, which *on other occasions* must be inter-'mitted on certain days.

107. 'For him, who shall persist a whole year in 'reading the *Veda*, his organs being kept in subjection, 'and his body pure, there will always rise good fruit 'from his *offerings of* milk and curds, *of* clarified butter 'and honey.

108. 'Let the twice-born youth, who has been girt 'with the sacrificial cord, collect wood for the holy fire, 'beg food of his relations, sleep on a low bed, and per-'form such offices as may please his preceptor, until his 'return to the house of his natural father.

109. 'Ten persons may legally be instructed in the '*Veda*; the son of a spiritual teacher; a boy who is 'assiduous; one who can impart other knowledge; one 'who is just; one who is pure; one who is friendly; 'one who is powerful; one who can bestow wealth; 'one who is honest; and one who is related by blood.

110. 'Let not a sensible teacher tell any *other* what 'he is not asked, nor what he is asked improperly; but 'let him, however intelligent, act in the multitude as if 'he were dumb:

111. 'Of the two persons, him, who illegally asks, 'and him, who illegally answers, one will die, or incur 'odium.

112. 'Where virtue, and wealth *sufficient to secure it*, 'are not found, or diligent attention, *at least* proportioned *to the holiness of the subject*, in that soil divine 'instruction must not be sown: it would perish like 'fine seed in barren land.

113. 'A teacher of the *Veda* should rather die with 'his learning, than sow it in sterile soil, even though 'he be in grievous distress for subsistence.

114. 'Sacred Learning, having approached a *Bráhman*, said to him: "I am thy precious gem; preserve 'me with care; deliver me not to a scorner; (so *preserved* I shall become supremely strong.)

115. 'But communicate me, as to a vigilant depository of thy gem, to that student, whom thou shalt 'know to be pure, to have subdued his passions, to perform the duties of his order."

116. 'He who shall acquire *knowledge of* the *Veda* 'without the assent of his preceptor, incurs the guilt of 'stealing the scripture, and shall sink to the region of 'torment.

117. 'From whatever teacher a student has received 'instruction, either popular, ceremonial, or sacred, let 'him first salute his instructor, when they meet.

118. 'A *Bráhman*, who completely governs his passions, though he know the *gáyatrì* only, is more 'honourable than he, who governs not his passions, 'who eats all *sorts of food*, and sells all *sorts of commodities*, even though he know the three *Vedas*.

119. 'When a superior sits on a couch or bench, 'let not an inferior sit on it with him; and, if an in-

'ferior be sitting on a couch, let him rise to salute a 'superior.

120. 'The vital spirits of a young man mount up-'wards *to depart from him,* when an elder approaches; 'but by rising and salutation he recovers them.

121. 'A youth who habitually greets and constantly 'reveres the aged, obtains an increase of four things; 'life, knowledge, fame, strength.

122. 'After the word of salutation, a *Bráhman* must 'address an elder; saying, "I am such an one," pro-'nouncing his own name.

123. 'If any persons, *through ignorance of the* San-'skrit *language,* understand not the import of his name, 'to them should a learned man say, "It is I;" and in 'that manner he should address all *classes of* women.

124. 'In the salutation he should pronounce, after 'his own name, the vocative particle *bhós;* for the par-'ticle *bhós* is held by the wise to have the same proper-'ty with names *fully expressed.*

125. 'A *Bráhman* should thus be saluted in return: '"May'st thou live long, excellent man!" and at the 'end of his name, the vowel and preceding consonant 'should be lengthened, *with an acute accent,* to three 'syllabic moments *or short vowels.*

126. 'That *Bráhman,* who knows not the form of 'returning a salutation, must not be saluted by a man of 'learning: as a *Súdra,* even so is he.

127. 'Let a learned man ask a priest, when he meets 'him, if his devotion prospers; a warrior, if he is un-'hurt; a merchant, if his wealth is secure; and one of 'the servile class, if he enjoys good health; *using res-'pectively the words,* kusalam, anámayam, kshémam, *and* 'árógyam.

128. 'He, who has just performed a solemn sacrifice 'and ablution, must not be addressed by his name, even 'though he be a younger man ; but he, who knows the 'law, should accost him with the vocative particle, or 'with *bhavat, the pronoun of respect.*

129. 'To the wife of another, and to any woman 'not related by blood, he must say, "*bhavati,* and 'amiable sister."

130. 'To his uncle's paternal and maternal, to his 'wife's father, to performers of the sacrifice, and to 'spiritual teachers ; he must say, "I am such an one" '—rising up to salute them, even though younger 'than himself.

131. 'The sister of his mother, the wife of his ma- 'ternal uncle, his own wife's mother, and the sister of 'his father, must be saluted like the wife of his *father* '*or* preceptor : they are equal to his *father's or his* pre- 'ceptor's wife.

132. 'The wife of his brother, if she be of the same 'class, must be saluted every day ; but his paternal 'and maternal kinswomen need only be greeted on his 'return from a journey.

133. 'With the sister of his father and of his mother, 'and with his own elder sister, let him demean himself 'as with his mother ; though his mother be more 'venerable than they.

134. 'Fellow citizens are equal for ten years ; dancers 'and singers, for five ; learned theologians, for less than 'three ; but persons related by blood, for a short time : *that is, a greater difference of age destroys their equality.*

135. 'The Student must consider a *Bráhman,* though 'but ten years old, and a *Kshatriya,* though aged a hun- 'dred years, as father and son ; as between those two, 'the young *Bráhman* is *to be respected as* the father.

136. 'Wealth, kindred, age, moral conduct, and, 'fifthly, divine knowledge, entitle men to respect; but 'that which is last mentioned in order, is the most 'respectable.

137. 'Whatever man of the three *highest* classes 'possesses the most of those five, both in number and 'degree, that man is entitled to most respect; even a '*Súdra*, if he have entered the tenth decade of his age.

138. 'Way must be made for a man in a wheeled 'carriage, or above ninety years old, or afflicted with 'disease, or carrying a burthen; for a woman; for a 'priest just returned from the mansion of his precep-'tor; for a prince, and for a bridegroom.

139. 'Among all those, if they be met at one time, 'the priest just returned home and the prince are most 'to be honored; and of those two, the priest just re-'turned, should be treated with more respect than the 'prince.

140. 'That priest who girds his pupil with the sacri-'ficial cord, and afterwards instructs him in the whole '*Veda*, with the law of sacrifice and the sacred *Upa-'nishads*, holy sages call an *áchárya*:

141. 'But, he, who for his livelihood, gives instruc-'tion in a part only of the *Veda*, or in grammar, and 'in other *Vedángas*, is called an *upádhya*, or sub-'lecturer.

142. 'The father, who performs the ceremonies on 'conception and the like, according to law, and who 'nourishes the child with his first rice, has the epithet 'of *guru*, or venerable.

143. 'He, who receives a stipend for preparing the 'holy fire, for conducting the *páka* and *agnishtóma*, and 'for performing other sacrifices, is called in this code 'the *ritwij* of his employer.

5

144. 'He, who truly and faithfully fills both ears 'with the *Veda*, must be considered as equal to a 'mother ; he must be revered as a father ; him the pupil 'must never grieve.

145. 'A *mere áchárya*, or *a teacher of the gáyatrì* '*only*, surpasses ten *upádhyáyas ;* a father, a hundred 'such *ácháryas ;* and a mother, a thousand *natural* 'fathers.

146. 'Of him, who gives natural birth, and him, who 'gives knowledge of the whole *Veda*, the giver of 'sacred knowledge is the more venerable father ; since 'the *second or* divine birth ensures life to the twice-born 'both in this world and hereafter eternally.

147. 'Let a man consider that as a mere human 'birth, which his parents gave him for their mutual 'gratification, and which he receives after lying in the 'womb.

148. 'But that birth which his *principal áchárya*, 'who knows the whole *Veda*, procures for him by *his* '*divine mother* the *gáyatrì*, is a true birth : that birth 'is exempt from age and from death.

149. 'Him, who confers on a man the benefit of sa-'cred learning, whether it be little or much, let him 'know to be here named *guru* or *venerable father*, in 'consequence of that heavenly benefit.

150. 'A *Bráhman*, who is the giver of spiritual birth, 'the teacher of prescribed duty, is by right *called* the 'father of an old man, though himself be a child.

151. 'KAVI, or *the learned*, child of ANGIRAS, taught 'his paternal uncles and cousins to read the *Veda*, and, 'excelling them in divine knowledge, said to them, '"little sons :"

152. 'They, moved with resentment, asked the gods

'the meaning of that *expression*; and the gods, being 'assembled, answered them: "The child has addressed 'you properly;

153. 'For an unlearned man is in truth a child; and 'he who teaches him the *Veda*, is his father: holy 'sages have always said child to an ignorant man, and 'father to a teacher of scripture."

154. 'Greatness is not conferred by years, not by 'grey hairs, not by wealth, not by powerful kindred: 'the divine sages have established this rule; "Who-'ever has read the *Vedas* and their *Angas*, he among 'us is great."

155. 'The seniority of priests is from sacred learn-'ing; of warriors from valour; of merchants from 'abundance of grain; of the servile class only from 'priority of birth.

156. 'A man is not therefore aged, because his head 'is grey: him, surely, the gods considered as aged, who, 'though young in years, has read *and understands* the '*Veda*.

157. 'As an elephant made of wood, as an antelope 'made of leather, such is an unlearned *Bráhman*: those 'three have nothing but names.

158. 'As an eunuch is unproductive with women, as 'cow with a cow is unprolific, as liberality to a fool 'is fruitless, so is a *Bráhman* useless, if he read not the 'holy texts.

159. 'Good instruction must be given without pain 'to the instructed; and sweet gentle speech must be 'used by a preceptor, who cherishes virtue.

160. 'He, whose discourse and heart are pure, and

'ever perfectly guarded, attains all the fruit arising from 'his complete course of studying the *Veda*.

161. 'Let not a man be querulous even though in 'pain; let him not injure another in deed or in thought; 'let him not even utter a word, by which his fellow 'creature may suffer uneasiness; since that will ob-'struct his own progress to future beatitude.

162. 'A *Bráhman* should constantly shun worldly 'honor, as he would shun poison; and rather constant-'ly seek disrespect, as he would seek nectar;

163. 'For though scorned, he may sleep with plea-'sure; with pleasure may he awake; with pleasure may 'he pass through this life: but the scorner utterly 'perishes.

164. 'Let the twice-born youth, whose soul has been 'formed by this regular succession of prescribed acts, 'collect by degrees, while he dwells with his preceptor, 'the devout habits proceeding from the study of scrip-'ture.

165. 'With various modes of devotion, and with aus-'terities ordained by the law, must the whole *Veda* 'be read, and above all the sacred *Upanishads*, by him, 'who has received a new birth.

166. 'Let the best of the twice-born classes, intend-'ing to practise devotion, continually repeat the read-'ing of scripture; since a repetition of reading the scrip-'ture is here styled the highest devotion of a *Bráhman*.

167. 'Yes verily; that student in theology performs 'the highest act of devotion *with his whole body*, to the 'extremities of his nails, even though he *be so far sen-'sual as to* wear a chaplet of sweet flowers, who to the 'utmost of his ability daily reads the *Veda*.

168. 'A twice-born man, who not having studied

'the *Veda*, applies diligent attention to a different *and* 'worldly study, soon falls, even when living, to the condition of a *Súdra*; and his descendants after him.

169. 'The first birth is from a natural mother; the 'second, from the ligation of the zone; the third from 'the due performance of the sacrifice; such are the births 'of him who is usually called twice-born, according to 'a text of the *Veda*:

170. 'Among them his divine birth is that, which 'is distinguished by the ligation of the zone, *and sacrificial cord*; and in that *birth* the *Gáyatri* is his mother, 'and the *A'chárya*, his father.

171. 'Sages call the *A'chárya* father, from his giving 'instruction in the *Veda*: nor can any holy rite be performed by a young man, before his investiture.

172. '*Till he be invested with the signs of the class*, 'he must not pronounce any sacred text, except what 'ought to be used in obsequies to an ancestor; since he 'is on a level with a *Súdra* before his new birth from 'the revealed scripture:

173. 'From him, who has been duly invested, are 'required both the performance of devout acts and the 'study of the *Veda* in order, preceded by stated ceremonies.

174. 'Whatever sorts of leathern mantle, sacrificial 'thread, and zone, whatever staff, and whatever under-apparel are ordained, *as before-mentioned*, for a youth 'of each class, the like must also be used in his religious acts.

175. 'These *following* rules must a *Brahmachári*, or '*student in theology*, observe, while he dwells with his 'preceptor; keeping all his members under control, 'for the sake of increasing his habitual devotion.

176. 'Day by day, having bathed and being purified, let him offer fresh water to the gods, the sages, 'and the manes; let him show respect to the images 'of the deities, and bring wood for the oblation to fire.

177. 'Let him abstain from honey, from flesh meat, 'from perfumes, from chaplets of flowers, from sweet 'vegetable juices, from women, from all sweet substances turned acid, and from injury to animated 'beings;

178. 'From unguents for his limbs, and from black 'powder for his eyes, from wearing sandals, and carrying an umbrella, from sensual desires, from wrath, 'from covetousness, from dancing, and from vocal and 'instrumental music;

179. 'From gaming, from disputes, from detraction, 'and from falsehood, from embracing or wantonly looking at women, and from disservice to other men.

180. 'Let him constantly sleep alone: let him never 'waste his own manhood; for he, who voluntarily 'wastes his manhood, violates the rule of his order, '*and becomes an* avakírní:

181, 'A twice-born youth, who has involuntarily 'wasted his manly strength during sleep, must repeat 'with reverence, having bathed and paid homage to 'the sun, the text of Scripture: "*Again let my 'strength return to me.*"

182. 'Let him carry water-pots, flowers, cow-dung, 'fresh earth, and *kusa*-grass, as much as may be useful 'to his preceptor; and let him perform every day the 'duty of a religious mendicant.

183. 'Each day must a *Bráhman* student receive his 'food by begging, with due care, from the houses of 'persons renowned for discharging their duties, and

'not deficient in performing the sacrifices which the '*Veda* ordains.

184. 'Let him not beg from the cousins of his pre-'ceptor; nor from his own cousins; nor from other 'kinsmen by the father's side, or by the mother's; 'but, if other houses be not accessible, let him begin 'with the last of those in order, avoiding the first;

185. 'Or, if none of those *houses* just mentioned can 'be found, let him go begging through the whole dis-'trict round the village, keeping his organs in subjec-'tion, and remaining silent; but let him turn away 'from such as have committed any deadly sin.

186. 'Having brought logs of wood from a distance, 'let him place them in the open air; and with them 'let him make an oblation to fire without remissness, 'both evening and morning.

187. 'He, who for seven successive days omits the 'ceremony of begging food, and offers not wood to the 'sacred fire, must perform the penance of an *avakírní*, 'unless he be afflicted with illness.

188. 'Let the student persist constantly in such beg-'ging, but let him not eat the food of one person only: 'the subsistence of a student by begging is held equal 'to fasting *in religious merit*.

189. 'Yet, when he is asked in a solemn act in 'honor of the gods or the manes, he may eat at his 'pleasure the food of a single person; observing, how-'ever, the laws of abstinence and the austerity of an 'anchoret: thus the rule of his order is kept inviolate.

190. 'This duty of a mendicant is ordained by the 'wise for a *Bráhman* only; but no such act is appointed 'for a warrior, or for a merchant.

191. 'Let the scholar, when commanded by his pre-

'ceptor, and even when he has received no command, 'always exert himself in reading, and in all acts useful 'to his teacher.

192. 'Keeping in due subjection his body, his speech, 'his organs of sense, and his heart, let him stand with 'the palms of his hands joined, looking at the face of 'his preceptor.

193. 'Let him always keep his right arm uncovered, 'be always decently apparelled, and properly compos-'ed; and when his instructor says, "be seated," let 'him sit opposite to his venerable guide.

194. 'In the presence of his preceptor let him always 'eat less, and wear a coarser mantle with worse appen-'dages; let him rise before, and go to rest after his 'tutor.

195. 'Let him not answer his teacher's orders, or 'converse with him, reclining on a bed; nor sitting, 'nor eating, nor standing, nor with an averted face:

196. 'But let him both *answer and converse*, if his 'preceptor sit, standing up; if he stand, advancing 'towards him; if he advance, meeting him; if he run, 'hastening after him.

197. 'If his face be averted, going round to front 'him, *from left to right*; if he be at a little distance, 'approaching him; if reclined, bending to him; and, if 'he stand ever so far off running toward him.

198. 'When his teacher is nigh, let his couch or 'his bench be always placed low: when his precep-'tor's eye can observe him, let him not sit carelessly 'at ease.

199. 'Let him never pronounce the mere name of 'his tutor, even in his absence; nor ever mimic his 'gait, his speech, or his manner.

200. 'In whatever place, either true but censorious, 'or false and defamatory, discourse is held concerning 'his teacher, let him there cover his ears or move to 'another place:

201. 'By censuring his preceptor, though justly, he 'will be born an ass; by falsely defaming him, a dog; 'by using his goods without leave, a small worm; by 'envying his merit, a larger insect or reptile.

202. 'He must not serve his tutor by the interven-'tion of another, while himself stands aloof; nor must 'he attend him in a passion, nor when a woman is 'near; from a carriage or raised seat he must descend 'to salute his heavenly director.

203. 'Let him not sit with his preceptor to the lee-'ward, or to the windward of him; nor let him say 'any thing which the venerable man cannot hear.

204. 'He may sit with his teacher in a carriage 'drawn by bulls, horses, or camels; on a terrace, on 'a pavement of stones, or on a mat of *woven* grass; 'on a rock, on a wooden bench, or in a boat.

205. 'When his tutor's tutor is near, let him demean 'himself as if his own were present; nor let him, unless 'ordered by his spiritual father, prostrate himself *in his* '*presence* before his natural father, or paternal uncle.

206. 'This is likewise ordained as his constant be-'haviour toward his other instructors in science; to-'ward his elder paternal kinsmen; toward all who may 'restrain him from sin, and all who give him salutary 'advice.

207. 'Toward men also, who are truly virtuous, let 'him always behave as toward his preceptor; and, in 'like manner, toward the sons of his teacher, who are 'entitled to respect *as older men, and are not students*;

'and toward the paternal kinsmen of his venerable 'tutor.

208. 'The son of his preceptor, whether younger or 'or of equal age, or a student, if he be capable of teach- 'ing the *Veda*, deserves the same honor with the pre- 'ceptor himself, *when he is present* at any sacrificial act:

209. 'But he must not perform for the son of his 'teacher, the duty of rubbing his limbs, or of bathing 'him, or of eating what he leaves, or of washing his 'feet.

210. 'The wives of his preceptor, if they be of the 'same class, must receive equal honor with their 'venerable husband; but if they be of a different 'class, they must be honored only by rising and salu- 'tation.

211. 'For no wife of his teacher must he perform 'the offices of pouring scented oil on them, of attend- 'ing them while they bathe, of rubbing their legs and 'arms, or of decking their hair ;

212. 'Nor must a young wife of his preceptor be 'greeted even by the ceremony of touching her feet, if 'he have completed his twentieth year, or can dis- 'tinguish virtue from vice.

213. 'It is the nature of women in this world to 'cause the seduction of men ; for which reason the wise 'are never unguarded in the company of females ;

214. 'A female indeed, is able to draw from the right 'path in this life not a fool only, but even a sage, and 'can lead him in subjection to desire or to wrath.

215. 'Let no man, therefore, sit in a sequestered 'place with his nearest female relations : the assemblage 'of corporeal organs is powerful enough to snatch wis- 'dom from the wise.

216. 'A young student may, as the law directs, 'make prostration at his pleasure on the ground before 'a young wife of his tutor, saying, "I am such an 'one;"

217. 'And on his return from a journey, he must 'once touch the feet of his preceptor's *aged* wife, and 'salute her each day by prostration, calling to mind the 'practice of virtuous men.

218. 'As he who digs deep with a spade comes to a 'spring of water, so the student, who humbly serves his 'teacher, attains the knowledge *which lies deep* in his 'teacher's mind.

219. 'Whether his head be shorn, or his hair long, 'or one lock be bound above in a knot, let not the sun 'ever set or rise while he lies asleep in the village.

220. 'If the sun should rise or set, while he sleeps 'through sensual indulgence, and knows it not, he must 'fast a whole day, repeating the *gáyatrì:*

221. 'He, who has been surprised asleep by the set'ting or by the rising sun, and performs not that pen'ance, incurs great guilt.

222. 'Let him adore GOD both at sunrise and at 'sunset, as the law ordains, having made his ablution 'and keeping his organs controlled; and, with fixed at'tention, let him repeat the text, which he ought to re'peat, in a place free from impurity.

223. 'If a woman or a *Súdra* perform any act lead'ing to the chief temporal good, let the student be 'careful to emulate it; and he may do whatever grati'fies his heart, unless it be forbidden by law:

224. 'The chief temporal good is by some declared 'to consist in virtue and wealth; by some, in wealth 'and lawful pleasure; by some, in virtue alone; by

'others, in wealth alone; but the chief good here below 'is an assemblage of all three: this is a true decision.

225. 'A teacher of the *Veda* is the image of GOD; 'a natural father, the image of BRAHMA'; a mother, 'the image of the earth; an elder whole brother, the 'image of the soul.

226. 'Therefore a spiritual and a natural father, a 'mother and the elder brother, are not to be treated 'with disrespect, especially by a *Bráhman*, though the 'student be grievously provoked.

227. 'That pain and care which a mother and father 'undergo in producing and rearing children, cannot be 'compensated in a hundred years.

228. 'Let every man constantly do what may please 'his parents: and, on all occasions, what may please 'his preceptor: when those three are satisfied, his 'whole course of devotion is accomplished.

229. 'Due reverence to those three is considered as 'the highest devotion; and without their approbation 'he must perform no other duty.

230. 'Since they alone are held equal to the three 'worlds; they alone, to the three principal orders; 'they alone, to the three *Vedas*; they alone, to the 'three fires.

231. 'The natural father is considered as the *gár-'hapatya*, or nuptial fire; the mother as the *dakshina*, 'or ceremonial; the spiritual guide, as the *áhavaniya*, 'or sacrificial: this triad of fires is most venerable.

232. 'He, who neglects not those three, when he 'becomes a house-keeper, will ultimately obtain domi-'nion over the three worlds; and his body being irra-'diated like a god, he will enjoy supreme bliss in 'heaven.

233. 'By honoring his mother he gains this *terrestrial* world; by honoring his father, the intermediate, 'or *etherial;* and, by assiduous attention to his preceptor, even the *celestial* world of BRAHMA':

234. 'All duties are completely performed by that 'man, by whom those three are completely honored; 'but to him by whom they are dishonored, all other 'acts of duty are fruitless.

235. 'As long as those three live, so long he must 'perform no other duty *for his own sake:* but delighting in what may conciliate their affections and gratify 'their wishes, he must from day to day assiduously 'wait on them:

236. 'Whatever duty he may perform in thought, 'word, or deed, with a view to the next world, without 'derogation from his respect to them; he must declare 'to them his entire performance of it.

237. 'By honoring those three, without more, a 'man effectually does whatever ought to be done: 'this is the highest duty, appearing before us like 'DHARMA himself, and every other act is an *upadharma,* or subordinate duty.

238. 'A believer in scripture may receive pure 'knowledge even from a *Súdra;* a lesson of the highest 'virtue, even from a *Chandála;* and a woman, bright 'as a gem, even from the basest family:

239. 'Even from poison may nectar be taken; even 'from a child, gentleness of speech; even from a foe, 'prudent conduct; and even from an impure substance, 'gold.

240. 'From every quarter, therefore, must be selected women bright as gems, knowledge, virtue, purity, 'gentle speech, and various liberal arts.

241. 'In case of necessity, a student is required to 'learn the *Veda* from one who is not a *Bráhman*, and, as 'long as that instruction continues, to honor his in-'structor with obsequious assiduity;

242. 'But a pupil who seeks the incomparable path 'to heaven, should not live to the end of his days in 'the dwelling of a preceptor who is no *Bráhman*, or 'who has not read all the *Vedas*, with their *Angas*.

243. 'If he anxiously desire to pass his whole life in 'the house of a sacerdotal teacher, he must serve him 'with assiduous care, till he be released from his mortal 'frame:

244. 'That *Bráhman*, who has dutifully attended his 'preceptor, till the dissolution of his body, passes direct-'ly to the eternal mansion of God.

245. 'Let not a student, who knows his duty, pre-'sent any gift to his preceptor *before his return home;* 'but when, by his tutor's permission, he is going to 'perform the ceremony on his return, let him give the 'venerable man some valuable thing to the best of his 'power;

246. 'A field, or gold, a jewel, a cow, or a 'horse, an umbrella, a pair of sandals, a stool, corn, 'cloths, or even any *very excellent* vegetable: thus will 'he gain the affectionate remembrance of his instructor.

247. 'The student for life must, if his teacher die, 'attend on his virtuous son, or his widow, or on one of 'his paternal kinsmen, with the same respect which he 'showed to the living:

248. 'Should none of those be alive, he must occupy 'the station of his preceptor, the seat, and the place of 'religious exercises; must continually pay due attention

'to the fires, which he had consecrated; and must prepare his own soul for heaven.

249. 'The twice-born man, who shall thus without intermission have passed the time of his studentship, shall ascend, after death, to the most exalted of regions, and no more again spring to birth in this lower world.

CHAP. III.

On Marriage; or on the Second Order.

1. 'THE discipline of a student in the three *Vedas* may be continued for thirty-six years, in the house of his preceptor; or for half that time, or for a quarter of it, or until he perfectly comprehend them:

2. 'A student, whose rules have not been violated, may assume the order of a married man, after he has read in succession a *sákhá*, or branch from each of the three, or from two, or from any one of them.

3. 'Being justly applauded for the strict performance of his duty, and having received from his *natural or spiritual* father the sacred gift of the *Veda*, let him sit on an elegant bed, decked with a garland of flowers, and let his father honor him, before his nuptials, with a present of a cow.

4. 'Let the twice-born man, having obtained the consent of his venerable guide, and having performed his ablution with stated ceremonies, on his return home, as the law directs, espouse a wife of the same class with himself and endued with the marks of excellence.

5. 'She, who is not descended from his *paternal or*

'*maternal* ancestors, within the sixth degree, and who 'is not *known by her family name to be* of the same pri- 'mitive stock with his father *or mother*, is eligible by a 'twice-born man for nuptials and holy union:

6. 'In connecting himself with a wife, let him stu- 'diously avoid the ten following families, be they ever 'so great, or ever so rich in kine, goats, sheep, gold 'and grain:

7. 'The family which has omitted prescribed acts of religion; that which has produced no male children; 'that, in which the *Veda* has not been read; that, which 'has thick hair on the body; and those, which have 'been subject to hemorrhoids, to phthisis, to dyspepsia, 'to epilepsy, to leprosy, and to elephantiasis.

8. 'Let him not marry a girl with reddish hair, nor 'with any deformed limb; nor one troubled with habi- 'tual sickness; nor one either with no hair or with too 'much; nor one immoderately talkative; nor one with 'inflamed eyes;

9. 'Nor one with the name of a constellation, or of 'a tree, or of a river, of a barbarous nation, or of a 'mountain, of a winged creature, a snake, or a slave; 'nor with any name raising an image of terror.

10. 'Let him choose for his wife a girl, whose form 'has no defect; who has an agreeable name; who 'walks *gracefully* like a phenicopteros, or like a young 'elephant; whose hair and teeth are moderate respec- 'tively in quantity and in size; whose body has ex- 'quisite softness.

11. 'Her, who has no brother, or whose father is 'not well known, let no sensible man espouse, through 'fear lest, *in the former case*, her father should take 'her first son as his own *to perform his obsequies*; or, '*in the second case*, lest an illicit marriage should be 'contracted.

12. 'For the first marriage of the twice-born classes, 'a woman of the same class is recommended; but for 'such as are impelled by inclination to marry again, 'women in the direct order of the classes are to be 'preferred:

13. 'A *Súdra* woman only must be the wife of a '*Súdra;* she and a *Vaisyà,* of a *Vaisya;* they two and 'a *Kshatriyà,* of a *Kshatriya;* those two and a *Bráh-'manì* of a *Bráhman.*

14. 'A woman of the servile class is not mentioned, 'even in the recital of any ancient story, as the first 'wife of a *Bráhman* or of a *Kshatriya,* though in the 'greatest difficulty, to find a suitable match.

15. 'Men of the twice-born classes, who through 'weakness of intellect, irregularly marry women of the 'lowest class, very soon degrade their families and 'progeny to the state of *Súdras:*

16. 'According to ATRI and to (GO'TAMA) the son of 'UTAT'HYA, he who *thus* marries a woman of the servile 'class, *if he be a priest,* is degraded instantly; accord-'ing to SAUNAKA, on the birth of a son, *if he be a war-'rior;* and, *if he be a merchant,* on the birth of a son's 'son, according to (me) BHRIGU.

17. 'A *Bráhman,* if he take a *Súdrà* to his bed, *as 'his first wife,* sinks to the regions of torment; if he 'beget a child by her, he loses even his priestly rank:

18. 'His sacrifices to the gods, his oblations to the 'manes, and his hospitable attentions to strangers, 'must be supplied principally by her; but the gods and 'manes will not eat such offerings; nor can heaven 'be attained by such hospitality.

19. 'For the crime of him, who *thus illegally* drinks the moisture of a *Súdrà's* lips, who is tainted by her

'breath, and who even begets a child on her body, the 'law declares no expiation.

20. 'Now learn compendiously the eight forms of 'the nuptial ceremony, used by the four classes, some 'good and some bad in this world, and in the next:

21. 'The ceremony of BRAHMA', of the *Dévas*, of the '*Rishis*, of the *Prajápatis*, of the *Asuras*, of the *Gand-'harvas*, and of the *Rakshases;* the eighth and basest is 'that of the *Pisáchas*.

22. 'Which of them is permitted by law to each 'class and what are the good and bad properties of 'each ceremony, all this I will fully declare to you, 'together with the qualities, good and bad, of the 'offspring.

23. 'Let mankind know, that *the* six *first* in direct 'order are *by some held* valid in the case of a priest; 'the four last, in that of a warrior; and the same 'four, except the *Rákshasa* marriage, in the cases of a 'merchant and a man of the servile class:

24. 'Some consider the four first only as approved 'in the case of a priest; one, that of *Rakshases*, as pe-'culiar to a soldier; and that of *Asuras*, to a mercan-'tile and a servile man.

25. 'But in this code, three of *the* five *last* are held 'legal, and two illegal: the ceremonies of *Pisáchas* and '*Asuras* must never be performed.

26. 'For a military man the before mentioned mar-'riages of *Gandharvas* and *Rakshases*, whether separate 'or mixed, *as when a girl is made captive by her lover,* '*after a victory over her kinsmen,* are permitted by law.

27. 'The gift of a daughter, clothed only with a sin-'gle robe, to a man learned in the *Veda*, whom her

'father voluntarily invites, and respectfully receives, is 'the nuptial right called *Bráhma*.

28. 'The right which sages call *Daiva*, is the gift of 'a daughter, whom her father has decked in gay attire, 'when the sacrifice is already begun, to the officiating 'priest, who performs that act of religion.

29. 'When the father gives his daughter away, after 'having received from the bridegroom one pair of kine, 'or two pairs, for uses prescribed by law, that marriage 'is termed *A'rsha*.

30. 'The nuptial rite called *Prájápatya*, is when the 'father gives away his daughter with due honor, saying 'distinctly, "May both of you perform together your 'civil and religious duties!"

31. 'When the bridegroom, having given as much 'wealth as he can afford to the father and paternal 'kinsmen, and to the damsel herself, takes her volunta-'rily as his bride, that marriage is named *A'sura*.

32. 'The reciprocal connexion of a youth and a dam-'sel, with mutual desire, is the marriage denominated '*Gándharva*, contracted for the purpose of amorous 'embraces, and proceeding from sensual inclination.

33. 'The seizure of a maiden by force from her 'house, while she weeps and calls for assistance, after 'her kinsmen and friends have been slain in battle, or 'wounded, and their houses broken open, is the mar-'riage styled *Rákshasa*.

34. 'When the lover secretly embraces the damsel, 'either sleeping or flushed with strong liquor, or disor-'dered in her intellect, that sinful marriage, called '*Paisácha*, is the eighth and the basest.

35. 'The gift of daughters in marriage by the sacer-'dotal class, is most approved, when they *previously*

'have poured water *into the hands of the bridegroom;* 'but the ceremonies of the other classes may be per- 'formed according to their several fancies.

36. 'Among these nuptial rites, what quality is 'ascribed by MANU to each, hear now ye *Bráhmans*, 'hear it all from me, who fully declare it!

37. 'The son of a *Bróhmì, or wife by the first ceremony*, redeems from sin, if he performs virtuous acts, ten 'ancestors, ten descendants, and himself the twenty-'first person.

38. 'A son, born of a wife by the *Daiva* nuptials, 'redeems seven and seven in higher and lower degrees; 'of a wife by the *A'rsha*, three and three; of a wife 'by the *Prajápatya*, six and six.

39. 'By four marriages, the *Brahma* and so forth, in 'direct order, or born sons illumined by the *Veda*, '*learned men*, beloved by the learned.

40. 'Adorned with beauty, and with the quality of 'goodness, wealthy, famed, amply gratified with lawful 'enjoyments, performing all duties, and living a hun-'dred years:

41. 'But in the other *four* base marriages, which 'remain, are produced sons acting cruelly, speaking 'falsely, abhorring the *Veda*, and the duties prescribed 'in it.

42. 'From the blameless nuptial rites of men spring 'a blameless progeny; from the reprehensible, a repre-'hensible offspring: let mankind, therefore, studiously 'avoid the culpable forms *of marriage*.

43. 'The ceremony of joining hands is appointed 'for those, who marry women of their own class; but, 'with women of a different class, the following nuptial 'ceremonies are to be observed:

44. 'By the *Kshatriyà* on her marriage with a *Bráhman*, an arrow must be held in her hand; by a '*Vaisyà* woman with a bridegroom *of the sacerdotal or military class*, a whip; *and* by a *Súdrà* bride, '*marrying a priest, a soldier, or a merchant*, must 'be held the skirt of a mantle.

45. 'Let the husband approach his wife in due season, *that is, at the time fit for pregnancy*; let him be 'constantly satisfied with her alone; but, except on the 'forbidden days of the moon, he may approach her, 'being affectionately disposed, *even out of due season*, 'with a desire of conjugal intercourse.

46. 'Sixteen days and nights in each month, with 'four distinct days neglected by the virtuous, are 'called the natural season of women:

47. 'Of those sixteen, the four first, the eleventh, 'and the thirteenth, are reprehended: the ten remaining nights are approved.

48. 'Some say, that on the even nights are conceived sons; on the odd nights daughters; therefore 'let the man, who wishes for a son, approach his wife 'in due season on the even nights;

49. 'But a boy is in truth produced by the greater 'quantity of the male strength; and a girl by a 'greater quantity of the female; by equality an hermaphrodite, or a boy and a girl; by weakness or deficiency, is occasioned a failure of conception.

50. 'He, who avoids conjugal embraces on the six 'reprehended nights and on eight others, is equal in 'chastity to a *Brahmachárì*, in whichever of the *two* '*next* orders he may live.

51. 'Let no father, who knows the law, receive a 'gratuity, however small, for giving his daughter in

'marriage; since the man, who, through avarice, takes 'a gratuity *for that purpose*, is a seller of his offspring.

52. 'Whatever male relations, through delusion of 'mind, take possession of a woman's property, be it only 'her carriages or her clothes, such offenders will sink 'to a region of torment.

53. 'Some say that the bull and cow *given* in the 'nuptial ceremony of the *Rihsis*, are a bribe to the 'father; but this is untrue; a bribe *indeed*, whether 'large or small, is an actual sale of *the daughter*.

54. 'When money or goods are given to damsels, 'whose kinsmen receive them not for their own use, it 'is no sale: it is merely a token of courtesy and affec'tion to the brides.

55. 'Married women must be honored and adorned 'by their fathers and brethren, by their husbands, and 'by the brethren of their husbands, if they seek abund'ant prosperity.

56. 'Where females are honored, there the deities 'are pleased; but where they are dishonored, there all 'religious acts become fruitless.

57. 'Where female relations are made miserable, the 'family of him who makes them so, very soon wholly 'perishes; but, where they are not unhappy, the family 'always increases.

58. 'On whatever houses the women of a family, not 'being duly honored, pronounce an imprecation, those 'houses, with all that belong to them, utterly perish, 'as if destroyed by a sacrifice for the death of an 'enemy.

59. 'Let those women, therefore, be continually sup'plied with ornaments, apparel and food, at festivals 'and at jubilees, by men desirous of wealth.

60. 'In whatever family the husband is contented 'with his wife, and the wife with her husband, in that 'house will fortune be assuredly permanent.

61. 'Certainly, if the wife be not elegantly attired, 'she will not exhilarate her husband; and if her lord 'want hilarity, offspring will not be produced.

62. 'A wife being gaily adorned, her whole house 'is embellished; but, if she be destitute of ornament, 'all will be deprived of decoration.

63. 'By culpable marriages, by omission of pre-'scribed ceremonies, by neglect of reading the *Veda*, 'and by irreverence toward a *Bráhman*, great families 'are sunk to a low state:

64. 'So they are by practising manual arts, by *lending* '*at interest and other* pecuniary transactions, by beget-'ting children on *Súdràs* only, by traffic in kine, 'horses, and carriages, by agriculture and by attendance 'on a king.

65. 'By sacrificing for such as have no right to sa-'crifice, and by denying a future compensation for 'good works, great families, being deprived of sacred 'knowledge, are quickly destroyed.

66. 'But families, enriched by a knowledge of the '*Veda*, though possessing little temporal wealth, are 'numbered among the great, and acquire exalted fame.

67. 'Let the house-keeper perform domestic reli-'gious rites, with the nuptial fire, according to law, and 'the ceremonies of the five great sacraments, and the 'several acts which must day by day be performed.

68. 'A house-keeper has five places of slaughter, *or* '*where small living creatures may be slain*; his kitchen-'hearth, his grindstone, his broom, his pestle and mor-

'tar, his water-pot; by using which, he becomes in 'bondage to sin:

69. 'For the sake of expiating *offences committed* '*ignorantly* in those places *mentioned* in order, the five 'great sacraments were appointed by eminent ages to 'be performed each day by such as keep house.

70. 'Teaching and studying the scripture is the sa'crament of the *Veda;* offering cakes and water, the 'sacrament of the manes; an oblation to fire, the sacra'ment of the deities; giving rice or other food to liv'ing creatures, the sacrament of spirits; receiving guests 'with honor, the sacrament of men:

71. 'Whoever omits not those five great ceremonies, 'if he have ability *to perform them,* is untainted by the 'sins of the *five* slaughtering-places, even though he 'constantly reside at home;

72. 'But whoever cherishes not five orders of beings, '*namely,* the deities; those, who demand hospitality; 'those, whom he ought by law to maintain; his de'parted forefathers; and himself; that man lives not 'even though he breathe.

73. 'Some call the five sacraments *ahuta* and *huta,* '*prahuta, bráhmya-huta* and *prásita:*

74. '*Ahuta,* or unoffered, is divine study; *huta,* or 'offered, is the oblation to fire; *prahuta,* or well offer'ed, is the food given to spirits; *bráhmya-huta,* is res'pect shown to twice-born guests; and *prásita,* or well 'eaten, is the offering of rice or water to the manes of 'ancestors.

75. 'Let every man in this second order employ 'himself daily in reading the scripture, and in perform'ing the sacrament of the gods; for, being employed 'in the sacrament of deities, he supports this whole ani'mal and vegetable world;

76. 'Since his oblation of clarified butter, duly cast 'into the flame, ascends *in smoke* to the sun; from the 'sun *it* falls *in* rain; from rain comes vegetable food; 'and from *such* food animals *derive their subsistence.*

77. 'As all creatures subsist by receiving support 'from air, thus all orders of men exist by receiving 'support from house-keepers;

78. 'And since men of the three other orders are 'each day nourished by them with divine learning and 'with food, a house-keeper is for this reason of the 'most eminent order:

79. 'That order, therefore, must be constantly sus'tained with great care by the man who seeks unperish'able bliss in heaven, and in this world pleasurable 'sensations; an order which cannot be sustained by men 'with uncontrolled organs.

80. 'The divine sages, the manes, the gods, the spi'rits, and guests, pray for benefits to masters of fami'lies; let these honors, therefore, be done to them by 'the house-keeper who knows his duty:

81. 'Let him honor the sages by studying the *Veda:* 'the gods, by oblations to fire ordained by law; the 'manes, by pious obsequies; men by supplying them 'with food; and spirits, by gifts to all animated crea'tures.

82. 'Each day let him perform a *śráddha* with boil'ed rice and the like, or with water, or with milk, roots, 'and fruit; for thus he obtains favor from departed 'progenitors.

83 'He may entertain one *Bráhman* in that sacra'ment among the five, which is performed for the '*Pitris;* but, at the oblation to all the Gods, let him 'not invite even a single priest.

84. 'In his domestic fire for dressing the food of all 'the gods, after the prescribed ceremony, let a *Bráhman* make an oblation each day to these *following* divinities;

85. 'First to AGNI, god of fire, and to the lunar 'god, severally; then, to both of them at once; next 'to the assembled gods; and afterwards, to DHANWANTARI, god of medicine;

86. 'To KUHU', goddess of the day, when the new 'moon is discernible; to ANUMATI, goddess of the day, 'after the opposition; to PRA'JAPATI, or the Lord of 'Creatures; to DYA'VA' and PRITHIWI', goddesses of sky 'and earth; and lastly, to the fire of the good sacrifice.

87. 'Having thus, with fixed attention, offered clarified butter in all quarters, proceeding *from the east* 'in a southern direction, to INDRA, YAMA, VARUNA, and 'the god SO'MA, let him offer his gift to animated 'creatures.

88. '*Saying*, "I salute the *Maruts*," or *Winds*, let 'him throw dressed rice near the door; *saying*, "I salute the water-gods," in water; and on his pestle and 'mortar, *saying*, "I salute the gods of large trees."

89. 'Let him do the like *in the north-east, or* near 'his pillow, to SRI', the goddess of abundance; *in the* '*south-west, or* at the foot *of his bed,* to the propitious 'goddess BHADRAKA'LI'; in the centre of his mansion, 'to BRAHMA' and his household god;

90. 'To all the gods assembled, let him throw up his 'oblation in the open air; by day, to the spirits who 'walk in light; and by night, to those who walk in 'darkness:

91. 'In the building on his house-top, *or behind his* '*back*, let him cast his oblation for the welfare of all

'creatures; and what remains let him give to the *Pitris* 'with his face toward the south:

92. 'The share of dogs, of outcasts, of dog-feeders, 'of sinful men, punished with elephantiasis or consump-'tion, of crows, and of reptiles, let him drop on the 'ground by little and little.

93. 'A *Bráhman*, who thus each day shall honor all 'beings, will go to the highest region in a straight path, 'in an irradiated form.

94. 'When he has performed his duty of making 'oblations, let him cause his guest to take food be-'fore himself; and let him give a portion of rice, 'as the law ordains, to the mendicant who studies the '*Veda*:

95. 'Whatever fruit shall be obtained by that stu-'dent, as the reward of his virtue, when he shall have 'given a cow to his preceptor, according to law, the 'like reward to virtue shall be obtained by the twice-'born house-keeper, when he has given a mouthful of 'rice *to the religious mendicant*.

96. 'To a *Bráhman* who knows the true principle 'of the *Veda*, let him present a portion of rice, or a pot 'of water, garnished with fruit and flowers, due cere-'monies having preceded:

97. 'Shares of oblations to the gods, or to the manes, 'utterly perish, when presented, through delusion of 'mind, by men regardless of duty, to such ignorant '*Bráhmans* as are mere ashes;

98. 'But an offering in the fire of a sacerdotal mouth, 'which richly blazes with true knowledge and piety, 'will release the giver from distress, and even from 'deadly sin.

99. 'To the guest who comes of his own accord, let

'him offer a seat and water, with such food as he is able 'to prepare, after the due rites of courtesy.

100. 'A *Bráhman* coming as a guest, and not received with just honor, takes to himself all the 'reward of the house-keeper's former virtue, even 'though he had been so temperate as to live on the 'gleanings of harvests, and so pious as to make oblations in five distinct fires.

101. 'Grass and earth to sit on, water to wash the 'feet, and, fourthly, affectionate speech are at no time 'deficient in the mansions of the good, *although they* '*may be indigent.*

102. 'A *Bráhman,* staying but one night as a guest, 'is called an *atit'hi;* since continuing so short a time, 'he is not even a sojourner for a whole *tit'hi*, or *day of* '*the moon.*

103. 'The house-keeper must not consider as an '*atit'hi* a mere visitor of the same town, or a *Bráh*-'*man,* who attends him on business, even though he 'come to the house where his wife dwells, and where 'his fires are kindled.

104. 'Should any house-keepers be so senseless, as 'to seek, on pretence of being guests, the food of 'others, they would fall after death, by reason of that 'baseness, to the condition of cattle belonging to the 'giver of such food.

105. 'No guest must be dismissed in the evening by 'a house-keeper; he is sent by the retiring sun; and, 'whether he come on fit season or unseasonably, he 'must not sojourn in the house without entertainment.

106. 'Let not himself eat any delicate food, without 'asking his guest to partake of it: the satisfaction of 'a guest will assuredly bring the house-keeper wealth, 'reputation, long life, and a place in heaven.

107. 'To the highest guests in the best form, to the 'lowest in the worst, to the equal, equally, let him 'offer seats, resting places, couches; giving them pro- 'portionable attendance, when they depart; and honor, 'as long as they stay.

108. 'Should another guest arrive, when the obla- 'tion to all the gods is concluded, for him also let the 'house-keeper prepare food, according to his ability; 'but let him not repeat his offerings to animated beings.

109. 'Let no *Bráhman* guest proclaim his family and 'ancestry for the sake of an entertainment; since he, 'who thus proclaims them, is called by the wise a '*vántásí*, or foul-feeding demon.

110. 'A military man is not denominated a guest in 'the house of a *Bráhman;* nor a man of the commer- 'cial or servile class; nor his familiar friend; nor his 'paternal kinsman; nor his preceptor:

111. 'But if a warrior come to his house in the 'form of a guest, let food be prepared for him, accord- 'ing to his desire, after the before-mentioned *Bráh- 'mans* have eaten.

112. 'Even to a merchant or a laborer, approach- 'ing his house in the manner of guests, let him give 'food, showing marks of benevolence at the same time 'with his domestics:

113. 'To others, as familiar friends, and the rest 'before-named, who come with affection to his place of 'abode, let him serve a repast at the same time with his 'wife *and himself,* having amply provided it according 'to his best means.

114. 'To a bride, and to a damsel, to the sick, and 'to pregnant women, let him give food, even before 'his guests, without hesitation.

115. 'The idiot, who first eats his own mess, without 'having presented food to the persons just enumerated, 'knows not, while he crams, that he will himself be 'food after death for bandogs and vultures.

116. 'After the repast of the *Bráhman* guest, of his 'kinsmen, and his domestics, the married couple may 'eat what remains untouched.

117. 'The house-keeper, having honored spirits, holy 'sages, men, progenitors, and household gods, may 'feed on what remains after those oblations.

118. 'He, who eats what has been dressed for him-'self only, eats nothing but sin: a repast on what re-'mains after the sacrament is called the banquet of the 'good.

119. 'After a year from the reception of a visitor, 'let the house-keeper again honor a king, a sacrificer, 'a student returned from his preceptor, a son-in-law, 'a father-in-law, and a maternal uncle, with a *madhu-'perka, or present of honey, curds, and fruit.*

120. 'A king or a *Bráhman* arriving at the celebra-'tion of the sacrament, are to be honored with a *mad-'huperka*; but not, if the sacrament be over: this is a 'settled rule.

121. 'In the evening let the wife make an offering 'of the dressed food, but without pronouncing any text 'of the *Veda*: one oblation to the assembled gods, 'thence named *Vaiswadéva,* is ordained both for even-'ing and morning.

122. 'From month to month, on the dark day of 'the moon, let a twice-born man, having finished the 'daily sacrament of the *Pitris,* and his fire being still 'blazing, perform the solemn *sráddha,* called *pindán-'wáhárya.*

123. 'Sages have distinguished the monthly *sráddha* 'by the title of *anwáhárya*, or *after eaten*, that is, eaten 'after the *pinda*, or ball of rice; and it must be performed with extreme care, and with flesh-meat in the 'best condition.

124. 'What *Bráhmans* must be entertained at that 'ceremony, and who must be excepted, how many are 'to be fed, and with what sorts of food, on all those 'articles, without omission, I will fully discourse.

125. 'At the *sraddha* of the gods he may entertain 'two *Bráhmans*; at that of his father, paternal grand-'father, and paternal great-grandfather, three; or one 'only at that of the gods, and one at that for his three 'paternal ancestors: though he abound in wealth, 'let him not be solicitous to entertain a large com-'pany.

126. 'A large company destroys these five advan-'tages; reverence to priests, propriety of time and 'place, purity, and the acquisition of virtuous *Bráh-'mans*: let him not therefore, endeavor to feed a su-'perfluous number.

127. 'This act of due honor to departed souls, on the 'dark day of the moon, is famed by the appellation of '*pitrya*, or ancestral: the legal ceremony, in honor of 'departed spirits, rewards with continual fruit, a man 'engaged in such obsequies.

128. 'Oblations to the gods and to ancestors should 'be given to a most reverend *Bráhman*, perfectly con-'versant with the *Veda*; since what is given to him 'produces the greatest reward.

129. 'By entertaining one learned man at the obla-'tion to the gods and at that to ancestors, he gains 'more exalted fruit than by feeding a multitude, who 'know not the holy texts.

130. 'Let him inquire into the ancestry, even in a 'remote degree, of a *Brahman*, who has advanced to 'the end of the *Veda*: such a man, if sprung from good 'men, is a fit partaker of oblations to gods and to an'cestors; such a man may justly be called an *atit'hi*, 'or guest.

131. 'Surely, though a million of men, unlearned 'in holy texts, were to receive food, yet a single man, 'learned in scripture, and fully satisfied with his en'tertainment, would be of more value than all of them 'together.

132. 'Food, consecrated to the gods and the manes, 'must be presented to a theologian of eminent learn'ing; for certainly, when hands are smeared with blood, 'they cannot be cleaned with blood only, *nor can sin 'be removed by the company of sinners.*

133. 'As many mouthsful as an unlearned man shall 'swallow at an oblation to the gods and to ancestors, 'so many *redhot* iron balls must the giver of the *ṣrad'dha* swallow in the next world.

134. 'Some *Bráhmans* are intent on scriptural know'ledge; others, on austere devotion; some are intent 'both on religious austerity and on the study of the '*Veda*; others on the performance of sacred rites:

135. 'Oblations to the manes of ancestors ought to 'be placed with care before such as are intent on sacred 'learning: but offerings to the gods may be presented, 'with due ceremonies, to *Bráhmans* of all the four des'criptions.

136. 'There may be a *Bráhman*, whose father had 'not studied the scripture, though the son has advanced 'to the end of the *Veda*; or there may be one, whose 'son has not read the *Veda*, though the father had tra'velled to the end of it:

137. 'Of those two let mankind consider him as the 'superior, whose father had studied the scripture, yet 'for the sake of performing rites with holy texts, the 'other is worthy of honor.

138. 'Let no man, at the prescribed obsequies, give 'food to an intimate friend; since advantage to a friend 'must be procured by gifts of different property; to 'that *Bráhman* let the performer of a *ṣráddha* give 'food, whom he considers neither as a friend nor as a 'foe.

139. 'For him, whose obsequies and offerings of cla-'rified butter are provided chiefly through friendship, 'no fruit is reserved in the next life, on account either 'of his obsequies or of his offerings.

140. 'The man, who, through delusion of intellect, 'forms temporal connexions by obsequies, is excluded 'from heavenly mansions, as a giver of the *ṣráddha* 'for the sake of friendship, and the meanest of twice-'born men:

141. 'Such a convivial present, by men of the three 'highest classes, is called the gift of *Pisáchas,* and 'remains fixed here below, like a blind cow in one 'stall.

142. 'As a husbandman, having sown seed in a bar-'ren soil, reaps no grain, thus a performer of holy rites, 'having given clarified butter to an unlearned *Bráhman,* 'attains no reward in heaven;

143. 'But a present made, as the law ordains, to a 'learned theologian, renders both the giver and the 'receiver partakers of good fruits in this world and in 'the next.

144. 'If no learned *Bráhman,* be at hand, he may at 'his pleasure invite a friend to the *ṣráddha,* but not a

'foe, be he ever so learned ; since the oblation, being 'eaten by a foe, loses all fruit in the life to come.

145. 'With great care let him give food at the *ṣrád-* '*dha* to a priest, who has gone through the scripture, 'but has chiefly studied the *Rig Veda ;* to one, who has 'read all the branches, but principally those of the '*Yajur ;* or to one who has finished the whole, with 'particular attention to the *Sáma :*

146. 'Of that man whose oblation has been eaten, 'after due honors, by any one of those three *Bráh-* '*mans,* the ancestors are constantly satisfied as high as 'the seventh person, *or to the sixth degree.*

147. 'This is the chief rule in offering the *ṣráddha* 'to the gods and to ancestors ; but the following may 'be considered as a subsidiary rule, *where no such* '*learned priests can be found,* and is ever observed by 'good men :

148. 'Let him entertain his maternal grandfather, his 'maternal uncle, the son of his sister, the father of his 'wife, the spiritual guide, the son of his daughter, or 'her husband, his maternal cousin, his officiating priest, 'or the performer of his sacrifice.

149. 'For an oblation to the gods, let not the man, 'who knows what is law, scrupulously inquire into the 'parentage of a *Bráhman ;* but for a prepared oblation 'to ancestors let him examine it with strict care.

150. 'Those *Bráhmans,* who have committed any *in-* '*ferior* theft *or any of the higher crimes,* who are de- 'prived of virility, or who profess a disbelief in a future 'state, MANU has pronounced unworthy of honor at a '*ṣráddha* to the gods or to ancestors.

151. 'To a student in theology, who has not read 'the *Veda,* to a man *punished for past crimes by being*

'born without a prepuce, to a gamester, and to such as 'perform many sacrifices for other men, let him never 'give food at the sacred obsequies.

152. 'Physicians, image-worshippers for gain, sellers 'of meat, and such as live by low traffic, must be 'shunned in oblations both to the deities and to pro-'genitors.

153. 'A public servant of the whole town, or of the 'prince, a man with whitlows on his nails, or with 'black-yellow teeth, an opposer of his preceptor, a de-'serter of the sacred fire, and an usurer,

154. 'A phthisical man, a feeder of cattle, one omit-'ting the five great sacraments, a contemner of *Bráh-mans*, a younger brother married before the elder, an 'elder brother not married before the younger, and a 'man who subsists by the wealth of many relations,

155. 'A dancer, one who has violated the rule of 'chastity in the first or fourth order, the husband of a '*Súdrà*, the son of a twice-married woman, a man who 'has lost one eye, and a husband in whose house an 'adulterer dwells,

156. 'One who teaches the *Veda* for wages, and one 'who gives wages to such a teacher, the pupil of a *Sú-dra*, and the *Súdra* preceptor, a rude speaker, and the 'son of an adulteress, born either before or after the 'death of the husband,

157. 'A forsaker, without just cause, of his mother, 'father or preceptor, and a man who forms a connexion, 'either by scriptural or connubial affinity, with great 'sinners,

'158. 'A house-burner, a giver of poison, an eater 'of food offered by the son of an adulteress, a seller of 'the moon-plant *(a species of mountain-rue)*, a naviga-

'tor of the ocean, a poetical encomiast, an oilman, and 'a suborner of perjury,

159. 'A wrangler with his father, an employer of 'gamesters for his own benefit, a drinker of intoxicating 'spirits, a man punished for sin with elephantiasis, one 'of evil repute, a cheat, and a seller of liquids,

160. 'A maker of bows and arrows, the husband of 'a younger sister married before the elder *of the whole 'blood*, an injurer of his friend, the keeper of a gam-'ing-house, and a father instructed in the *Veda* by his 'own son,

161. 'An epileptic person, who has the erysipe-'las or the leprosy, a common informer, a lunatic, 'a blind man, and a despiser of scripture, must all be 'shunned,

162. 'A tamer of elephants, bulls, horses, or camels, 'a man who subsists by astrology, a keeper of birds, 'and one who teaches the use of arms,

163. 'He, who diverts water-courses, and he, who 'is gratified by obstructing them, he, who builds houses 'for gain, a messenger, and a planter of trees *for pay*,

164. 'A breeder of sporting dogs, a falconer, a seduc-'er of damsels, a man delighting in mischief, a *Bráh-'man* living as a *Súdra*, a sacrificer to the inferior 'gods only,

165. 'He, who observes not approved customs, and 'he, who regards not prescribed duties, a constant 'importunate asker of favors, he, who supports him-'self by tillage, a club-footed man, and one despised 'by the virtuous,

166. 'A shepherd, a keeper of buffalos, the husband 'of a twice-married woman, and the remover of dead 'bodies *for pay*, are to be avoided with great care.

167. 'Those lowest of *Bráhmans,* whose manners 'are contemptible, who are not admissible into com-'pany at a repast, an exalted and learned priest must 'avoid at both *sráddhas.*

168. 'A *Bráhman* unlearned in holy writ, is extin-'guished in an instant like a fire of dry grass: to him 'the oblation must not be given; for the clarified butter 'must not be poured on ashes.

169. 'What retribution is prepared in the next life 'for the giver of food to men inadmissible into com-'pany, at the *ṣráddha* to the gods and to ancestors, 'I will now declare without omission.

170. On that food, which has been given to *Bráh-'mans* who have violated the rules of their order, to 'the younger brother married before the elder, and the '*Rakshases* eagerly feast.

171. 'He, who makes a marriage contract with the 'connubial fire, while his elder brother continues un-'married, is called a *parivéttri;* and the elder brother 'a *parivitti:*

172. 'The *parivéttri,* the *parivitti,* the damsel thus 'wedded, the giver of her in wedlock, and, fifthly, the 'performer of the nuptial sacrifice, all sink to a region 'of torment.

173. 'He, who lasciviously dallies with the widow 'of his deceased brother, though she be legally mar-'ried to him, is denominated the husband of a *di-'dhishú.*

174. 'Two sons, named a *kunda* and a *gólaka,* are 'born in adultery; the *kunda,* while the husband is 'alive, and the *gólaka,* when the husband is dead:

175. 'Those animals begotten by adulterers, destroy, 'both in this world and in the next, the food present-

'ed to them by such as make oblations to the gods or 'to the manes.

176. 'The foolish giver of a *śráddha* loses, in a future life, the fruit of as many admissible guests, as a '*thief or the like* person, inadmissible into company, 'might be able to see.

177. 'A blind man placed where one with eyes 'might have seen, destroys the reward of ninety; he, 'who has lost one eye, of sixty; a leper, of an hundred; 'one punished with elephantiasis, of a thousand.

178. 'Of the gift at a *śráddha*, to as many *Bráhmans*, as a sacrificer for a *Súdra* might be able to 'touch on the body, the fruit is lost to the giver, *if he 'invite such a wretch*;

179. 'And if a *Bráhman* who knows the *Veda*, 'receive through covetousness a present from such a 'sacrificer, he speedily sinks to perdition, like a figure 'of unburnt clay in water.

180. 'Food given to a seller of the moon-plant, becomes ordure in another world; to a physician purulent blood; *and the giver will be a reptile bred in them*; 'if offered to an image-worshipper, it is thrown away; 'if to an usurer, infamous.

181. 'That which is given to a trader, endures neither in this life nor in the next, and that bestowed on 'a *Bráhman*, who has married a widow, resembles clarified butter poured on ashes as an oblation to fire.

182. 'That food, which is given to other base, inadmissible men, before mentioned, the wise have pronounced to be no more than animal oil, blood, flesh, 'skin, and bones.

183. 'Now learn comprehensively, by what *Bráhmans* a company may be purified, when it has been

'defiled by inadmissible persons; *Bráhmans,* the chief 'of their class, the purifiers of every assembly.

184. 'Those priests must be considered as the purifiers 'of a company who are most learned in all the *Vedas* 'and in all their *Angas,* together with their descendants 'who have read the whole scripture:

185. 'A priest learned in a principal part of the '*Yajur Veda;* one who keeps the five fires constantly 'burning; one skilled in a principal part of the *Rig* '*Veda;* one who explains the six *Vedángas;* the son of a '*Bráhmì,* or woman married by the *Bráhma* ceremony; 'and one who chants the principal *Sáman;*

186. 'One who propounds the sense of the *Vedas,* 'which he learnt from his preceptor, a student who has 'given a thousand *cows for pious uses,* and a *Bráhman* 'a hundred years old, must all be considered as the 'purifiers of a party at a *ṣraddha.*

187. 'On the day before the sacred obsequies, or on 'the very day when they are prepared, let the performer 'of them invite, with due honor, such *Bráhmans* as 'have been mentioned; *usually* one superior, who has 'three inferior to him.

188. 'The *Bráhman,* who has been invited to a '*ṣráddha* for departed ancestors, must be continually 'abstemious; he must not even read the *Vedas;* and 'he, who performs the ceremony, must act in the same 'manner.

189. 'Departed ancestors, no doubt, are attendant 'on such invited *Bráhmans;* hovering around them like 'pure spirits, and sitting by them, when they are seated.

190. 'The priest, who having been duly invited to a '*ṣráddha,* breaks the appointment, commits a grievous 'offence, and, in his next birth, becomes a hog.

191. He, who caresses a *Súdrà* woman, after he has 'been invited to sacred obsequies, takes on himself all 'the sin, that has been committed by the giver of the 'repast.

192. 'The *Pitris* or *great progenitors*, are free from 'wrath, intent on purity, ever exempt from sensual 'passions, endued with exalted qualities: they are 'primeval divinities, who have laid arms aside.

193. 'Hear now completely, from whom they sprang; 'who they are; by whom, and by what ceremonies 'they are to be honored.

194. 'The sons of MARI'CHI and of all the other '*Rishis*, who were the offspring of MANU, son of BRAH-'MA', are called the companies of *Pitris*, or *forefathers*.

195. 'The *Sómasads*, who sprang from VIRA'J, are 'declared to be the ancestors of the *Sádhyas*; and the '*Agnishwáttas*, who are famed among created beings 'as the children of MARI'CHI, to be the progenitors of 'the *Devas*.

196. 'Of the *Daityas*, the *Dánavas*, the *Yakshas*, 'the *Gandharvas*, the *Uragas*, or *Serpents*, the *Rak-'shases*, the *Garudas*, and the *Kinnaras*, the ancestors 'are *Barhishads* descended from ATRI.

197. 'Of *Bráhmans*, those named *Sómapas*; of '*Kshatriyas*, the *Havishmats*; of *Vaisyas*, those called '*A'jyapas*; of *Súdras*, the *Sukálins*:

198. 'The *Sómapas* descended from *Me*, BHRIGU; 'the *Havishmats*, from ANGIRAS; the *A'jyapas*, from 'PULASTYA; the *Sukálins*, from VASISHT'HA.

199. 'Those who are, and those who are not, con-'sumable by fire, called *Agnidagdhas*, and *Anagni-'daghas*, the *Kavyas*, the *Barhishads*, the *Agnishwáttas*,

'and the *Saumyas,* let mankind consider as the chief 'progenitors of *Bráhmans.*

200. 'Of those just enumerated, who are generally 'reputed the principal tribes of *Pitris,* the sons and 'grandsons indefinitely, are also in this world consider-'ed as great progenitors.

201. 'From the *Rishis* come the *Pitris,* or patriarchs; 'from the *Pitris,* both *Devas* and *Dánavas;* from the '*Devas,* this whole world of animals and vegetables, 'in due order.

202. 'Mere water, offered with faith to the progeni-'tors of men, in vessels of silver, or adorned with sil-'ver, proves the source of incorruption.

203. 'An oblation by *Bráhmans* to their ancestors 'transcends an oblation to the deities; because that to 'the deities is considered as the opening and completion 'of that to ancestors.

204. 'As a preservative of the oblation to the patri-'archs, let the house-keeper begin with an offering to 'the gods; for the *Rakshases* rend in pieces an oblation 'which has no such preservative.

205. 'Let an offering to the gods be made at the 'beginning and end of the *sraddha:* it must not begin 'and end with an offering to ancestors; for he, who 'begins and ends it with an oblation to the *Pitris,* 'quickly perishes with his progeny.

206. 'Let the *Bráhman* smear with cow-dung a pu-'rified and sequestered piece of ground; and let him, 'with great care, select a place with a declivity toward 'the south:

207. 'The divine manes are always pleased with an 'oblation in empty glades, naturally clean, on the banks 'of rivers and in solitary spots.

208. 'Having duly made an ablution with water, let 'him place the invited *Bráhmans*, who have also per-'formed their ablutions, one by one, on allotted seats 'purified with *kuṣa*-grass.

209. 'When he has placed them with reverence on 'their seats, let him honor them, (having first honored 'the gods) with fragrant garlands and sweet odours.

210. 'Having brought water for them with *kuṣa*-'grass and *tila*, let the *Bráhman*, with the *Brahmans*, 'pour the oblation, as the law directs, on the holy fire.

211. 'First, as it is ordained, having satisfied AGNI, 'SÓMA, and YAMA, with clarified butter, let him proceed 'to satisfy the manes of his progenitors.

212. 'If he have no consecrated fire, *as if he be yet* '*unmarried, or his wife be just deceased*, let him drop 'the oblation into the hand of a *Bráhman*; since, what 'fire is, even such is a *Bráhman*; as priests, who know 'the *Veda* declare:

213. 'Holy sages call the chief of the twice-born 'the gods of obsequies, free from wrath, with placid as-'pects, of a primeval race, employed in the advance-'ment of human creatures.

214. 'Having walked in order from east to south, 'and thrown into the fire all the ingredients of his ob-'lation, let him sprinkle water on the ground with his 'right hand.

215. 'From the remainder of the clarified butter 'having formed three balls of rice, let him offer them, 'with fixed attention, in the same manner as the water, 'his face being turned to the south:

216. 'Then having offered those balls, after due 'ceremonies and with an attentive mind, *to the manes* '*of his father, his paternal grandfather, and great*

'*grandfather*, let him wipe the same hand with the 'roots of *kuṣa*, which he had before used, for the sake 'of *his paternal ancestors in the fourth, fifth, and sixth* '*degrees, who are* the partakers of the rice and clarified 'butter *thus* wiped off.

217. 'Having made an ablution, returning toward 'the north, and thrice suppressing his breath slowly, 'let him salute the gods of the six seasons, and the '*Pitris* also, being well acquainted with proper texts 'of the *Veda*.

218. 'Whatever water remains in his ewer, let him 'carry back deliberately near the cakes of rice; and, 'with fixed attention, let him smell those cakes, in 'order as they were offered:

219. 'Then, taking a small portion of the cakes in 'order, let him first, as the law directs, cause the *Brah*-'*mans* to eat of them, while they are seated.

220. 'If his father be alive, let him offer the *ṣráddha* 'to his ancestors in *three* higher degrees; or let him 'cause his own father to eat, as a *Bráhman* at the ob-'sequies:

221. 'Should his father be dead, and his grandfather 'living, let him, in celebrating the name of his father, '*that is, in performing obsequies to him*, celebrate also 'his paternal great grandfather;

222. 'Either the paternal grandfather may partake 'of the *ṣraddha* (so has MANU declared) or the grand-'son, authorized by him, may perform the ceremony at 'his discretion.

223. 'Having poured water, with *kuṣa*-grass and *tila*, 'into the hands of the *Bráhmans*, let him give them 'the upper part of the cakes, saying "*Swadhá* to the 'manes!"

224. 'Next, having himself brought with both hands, 'a vessel full of rice, let him, still meditating on the '*Pitris*, place it before the *Bráhmans* without precipi'tation.

225. 'Rice taken up, but not supported with both 'hands, the malevolent *Asuras* quickly rend in pieces.

226. 'Broths, potherbs, and other eatables accom'panying the rice, together with milk and curds, clari'fied butter and honey, let him first place on the ground, 'after he has made an ablution; and let his mind be 'intent on no other object:

227. 'Let him add spiced puddings, and milky messes 'of various sorts, roots of herbs and ripe fruits, savoury 'meats, and sweet smelling drinks.

228. 'Then being duly purified, and with perfect pre'sence of mind, let him take up all the dishes, one by 'one, and present them in order to *Bráhmans*, pro'claiming their qualities.

229. 'Let him at no time drop a tear; let him on no 'account be angry; let him say nothing false; let him 'not touch the eatables with his foot; let him not even 'shake the dishes:

230. 'A tear sends the messes to restless ghosts; 'anger, to foes; falsehood, to dogs; contact with his 'foot, to demons; agitation, to sinners.

231. 'Whatever is agreeable to the *Bráhmans*, let 'him give without envy; and let him discourse on the 'attributes of God: such discourse is expected by the 'manes.

232. 'At the obsequies to ancestors, he must let the '*Bráhmans* hear passages from the *Veda*, from the codes 'of law, from moral tales, from heroic poems, from the '*Puránas*, and from theological texts.

233. 'Himself being delighted, let him give delight 'to the *Bráhmans*, and invite them to eat of the provi'sions by little and little; attracting them often with 'the dressed rice and other eatables, and mentioning 'their good properties.

234. 'To the son of his daughter, though a student 'in theology, let him carefully give food at the *ṣraddha*; 'offering him a blanket *from Nepàl* as his seat, and 'sprinkling the ground with *tila*.

235. 'Three things are held pure at such obsequies, 'the daughter's son, the *Nepàl* blanket, and the *tila*; 'and three things are praised in it by the wise, clean'liness, freedom from wrath, and want of precipitate 'haste.

236. 'Let all the dressed food be very hot; and let 'the *Bráhmans* eat it in silence; nor let them declare 'the qualities of the food, even though asked by the 'giver.

237. 'As long as the messes continue warm, as 'long as they eat in silence, as long as the qualities of 'the food are not declared by them, so long the manes 'feast on it.

238. 'What a *Bráhman* eats with his head covered, 'what he eats with his face to the south, what he eats 'with sandals on his feet, the demons assuredly devour.

239. 'Let not a *Chandála*, a town-boar, a cock, a 'dog, a woman in her courses, or an eunuch, see the '*Bráhmans* eating:

240. 'That, which any of them sees at the oblation 'to fire, at a solemn donation of cows and gold, at a 'repast given to *Bráhmans*, at holy rites to the gods, 'and at the obsequies to ancestors, produces not the 'intended fruit:

241. 'The boar destroys it by his smell; the cock, 'by the air of his wings; the dog, by the cast of a 'look; the man of the lowest class, by the touch.

242. 'If a lame man, or a man with one eye, or 'a man with a limb defective or redundant, be even 'a servant of the giver, him also let his master remove 'from the place.

243. 'Should another *Bráhman*, or a mendicant, come '*to his house* for food, let him, having obtained permis'sion from the invited *Bráhmans*, entertain the stranger 'to the best of his power.

244. 'Having brought together all the sorts of food, 'as dressed rice and the like, and sprinkling them with 'water, let him place them before the *Bráhmans*, who 'have eaten; dropping some *on the blades of kuṣa-grass*, '*which have been spread* on the ground.

245. 'What remains in the dishes, and what has been 'dropped on the blades of *kuṣa*, must be considered as 'the portion of deceased *Bráhmans*, not girt with the 'sacrificial thread, and of such as have deserted unrea'sonably the women of their own tribe.

246. 'The residue, that has fallen on the ground at 'the *ṣráddha* to the manes, the wise have decided to be 'the share of all the servants, who are not crooked in 'their ways, nor lazy and ill-disposed.

247. 'Before the obsequies to ancestors as far as the 'sixth degree, they must be performed to a *Bráhman* 'recently deceased; but the performer of them must, '*in that case*, give the *ṣráddha* without the ceremony 'to the gods, and offer only one round cake; *and these* '*obsequies for a single ancestor should be annually per*'*formed on the day of his death:*

248. 'When, *afterwards*, the obsequies to ancestors

'as far as the sixth degree, inclusively of him, are performed according to law, then must the offering of cakes be made by the descendants in the manner before ordained *for the monthly ceremonies.*

249. 'That fool, who, having eaten of the *sráddha*, gives the residue of it to a man of the servile class, falls headlong down to the hell, named *Kálasútra.*

250. 'Should the eater of a *sráddha* enter, on the same day, the bed of a seducing woman, his ancestors would sleep for that month on her excrement.

251. 'Having, by the word *swaditam*, asked the *Bráhmans* if they have eaten well, let him give them, being satisfied, water for an ablution, and courteously say to them: "Rest either at home or here."

252. 'Then let the *Bráhmans* address him, saying *swadhá*; for in all ceremonies relating to deceased ancestors, the word *swadha* is the highest benison.

253. 'After that, let him inform those, who have eaten, of the food which remains; and, being instructed by the *Bráhmans*, let him dispose of it, as they may direct.

254. 'At the close of the *sráddha* to his ancestors, he must ask, if the *Bráhmans* are satisfied, by the word *swadita*; after that for his family, by the word *susruta*; after that for his own advancement, by the word *sampanna*; after that, which has been offered to the gods, by the word *ruchita.*

255. 'The afternoon, the *kusa*-grass, the cleansing of the ground, the *tilas*, the liberal gifts of food, the due preparation for the repast, and the company of most exalted *Bráhmans*, are true riches in the obsequies to ancestors.

256. 'The blades of *kusa*, the holy texts, the fore-

'noon, all the oblations, *which will presently be enumerated*, and the purification before-mentioned, are to be 'considered as wealth in the *sráddha* to the gods:

257. 'Such wild grains as are eaten by hermits, milk, 'the juice of the moon-plant, meat untainted, and salt 'unprepared by art, are held things fit, in their own 'nature, for the last mentioned offering.

258. 'Having dismissed the invited *Bráhmans*, keep'ing his mind attentive, and his speech suppressed, 'let him, after an ablution, look toward the south, and 'ask these blessings of the *Pitris:*

259. '"May generous givers abound in our house! 'may the scriptures be studied, and progeny increase, 'in it! may faith never depart from us! and may we 'have much to bestow on the needy!"

260. 'Thus having ended the *sráddha*, let him cause 'a cow, a priest, a kid, or the fire, to devour what 'remains of the cakes; or let him cast them into the 'waters.

261. 'Some make the offering of the round cakes 'after the repast of the *Bráhmans;* some cause the 'birds to eat what remains, or cast it into water or fire.

262. 'Let a lawful wife, ever dutiful to her lord, 'and constantly honoring his ancestors, eat the mid'dlemost of the three cakes, *or that offered to his paternal grandfather*, with due ceremonies, praying for 'offspring:

263. 'So may she bring forth a son, who will be 'long-lived, famed, and strong-minded, wealthy, having 'numerous descendants, endued with the best of quali'ties, and performing all duties religious and civil.

264. 'Then, having washed both his hands and 'sipped water, let him prepare some rice for his pater-

'nal kinsmen; and, having given it to them with due 'reverence, let him prepare food also for his maternal 'relations.

265. 'Let the residue continue in its place, until the '*Bráhmans* have been dismissed; and then let him 'perform the *remaining* domestic sacraments.

266. 'What sort of oblations, given duly to the 'manes, are capable of satisfying them, for a long 'time or for eternity, I will now declare without omis-'sion.

267. 'The ancestors of men are satisfied a whole 'month with *tila*, rice, barley, black lentils or vetches, 'water, roots, and fruit, given with prescribed cere-'monies;

268. 'Two months, with fish; three months, with 'venison; four, with mutton; five, with the flesh of '*such* birds, *as* the twice-born may eat;

'269. 'Six months, with the flesh of kids; seven, 'with that of spotted deer; eight, with that of the 'deer, or antelope, called *ena;* nine with that of the '*ruru:*

270. 'Ten months are they satisfied with the flesh of 'wild boars and wild buffaloes; eleven, with that of '*rabbits or* hares, and of tortoises;

271. 'A whole year with the milk of cows, and food 'made of that milk; from the flesh of the long-eared 'white goat, their satisfaction endures twelve years.

272. 'The potherb *kálasáka*, the fish *mahásalka*, or 'the *diodon*, the flesh of a rhinoceros, or of an iron-co-'lored kid, honey, and all such forest grains as are eaten 'by hermits, are formed for their satisfaction without 'end.

273. 'Whatever pure food, mixed with honey, a man 'offers on the thirteenth day of the moon, in the season 'of rain, and under the lunar asterism *Maghà*, has like- 'wise a ceaseless duration.

274. '"Oh! may that man, *say the manes*, be born 'in our line, who may give us milky food, with honey 'and pure butter, both on the thirteenth of the moon, 'and when the shadow of an elephant falls to the 'east!"

275. 'Whatever a man, endued with strong faith, 'piously offers, as the law has directed, becomes a per- 'petual unperishable gratification to his ancestors in the 'other world.

276. 'The tenth and so forth, except the fourteenth, 'in the dark half of the moon, are the lunar days most 'approved for sacred obsequies: as they *are*, so *are* not 'the others.

277. 'He, who does honor to the manes, on even 'lunar days, and under even lunar stations, enjoys all 'his desires; on odd lunar days, and under odd lunar 'asterisms, he procures an illustrious race.

278. 'As the latter, *or dark*, half of the month sur- 'passes, for the celebration of obsequies, the former, *or* '*bright* half, so the latter half of the day surpasses, '*for the same purpose*, the former half of it.

279. 'The oblation to ancestors must be duly made, 'even to *the conclusion of it with the distribution to* the 'servants (or even to the close of life), in the form 'prescribed, by a *Bráhman* wearing his thread on his 'right shoulder, proceeding from left to right, without 'remissness, and with *kuṣa*-grass in his hand.

280. 'Obsequies must not be performed by night; 'since the night is called *rakshasí*, or *infested by de-*

'*mons;* nor while the sun is rising or setting, nor when 'it has just risen.

281. 'A house-keeper, *unable to give a monthly repast,* may perform obsequies here below, according 'to the sacred ordinance, only thrice a year, in the seasons of *hémanta, grishma,* and *varshà;* but the five 'sacraments he must perform daily.

282. 'The sacrificial oblation at obsequies to ancestors, is ordained to be made in no vulgar fire; nor 'should the monthly *ṣráddha* of that *Bráhman,* who 'keeps a perpetual fire, be made on any day, except on 'that of the conjunction.

283. 'When a twice-born man, having performed his 'ablution, offers a satisfaction to the manes with water 'only, *being unable to give a repast,* he gains by that 'offering all the fruit of a *ṣraddha.*

284. 'The wise call our fathers, *Vasus;* our paternal 'grandfathers, *Rudras;* our paternal great grandfathers, '*Adityas* (that is, *all are to be revered as deities*); and 'to this effect there is a primeval text in the *Veda.*

285. 'Let a man, who is able, continually feed on '*vighasa,* and continually feed on *amrita:* by *vighasa* is 'meant the residue of a repast at obsequies; and by '*amrita,* the residue of a sacrifice to the gods.

286. 'This complete system of rules, for the five 'sacraments and the like, has been declared to you: 'now hear the law for those means of subsistence, which 'the chief of the twice-born may seek.

CHAP. IV.

On Economics; and Private Morals.

---

1. 'Let a *Bráhman*, having dwelt with a preceptor 'during the first quarter of a man's life, pass the second 'quarter of human life in his own house, when he has 'contracted a legal marriage.

2. 'He must live, with no injury, or with the least 'possible injury, to animated beings, by pursuing those 'means of gaining subsistence, which are strictly pre'scribed by law, except in times of distress:

3. 'For the sole purpose of supporting life, let him 'acquire property by those irreproachable occupations, 'which are peculiar to his class, and unattended with 'bodily pain.

4. 'He may live by *rita* and *amrita*, or, *if necessary*, 'by *mrita*, or *pramrita*, or even by *satyánrita*; but never 'let him subsist by *swavritti*:

5. 'By *rita*, must be understood lawful gleaning and 'gathering; by *amrita*, what is given unasked; by '*mrita*, what is asked as alms; tillage is called *pra'mrita*;

6. 'Traffic and money-lending are *satyánrita*; even 'by them, *when he is deeply distressed*, may he support 'life; but service for hire is named *swavritti* or *dog-liv'ing*, and of course he must by all means avoid it.

7. 'He may either store up grain for three years; or 'garner up enough for one year; or collect what may 'last three days; or make no provision for the mor'row.

8. 'Of the four *Bráhmans* keeping house, *who follow* '*those four different modes*, a preference is given to the 'last in order successively; as to him, who most com'pletely by virtue has vanquished the world:

9. 'One of them subsists by all the six means of live'lihood; another by three of them; a third, by two 'only; and a fourth lives barely on continually teach'ing the *Veda*.

10. 'He, who sustains himself by picking up grains 'and ears, must attach himself to some altar of conse'crated fire, but constantly perform those rites only, 'which end with the dark and bright fortnights and 'with the solstices.

11. 'Let him never, for the sake of a subsistence, 'have recourse to popular conversation; let him live 'by the conduct of a priest, neither crooked, nor artful, 'nor blended *with the manners of the mercantile class*.

12. 'Let him, if he seek happiness, be firm in per'fect content, and check all desire of acquiring more '*than he possesses*; for happiness has its root in content, 'and discontent is the root of misery.

13. 'A *Bráhman* keeping house, *and* supporting him'self by any of the *legal* means before-mentioned, must 'discharge these *following* duties, which conduce to 'fame, length of life, and beatitude.

14. 'Let him daily without sloth perform his pecu'liar duty, which the *Veda* prescribes; for he, who per'forms that *duty*, as well as he is able, attains the high'est path to supreme bliss.

15. 'He must not gain wealth *by music or dancing*, '*or* by any art that pleases the sense; nor by any pro'hibited art; nor whether he be rich or poor, *must he* '*receive gifts* indiscriminately.

16. 'Let him not, from a selfish appetite, be strongly addicted to any sensual gratification; let him, by improving his intellect, studiously preclude an excessive attachment to such pleasures, *even though lawful*.

17. 'All kinds of wealth, that may impede his reading the *Veda*, let him wholly abandon, persisting by all means in the study of scripture, for that will be found his most beneficial attainment.

18. 'Let him pass through this life, bringing his apparel, his discourse, and his frame of mind, to a conformity with his age, his occupations, his property, his divine knowledge, and his family.

19. 'Each day let him examine those holy books which soon give increase of wisdom; and those, which teach the means of acquiring wealth; those, which are salutary to life; and those *nigamas*, which are explanatory of the *Veda*;

20. 'Since, as far as a man studies completely the system of sacred literature, so far only can he become eminently learned, and so far may his learning shine brightly.

21. 'The sacramental oblations to sages, to the gods, to spirits, to men, and to his ancestors, let him constantly perform to the best of his power.

22. 'Some, who well know the ordinances for those oblations, perform not always externally the five great sacraments, but continually make offerings in their own organs *of sensation and intellect*:

23. 'Some constantly sacrifice their breath in their speech, *when they instruct others, or praise* GOD *aloud*, and their speech in their breath, *when they meditate in silence*; perceiving in their speech and breath, *thus*

'*employed*, the unperishable fruit of a sacrificial offer-'ing:

24. 'Other *Bráhmans* incessantly perform those sa-'crifices with scriptural knowledge only; seeing with 'the eye of divine learning, that scriptural knowledge 'is the root of every ceremonial observance.

25. 'Let a *Bráhman* perpetually make oblations to 'consecrated fire at the beginning and end of day and 'night, and at the close of each fortnight, or at the 'conjunction and opposition:

26. 'At the season, when old grain is usually con-'sumed, let him offer new grain for a plentiful harvest; 'and at the close of the season, let him perform the 'rites called *adhwara:* at the solstices let him sacrifice 'cattle; at the end of the year, let his oblations be 'made with the juice of the moon-plant.

27. 'Not having offered grain for the harvest, nor 'cattle *at the time of the solstice*, let no *Bráhman*, who 'keeps hallowed fire, and wishes for long life, taste rice 'or flesh;

28. 'Since the holy fires, not being honored with 'new grain and with a sacrifice of cattle, are greedy for 'rice and flesh, and seek to devour his vital spirits.

29. 'Let him take care, to the utmost of his power, 'that no guest sojourn in his house unhonored with a 'seat, with food, with a bed, with water, with esculent 'roots, and with fruit:

30. 'But let him not honor with his conversation 'such as do forbidden acts; such as subsist, like cats, '*by interested craft*; such as believe not the scripture; 'such as oppugn it by sophisms; or such as live like 'rapacious water-birds.

31. 'With oblations to the gods and to ancestors, let

'him do reverence to *Bráhmans* of the second order, 'who are learned in theology, who have returned home 'from their preceptors, after having performed their re-'ligious duties and fully studied the *Veda*; but men of 'an opposite description let him avoid.

32. 'Gifts must be made by each house-keeper, as 'far as he has ability, to religious mendicants, though 'heterodox; and a just portion must be reserved, with-'out inconvenience to his family, for all sentient beings, '*animal and vegetable.*

33. 'A priest, who is master of a family, and pines 'with hunger, may seek wealth from a king *of the mi-'litary class* from a sacrificer, or his own pupil, but 'from no person else, *unless all other helps fail*: thus '*will he show his* respect for the law.

34. 'Let no priest, who keeps house, *and is* able *to 'procure food,* ever waste himself with hunger; nor, 'when he has any substance, let him wear old or sordid 'clothes.

35. 'His hair, nails, and beard, being clipped; *his 'passions* subdued; his mantle, white; his body, pure; 'let him diligently occupy himself in reading the *Veda*, 'and be constantly intent on such acts, as may be salu-'tary to him.

36. 'Let him carry a staff of *Venu*, an ewer with 'water in it, a handful of *kuṣa*-grass, or *a copy of* the '*Veda*; with a pair of bright golden rings in his ears.

37. 'He must not gaze on the sun, whether rising or 'setting, or eclipsed, or reflected in water, or advanced 'to the middle of the sky.

38. 'Over a string, to which a calf is tied, let him 'not step; nor let him run, while it rains; nor let him 'look on his image in water: this is a settled rule.

39. 'By a mound of earth, by a cow, by an idol, by 'a *Bráhman*, by *a pot of* clarified butter, or of honey, 'by a place where four ways meet, and by large trees 'well known in the district, let him pass with his right 'hand toward them.

40. 'Let him not, though mad with desire, approach 'his wife, when her courses appear; nor let him then 'sleep with her in the same bed;

41. 'Since the knowledge, the manhood, the strength, 'the eye-sight, even the vital spirit of him, who ap-'proaches his wife thus defiled, utterly perish;

42. 'But the knowledge, the manhood, the strength, 'the sight, and the life of him, who avoids her in that 'state of defilement, are greatly increased.

43. 'Let him neither eat with his wife, nor look at 'her eating, or sneezing, or yawning, or sitting careless-'ly at her ease;

44. 'Nor let a *Bráhman*, who desires manly strength, 'behold her setting off her eyes with black powder, or 'scenting herself with essences, or baring her bosom, or 'bringing forth a child.

45. 'Let him not eat his food, wearing only a single 'cloth: nor let him bathe quite naked; nor let him 'eject urine or feces in the highway, nor on ashes, nor 'where kine are grazing.

46. 'Nor on tilled ground, nor in water, nor on wood 'raised for burning, nor, *unless he be in great need*, on 'a mountain, nor on the ruins of a temple, nor at any 'time on a nest of white ants;

47. 'Nor in ditches with living creatures in them, 'nor walking, nor standing, nor on the bank of a river, 'nor on the summit of a mountain;

48. 'Nor let him ever eject them, looking at *things* '*moved by* the wind, or at fire, or at a priest, or at the 'sun, or at water, or at cattle;

49. 'But let him void his excrements, having cover- 'ed the earth with wood, potsheds, *dry* leaves and grass, 'or the like, carefully suppressing his utterance, wrap- 'ping up his breast and his head:

50. 'By day let him void them with his face to the 'north; by night, with his face to the south; at sunrise 'and at sunset, in the same manner as by day;

51. 'In the shade or in darkness, whether by day or 'by night, let a *Bráhman* ease nature with his face 'turned as he pleases; and in places where he fears in- 'jury to life *from wild beasts or from reptiles.*

52. 'Of him, who should urine against fire, against 'the sun or the moon, against a twice-born man, a cow, 'or the wind, all the sacred knowledge would perish.

53. 'Let him not blow the fire with his mouth; let 'him not see his wife naked; let him not throw any 'foul thing into the fire; nor let him warm his feet 'in it;

54. 'Nor let him place it *in a chafing dish* under *his* '*bed;* nor let him stride over it; nor let him keep it, '*while he sleeps,* at his feet: let him do nothing that 'may be injurious to life.

55. 'At the time of sunrise or sunset, let him not 'eat, nor travel, nor lie down to rest; let him not idly 'draw lines on the ground; nor let him take off his 'own chaplet of flowers.

56. 'Let him not cast into the water either urine or 'ordure, nor saliva, nor cloth, nor any other thing, soil- 'ed with impurity, nor blood, nor any other kinds of 'poison.

57. 'Let him not sleep alone in an empty house; 'nor let him wake a sleeping man *superior to himself in* '*wealth and in learning;* nor let him speak to a woman 'at the time of her courses; nor let him go to *perform* 'a sacrifice, unattended *by an officiating priest.*

58. In a temple *of consecrated fire,* in the pasture of 'kine, in the presence of *Bráhmans,* in reading the *Veda,* 'and in eating his food, let him hold out his right arm 'uncovered.

59. 'Let him not interrupt a cow *while she is* drink-'ing, nor give notice to any, *whose milk or water she* '*drinks;* nor let him, who knows *right from wrong,* and 'sees in the sky the bow of INDRA, show it to any man.

60. 'Let him not inhabit a town, in which civil 'and religious duties are neglected; nor, for a long 'time, one in which diseases are frequent; let him 'not begin a journey alone: let him not reside long on 'a mountain.

61. 'Let him not dwell in a city governed by a '*Súdra* king, nor in one surrounded with men unobser-'vant of their duties, nor in one abounding with pro-'fessed heretics, nor in one swarming with low-born 'outcasts.

62. 'Let him eat no vegetable, from which the oil 'has been extracted; nor indulge his appetite to sa-'tiety; nor eat either too early or too late; nor *take* '*any food* in the evening, if he have eaten to fulness in 'the morning.

63. 'Let him make no vain corporeal exertion: let 'him not sip water *taken up* with his *closed* fingers: 'let him eat nothing *placed* in his lap: let him never 'take pleasure in asking idle questions.

64. 'Let him neither dance nor sing, nor play on 'musical instruments, *except in religious rites;* nor let

'him strike his arm, or gnash his teeth, or make a 'braying noise, though agitated by passion.

65. 'Let him not wash his feet in a pan of mixed 'yellow metal; nor let him eat from a broken dish, 'nor where his mind is disturbed with anxious appre- 'hensions.

66. 'Let him not use either slippers or clothes, or a 'sacerdotal string, or an ornament, or a garland, or a 'waterpot, which before have been used by another.

67. 'With untrained beasts of burden let him not 'travel; nor with such, as are oppressed by hunger or 'by disease; nor with such as have imperfect horns, 'eyes, or hoofs; nor with such as have ragged tails:

68. 'But let him constantly travel with beasts well 'trained, whose pace is quick, who bear all the marks 'of a good breed, who have an agreeable colour, and a 'beautiful form; giving them very little pain with his 'whip.

'69. The sun in the sign of *Kanyà*, the smoke of a 'burning corpse, and a broken seat, must be shunned: 'he must never cut his own hair and nails, nor ever tear 'his nails with his teeth.

70. 'Let him not break mould or clay *without cause*: 'let him not cut grass with his nails; let him neither 'indulge any vain fancy, nor do any act, that can bring 'no future advantage:

71. 'He, who *thus idly* breaks clay, or cuts grass, or 'bites his nails, will speedily sink to ruin; and *so shall* 'a detractor, and an unclean person.

72. 'Let him use no contumelious phrase: let him 'wear no garland except on his hair: to ride on the 'back of a bull or a cow, is in all modes culpable.

73. 'Let him not pass, otherwise than by the gate, 'into a walled town, or an inclosed house; and by 'night let him keep aloof from the roots of trees.

74. 'Never let him play with dice; let him not put 'off his sandals with his hand: let him not eat, while 'he reclines on a bed, nor what is placed in his hand, or 'on a bench;

75. 'Nor, when the sun is set, let him eat any thing 'mixed with *tila*; nor let him ever in this world sleep 'quite naked; nor let him go any whither with a rem-'nant of food in his mouth.

76. 'Let him take his food, having sprinkled his 'feet with water; but never let him sleep with his 'feet wet: he, who takes his food with his feet so 'sprinkled, will attain long life.

77. 'Let him never advance into a place undistin-'guishable by his eye, or not easily passable: never let 'him look at urine or ordure; nor let him pass a river '*swimming* with his arms.

78. 'Let not a man, who desires to enjoy long life, 'stand upon hair, nor upon ashes, bones, or potsherds, 'nor upon seeds of cotton, nor upon husks of grain.

79. 'Nor let him tarry *even under the shade of the* '*same tree* with outcasts for great crimes, nor with '*Chandálas*, nor with *Pukkasas*, nor with idiots, nor 'with men proud of wealth, nor with *washermen and* '*other* vile persons, nor with *Antyavasáyins*.

80. 'Let him not give *even temporal* advice to a *Sú-*'*dra*; nor, *except to his own servant*, what remains 'from his table; nor clarified butter, of which part has 'been offered *to the gods*; nor let him *in person* give 'spiritual counsel to such a man, nor *personally* inform 'him of the legal expiation for his sin:

81. 'Surely he, who declares the law to a servile 'man, and he, who instructs him in the mode of expiating sin, *except by the intervention of a priest*, sinks with 'that very man into the hell named *Asamvrita*.

82. 'Let him not stroke his head with both hands; 'nor let him even touch it, while food remains in his 'mouth; nor without *bathing it*, let him bathe his body.

83. 'Let him not *in anger* lay hold of hair, or smite 'any one on the head; nor let him, after his head has 'been rubbed with oil, touch with oil any of his limbs.

84. 'From a king, not born in the military class, let 'him accept no gift, nor from such as keep a slaughter-'house, or an oil-press, or put out a vintner's flag, or 'subsist by the gain of prostitutes:

85. 'One oil-press is as bad as ten slaughter-houses; 'one vintner's flag, as ten oil-presses; one prostitute, as 'ten vintner's flags; one *such* king, as ten prostitutes;

86. 'With a slaughterer, *therefore*, who employs 'ten thousand slaughter-houses, a king, *not a soldier* '*by birth*, is declared to be on a level; *and* a gift from 'him is tremendous.

87. 'He, who receives a present from an avaricious 'king and a transgressor of the sacred ordinances, goes 'in succession to the following twenty-one hells:

88. '*Tamisra, Andhatámisra, Mahúraurava, Raurava, Naraka, Kálasútra,* and *Mahánaraka;*

89. '*Sanjívana, Mahavíchi, Tapana, Sampratápana,* '*Sanhâta, Sakákóla, Kudmala, Pútimrittika;*

90. '*Lóhasanku*, or *iron-spiked*, and *Rijísha, Pant'hána*, the river *Sálmalì, Asipatravana*, or *the sword-*'*leaved forest*, and *Lóhángáraka*, or *the pit of red-hot* '*charcoal.*

91. '*Bráhmans,* who know this *law,* who speak the 'words of the *Veda,* and who seek bliss after death, 'accept no gifts from a king.

92. 'Let the house-keeper wake in the time sacred 'to BRA'HMI', *the goddess of speech, that is, in the last* '*watch of the night:* let him then reflect on virtue and 'virtuous emoluments, on the bodily labor, which they 'require, and on the whole meaning and very essence of 'the *Veda.*

93. 'Having risen, having done what nature makes 'necessary, having then purified himself and fixed his 'attention, let him stand a long time repeating the '*gayatrí* for the first *or morning* twilight; as he must, 'for the last *or evening* twilight in its proper time.

94. 'By continued repetition of the *gayatrí,* at the 'twilights, the holy sages acquire length of days, per-'fect knowledge, reputation during life, fame after 'death, and celestial glory,

95. 'Having duly performed the *upákarma,* or *do-*'*mestic ceremony with sacred fire,* at the full moon of '*Srávana,* or of *Bhádra,* let the *Bráhman,* fully exert-'ing his intellectual powers, read the *Vedas* during four 'months and one fortnight:

96. 'Under the lunar asterism *Pushya,* or on the 'first day of the bright half of *Mágha,* and in the first 'part of the day, let him perform, out of the town, *the* '*ceremony called* the *utsarga* of the *Vedas.*

97. 'Having performed that ceremony out of town, 'as the law directs, let him desist from reading for one '*intermediate* night winged *with two days,* or for that 'day and *that following* night only;

98. 'But after that *intermission,* let him attentively 'read the *Vedas* in the bright fortnights; and in the

'dark fortnights let him constantly read all the *Vedán-*
'*gas*.

99. 'He must never read the *Veda* without accents 'and letters well pronounced; nor ever in the presence 'of *Súdras;* nor, *having begun to read it* in the last 'watch of the night, must he, though fatigued, sleep 'again.

100. 'By the rule just mentioned let him con- 'tinually, with his faculties exerted, read the *Mantras,* 'or holy texts, composed in regular measures; and, 'when he is under no restraint, let him read both the '*Mantras* and the *Bráhmanas,* or chapters on the attri- 'butes of GOD.

101. 'Let a reader of the *Veda,* and a teacher of it 'to his pupils, in the form prescribed, always avoid 'reading on the following prohibited days.

102. 'By night, when the winds meets his ear, and 'by day when the dust is collected, *he must not read* 'in the season of rain; since both those times are de- 'clared unfit for reading, by such as know when the '*Veda* ought to be read.

103. 'In lightning, thunder, *and* rain, or during the 'fall of large fireballs on all sides, at such times MANU 'has ordained the reading of scripture to be deferred 'till the same time next day.

104. 'When the priest perceives those accidents oc- 'curring at once, while his fires are kindled for *morning* '*and evening* sacrifices, then let him know, that the '*Veda* must not be read; and when clouds are seen ga- 'thered out of season.

105. 'On the occasion of a preternatural sound from 'the sky, of an earthquake, or an obscuration of the hea- 'venly bodies, even in due season, let him know, that 'his reading must be postponed till the proper time:

106. 'But if, while his fires are blazing, the sound of 'lightning and thunder is heard *without rain*, his reading must be discontinued, only while the phenomenon 'lasts; the remaining event, *or rain also*, happening, it 'must cease for a night and a day.

107. 'The reading of such, as wish to attain the excellent reward of virtue, must continually be suspended in towns and in cities, and always where an offensive smell prevails.

108. 'In a district, through which a corpse is carried, 'and in the presence of an unjust person, the reading 'of scripture must cease; *and* while the sound of 'weeping is heard; and in a promiscuous assembly of 'men.

109. 'In water, near midnight, and while the two 'natural excretions are made, or with a remnant of 'food in the mouth, or when the *sráddha* has recently 'been eaten, let no man even meditate in his heart *on the holy texts*.

110. 'A learned *Bráhman*, having received an invitation to the obsequies of a single ancestor, must not 'read the *Veda* for three days; nor when the king has 'a son born; nor when the dragon's head causes an 'eclipse.

111. 'As long as the scent and unctuosity of perfumes remain on the body of a learned priest, who has 'partaken of an entertainment, so long he must abstain 'from pronouncing the texts of the *Veda*.

112. 'Let him not read lolling on a couch, nor 'with his feet raised on a bench, nor with his thighs 'crossed, nor having lately swallowed meat, or the rice 'and other food *given* on the birth or death of a relation:

113. 'Nor in a cloud of dust, nor while arrows whiz, '*or a lute sounds*, nor in either of the twilights, nor at

'the conjunction, nor on the fourteenth day, nor at the 'opposition, nor on the eighth day, of the moon:

114. 'The dark lunar day destroys the spiritual 'teacher; the fourteenth destroys the learner; the eighth 'and the day of the full moon destroy *all remembrance 'of* scripture; for which reasons he must avoid reading 'on those lunar days.

115. 'Let no *Bráhman* read, while dust falls like a 'shower, nor while the quarters of the firmament are 'inflamed, nor while the shakals yell, nor while dogs 'bark or yelp, nor while asses or camels bray, *nor while 'men in company chatter.*

116. 'He must not read near a cemetery, near a town, 'or in a pasture for kine; nor in a mantle worn before 'at a time of dalliance; nor having just received the 'present usual at obsequies:

117. 'Be it an animal, or a thing inanimate, or what-'ever be the gift at a *sráddha,* let him not, having 'lately accepted it, read the *Veda;* for such a *Brahman* 'is said to have his mouth in his hand.

118. 'When the town is beset by robbers, or an 'alarm has been raised by fire, and in all terrors from 'strange phenomena, let him know, that his lecture 'must be suspended till the due time *after the cause of 'terror be ceased.*

119. 'The suspension of reading scripture, after a 'performance of the *upákarma* and *utsarga,* must be for 'three whole nights, *by the man who seeks virtue more 'than knowledge;* also for one day and night, on the 'eighth lunar days which follow those ceremonies, and 'on the nights at the close of the seasons.

120. 'Never let him read on horseback, nor on a tree, 'nor on an elephant, nor in a boat, nor on an ass, nor

'on a camel, nor standing on barren ground, nor borne 'in a carriage;

121. 'Nor during a verbal altercation, nor during a 'mutual assault, nor with an army, nor in battle, nor 'after food, *while his hand is moist from washing*, nor 'with an indigestion, nor after vomiting, nor with sour 'eructations;

122. 'Nor without notice to a guest just arrived, nor 'while the wind vehemently blows, nor when blood 'gushes from his body, nor when it is wounded by a 'weapon.

123. 'While the strain of the *Sáma* meets his ear, he 'shall not read the *Rig*, or the *Yajur*; nor any part 'of the *Veda*, when he has just concluded the whole; 'nor *any other part*, when he has just finished the book 'entitled *A'ranyaka*:

124. 'The *Rig Veda* is held sacred to the gods; the *Yajur Veda* relates to mankind; the *Sáma Veda* con-'cerns the manes of ancestors, and the sound of it, '*when chanted*, raises therefore a notion of something 'impure.

125. 'Knowing this *collection of rules*, let the learn-'ed read the *Veda* on every *lawful* day, having first 'repeated in order the pure essence of the three *Vedas*, 'namely, the *pranava*, the *vyáhritis*, and the *gáyatrí*.

126. 'If a beast used in agriculture, a frog, a cat, a 'dog, a snake, an ichneumon, or a rat, pass between *the 'lecturer and his pupil*, let him know, that the lecture 'must be intermitted for a day and a night.

127. 'Two occasions, when the *Veda* must not be 'read, let a *Bráhman* constantly observe with great 'care; *namely*, when the place for reading it is impure, 'and when he is himself unpurified.

128. 'On the dark night of the moon, and on the 'eighth, on the night of the full moon, and on the four-'teenth, let a *Bráhman,* who keeps house, be continual-'ly chaste as a student in theology, even in the season 'of nuptial embraces.

129. 'Let him not bathe, having just eaten; nor 'while he is afflicted with disease; nor in the middle of 'the night; nor with many clothes; nor in a pool of 'water imperfectly known.

130. 'Let him not intentionally pass over the shadow 'of sacred images, of a *natural or spiritual* father, of 'a king, of a *Bráhman,* who keeps house, or of any 'reverend personage; nor of a red-haired *or copper-'colored* man; nor of one who has just performed a 'sacrifice.

131. 'At noon or at midnight, or having eaten flesh 'at a *ṣráddha,* or in either of the twilights, let him not 'long tarry, where four ways meet.

132. 'He must not stand knowingly near oil and 'other things, with which a man has rubbed his body, 'or water, in which he has washed himself, or feces and 'urine, or blood, or mucus, or any thing chewed and 'spitten out, or any thing vomited.

133. 'Let him show no particular attention to his 'enemy, or his enemy's friend, to an unjust person, to a 'thief, or to the wife of another man;

134. 'Since nothing is known in this world so ob-'structive to length of days, as the culpable attention 'of a man to the wife of another.

135. 'Never let him, who desires an increase of 'wealth, despise a warrior, a serpent, or a priest versed 'in scripture, how mean soever *they may appear;*

136. 'Since those three, when contemned, may de-

'stroy a man; let a wise man therefore always beware 'of treating those three with contempt:

137. 'Nor should he despise *even* himself on account 'of previous miscarriages: let him pursue fortune till 'death, nor ever think her hard to be attained.

138. 'Let him say what is true, but let him say 'what is pleasing; let him speak no disagreeable truth, 'nor let him speak agreeable falsehood: this is a prim'eval rule.

139. 'Let him say "well and good," or let him say '"well" only; but let him not maintain fruitless 'enmity and altercation with any man.

140. 'Let him not journey too early in the morn'ing or too late in the evening, nor too near the mid'day, nor with an unknown companion, nor alone, nor 'with men of the servile class.

141. 'Let him not insult those, who want a limb, or 'have a limb redundant, who are unlearned, who are 'advanced in age, who have no beauty, who have no 'wealth, or who are of an ignoble race.

142. 'Let no priest, unwashed after food, touch with 'his hand a cow, a *Bráhman*, or fire; nor being in good 'health *and* unpurified, let him even look at the lumi'naries in the firmament:

143. 'But, having accidentally touched them before 'his purification, let him ever sprinkle, with water in 'the palm of his hand, his organs of sensation, all his 'limbs, and his navel.

144. 'Not being in pain from disease, let him never 'without cause touch the cavities of his body; and care'fully let him avoid his concealed hair.

145. 'Let him be intent on *those propitious observ-*

'*ances which lead to* good fortune, and on the discharge 'of his customary duties, his body and mind being pure, 'and his members kept in subjection; let him constant'ly without remissness repeat the *gáyatrì*, and present 'his oblation to fire:

146. 'To those, who are intent on good fortune and 'on the discharge of their duties, who are always pure, 'who repeat the holy text and make oblations to fire, 'no calamity happens.

147. 'In due season let him ever study the scripture 'without negligence; for the sages call that his princi'pal duty: every other duty is declared to be subordi'nate.

148. 'By reading the *Veda* continually, by purity of 'body and mind, by rigorous devotion, and by doing no 'injury to animated creatures, he brings to remem'brance his former birth:

149. 'A *Bráhman*, remembering his former birth, 'again reads the *Veda*, and, by reading it constantly, 'attains bliss without end.

150. 'On the days of the conjunction and opposition, 'let him constantly make those oblations, which are 'hallowed by the *gáyatrì*, and those, which avert mis'fortune; but on the eighth and ninth lunar days *of the* '*three dark fortnights after the end of Agraháyan*, let 'him always do reverence to the manes of ancestors.

151. 'Far from the mansion of holy fire, let him re'move all ordure; far *let him remove* water, in which 'feet have been washed; far *let him remove* all rem'nants of food, and all seminal impurity.

152. 'At the beginning of each day let him discharge 'his feces, bathe, rub his teeth, apply a collyrium to his 'eyes, adjust his dress, and adore the gods.

153. '*On the dark lunar day, and* on the *other* '*monthly* parvans let him visit the images of deities, 'and *Bráhmans* eminent in virtue, and the ruler of the 'land, for the sake of protection, and those whom he is 'bound to revere.

'154. 'Let him humbly greet venerable men, *who* '*visit him,* and give them his own seat; let him sit 'near them, closing the palms of his hands; and when 'they depart, let him walk some way behind them.

155. 'Let him practise without intermission that 'system of approved usages, which is the root of all 'duty religious and civil, declared at large in the scrip'ture and sacred law tracts, together with the ceremo'nies peculiar to each act:

156. 'Since by such practice long life is attained; by 'such practice *is gained* wealth unperishable; such 'practice baffles every mark of ill fortune:

157. 'But, by an opposite practice, a man surely 'sinks to contempt in this world, has always a large 'portion of misery, is afflicted with disease and short'lived;

158. 'While the man, who is observant of approved 'usages, endued with faith in scripture, and free from a 'spirit of detraction, lives a hundred years, even though 'he bear no bodily mark of a prosperous life.

159. 'Whatever act depends on another man, that 'act let him carefully shun; but whatever depends on 'himself, to that let him studiously attend;

160. 'ALL THAT DEPENDS ON ANOTHER, GIVES PAIN; 'AND ALL, THAT DEPENDS ON HIMSELF, GIVES PLEASURE; 'let him know this to be in few words the definition of 'pleasure and pain.

161. 'When an act, *neither prescribed nor prohibited,*

'gratifies the mind of him who performs it, let him 'perform it with diligence; but let him avoid its opposite.

162. 'Him, by whom he was invested with the sacri'ficial thread, him, who explained the *Veda*, or even a 'part of it, his mother, and his father, natural, or spiri'tual, let him never oppose; nor priests, nor cows, nor 'persons truly devout.

163. 'Denial of a future state, neglect of the scrip'ture, and contempt of the deities, envy and hatred, 'vanity and pride, wrath and severity, let him *at all* '*times* avoid.

164. 'Let him not, when angry, throw a stick at 'another man, nor smite him with any thing; unless he 'be a son or a pupil; those two he may chastise for 'their *improvement* in learning.

165. 'A twice-born man, who barely assaults a *Bráh*'*man* with intention to hurt him, shall be whirled about 'for a century in the hell named *Támisra*;

166. '*But*, having smitten him in anger and by de'sign, even with a blade of grass, he shall be born, in 'one and twenty transmigrations, from the wombs of 'impure quadrupeds.

167. 'He, who, through ignorance of law, sheds 'blood from the body of a *Bráhman*, not engaged in 'battle, shall feel excessive pain in his future life:

168. 'As many particles of dust as the blood shall 'roll up from the ground, for so many years shall the 'shedder of that blood be mangled by other animals in 'his next birth.

169. 'Let not him then, who knows *this law*, even 'assault a *Bráhman* at any time, nor strike him even 'with grass, nor cause blood to gush from his body.

170. 'Even here below an unjust man attains no 'felicity; nor he, whose wealth proceeds from giving 'false evidence; nor he, who constantly takes delight 'in mischief.

171. 'Though oppressed by penury, in consequence 'of his righteous dealings, let him never give his mind 'to unrighteousness; for he may observe the speedy 'overthrow of iniquitous and sinful men.

172. 'Iniquity, committed in this world, produces 'not fruit immediately, *but*, like the earth *in due season*: 'and, advancing by little and little, it eradicates the 'man who committed it.

173. 'Yes; iniquity, once committed, fails not of 'producing fruit to him, who wrought it; if not in his 'own person, yet in his sons; or, if not in his sons, 'yet in his grandsons:

174. 'He grows rich for a while through unrighteous'ness; then he beholds good things; then it is, that 'he vanquishes his foes; but he perishes at length from 'his whole root upwards.

175. 'Let a man continually take pleasure in truth, 'in justice, in laudable practices, and in purity; let 'him chastise those, whom he may chastise, in a legal 'mode; let him keep in subjection his speech, his arm, 'and his appetite:

176. 'Wealth and pleasures, repugnant to law, let 'him shun; and even lawful acts, which may cause fu'ture pain, or be offensive to mankind.

177. 'Let him not have nimble hands, restless feet, 'or voluble eyes; let him not be crooked in his ways; 'let him not be flippant in his speech, nor intelligent 'in doing mischief.

'178. 'Let him walk in the path of good men; the

'path, in which his parents and forefathers walked: 'while he moves in that path, he can give no offence.

179. 'With an attendant on consecrated fire, a performer of holy rites, and a teacher of the *Veda*, with his 'maternal uncle, with his guest or a dependant, with a 'child, with a man either aged or sick, with a physician, 'with his paternal kindred, with his relations by marriage, and with cousins on the side of his mother,

180. 'With his mother herself, or with his father, 'with his kinswomen, with his brother, with his son, his 'wife, or his daughter, and with his whole set of servants let him have no strife.

181. 'A house-keeper, who shuns altercation with 'those *just mentioned*, is released from all *secret* faults; 'and, by suppressing all such disputes, he obtains a victory over the following worlds:

182. 'The teacher of the *Veda* secures him the world 'of BRAHMA'; his father, the world *of the Sun, or* of the '*Prajápatis;* his guest, the world of INDRA; his attendance on holy fire, the world of *Devas;*

183. 'His female relations, the world of celestial 'nymphs; his maternal cousins, the world of the *Viswadévas;* his relations by affinity, the world of waters; 'his mother and maternal uncle give him power on 'earth;

184. 'Children, old men, poor dependants, and sick 'persons, must be considered as rulers of the pure 'ether; his elder brother, as equal to his father; his 'wife and son, as his own body;

185. 'His assemblage of servants, as his own shadow; 'his daughter, as the highest object of tenderness; let 'him, therefore, when offended by any of those, bear 'the offence without indignation.

186. 'Though permitted to receive presents, let him 'avoid a habit of taking them; since, by taking many 'gifts, his divine light soon fades.

187. 'Let no man of sense, who has not fully informed himself of the law concerning gifts of *particular* 'things, accept a present, even though he pine with 'hunger.

188. 'The man who knows not that law, yet accepts 'gold or gems, land, a horse, a cow, food, raiment, oils 'or clarified butter, becomes mere ashes, like wood *con*'*sumed by fire:*

189. 'Gold and gems burn up his nourishment and 'life: land and a cow, his body; a horse, his eyes; rai'ment, his skin; clarified butter, his manly strength; 'oils, his progeny.

190. 'A twice-born man, void of true devotion, and 'not having read the *Veda,* yet eager to take a gift, 'sinks down together with it, as with a boat of stone 'in deep water.

191. 'Let him then, who knows not the law, be 'fearful of presents from this or that giver; since an 'ignorant man, even by a small gift, may become help'less as a cow in a bog.

192. 'Let no man, apprized of this law, present even 'water to a priest, who acts like a cat, nor to him, who 'acts like a bittern, nor to him, who is unlearned in 'the *Veda;*

193. 'Since property, though legally gained, if it be 'given to either of those three, becomes prejudicial in 'the next world, both to the giver and receiver:

194. 'As he, who tries to pass over deep water in a 'boat of stone, sinks to the bottom, so those two igno-

'rant men, the receiver and the giver, sink to a region 'of torment.

195. 'A covetous wretch, who continually displays 'the flag of virtue, a pretender, a deluder of the people, 'is declared to be the man who acts like a cat: he is 'an injurious hypocrite, a detractor from the merits of 'all men.

196. 'A twice-born man, with his eyes dejected, 'morose, intent on his own advantage, sly, and falsely 'demure, is he, who acts like a bittern.

197. 'Such priests, as live like bitterns, and such as 'demean themselves like cats, fall by that sinful conduct 'into the hell called *Andhatámisra*.

198. 'Let no man, having committed sin, perform a 'penance, under the pretext of austere devotion, dis'guising his crime under fictitious religion, and deceiv'ing both women and low men:

199. 'Such impostors, though *Bráhmans*, are despis'ed in the next life and in this, by all who pronounce 'holy texts; and every religious act fraudulently per'formed goes to evil beings.

200. 'He, who has no right to distinguishing marks, 'yet gains a subsistence by wearing false marks of dis'tinction, takes to himself the sin committed by those 'who are entitled to such marks, and shall again be 'born from the womb of a brute animal.

201. 'Never let him bathe in the pool of another 'man; for he, who bathes in it *without licence*, takes 'to himself a small portion of the sins, which the maker 'of the pool has committed.

202. 'He, who appropriates to his own use the car'riage, the bed, the seat, the well, the garden, or the

'house of another man, who has not delivered them to 'him, assumes a fourth part of the guilt of their 'owner.

203. 'In rivers, in ponds dug by holy persons, and 'in lakes, let him always bathe ; in rivulets also, and 'in torrents.

204. 'A WISE man should constantly discharge all 'the moral duties, though he perform not constantly 'the ceremonies of religion ; since he falls low, if, while 'he performs ceremonial acts only, he discharge not his 'moral duties.

205. 'Never let a priest eat part of a sacrifice not 'begun with texts of the *Veda*, nor of one performed 'by a common sacrifice, by a woman, or by an eunuch :

206. 'When those persons offer the clarified butter, 'it brings misfortune to good men, and raises aversion 'in the deities ; such *oblations*, therefore, he must care-'fully shun.

207. 'Let him never eat the food of the insane, the 'wrathful, or the sick ; nor that, on which lice have 'fallen ; nor that, which has designedly been touched 'by a foot ;

208. 'Nor that, which has been looked at by the 'slayer of a priest, *or by any other deadly sinner*, or has 'even been touched by a woman in her courses, or peck-'ed by a bird, or approached by a dog :

209. 'Nor food which has been smelled by a cow ; 'nor particularly that which has been proclaimed *for all* '*comers* ; nor the food of associated knaves, or of har-'lots ; nor that, which is contemned by the learned in 'scripture :

210. 'Nor that of a thief or a public singer, of a 'carpenter, of an usurer, of one who has recently come

'from a sacrifice, of a niggardly churl, or of one bound 'with fetters;

211. 'Of one publicly defamed, of an eunuch, of an 'unchaste woman, or of a hypocrite: nor any sweet 'thing turned acid, nor what has been kept a whole 'night; nor the food of a servile man, nor the orts of 'another;

212. 'Nor the food of a physician, or of a hunter, or 'of a dishonest man, or of an eater of orts; nor that of 'any cruel person; nor of a woman in child-bed; nor of 'him, who rises prematurely from table to make an ab-'lution; nor of her, whose ten days of purification have 'not elapsed;

213. 'Nor that, which is given without due honor 'to honorable men; nor any flesh, which has not been 'sacrified; nor the food of a woman, who has neither a 'husband nor a son; nor that of a foe, nor that of the 'whole town, nor that of an outcast, nor that on which 'any person has sneezed;

214. 'Nor that of a backbiter, or of a false witness; 'nor of one, who sells the reward of his sacrifice; nor 'of a public dancer, or a tailor; nor of him who has re-'turned evil for good;

215. 'Nor that of a blacksmith, or a man of the 'tribe called *Nisháda*, nor of a stage-player, nor of a 'worker in gold or in cane, nor of him who sells wea-'pons;

216. 'Nor of those, who train hunting-dogs, or sell 'fermented liquor; nor of him who washes clothes, or 'who dyes them; nor of any malevolent person; nor of 'one, who ignorantly suffers an adulterer to dwell under 'his roof;

217. 'Nor of those, who knowingly bear with the

'paramours of their own wives, or are constantly in 'subjection to women; nor food given for the dead 'before ten days of purification have passed; nor any 'food whatsoever, but that which satisfies him.

218. 'Food given by a king, impairs his manly vi'gour; by one of the servile class, his divine light; by 'goldsmiths, his life; by leather-cutters, his good name:

219. 'Given by *cooks and the like* mean artizans, it 'destroys his offspring; by a washerman, his muscular 'strength; but the food of knavish associates and har'lots excludes him from heaven:

220. 'The food of a physician is purulent; that of 'a libidinous woman, seminal; that of an usurer, fecu'lent; that of a weapon-seller, filthy:

221. 'That of all others, mentioned in order, whose 'food must never be tasted, is held equal by the wise to 'the skin, bones, and hair of the dead.

222. 'Having unknowingly swallowed the food of 'any such persons, he must fast during three days; but, 'having eaten it knowingly, he must perform the same 'harsh penance, as if he had tasted any seminal impu'rity, ordure, or urine.

223. 'Let no learned priest eat the dressed grain of 'a servile man, who performs no parental obsequies; 'but, having no other means to live, he may take from 'him raw grain enough for a single night.

224. 'The deities, having well considered the food of 'a niggard, who has read the scripture, and that of an 'usurer, who bestows gifts liberally, declared the food 'of both to be equal in quality;

225. 'But BRAHMA', advancing towards the gods, 'thus addressed them: "Make not that equal, which 'in truth is unequal; since the food of a liberal man

'is purified by faith, while that of a learned miser is 'defiled by his want of faith in what he has read."

226. 'Let each *wealthy* man continually and sedulously perform sacred rites, and consecrate pools or 'gardens with faith; since those two acts, accomplished with faith and with riches honestly gained, procure 'an unperishable reward:

227. 'If he meet with fit objects of benevolence, let 'him constantly bestow gifts on them, both at sacrifices 'and consecrations, to the best of his power and with 'a cheerful heart;

228. 'Such a gift, how small soever, bestowed on 'request without grudging, passes to a worthy object, 'who will secure the giver from all evil.

229. 'A giver of water obtains content; a giver of 'food, extreme bliss; a giver of *tila*, desired offspring; 'a giver of a lamp, unblemished eyesight;

230. 'A giver of land obtains landed property; a 'giver of gems or gold, long life; a giver of a house, 'the most exalted mansion; a giver of silver, exquisite 'beauty;

231. 'A giver of clothes, the same station with 'CHANDRA; a giver of a horse, the same station with 'ASWI; a giver of a bull, eminent fortune; a giver of a 'cow, the mansion of SU'RYA;

232. 'A giver of a carriage or a bed, an excellent 'consort; a giver of safety, supreme dominion; a giver 'of grain, perpetual delight; a giver of scriptural knowledge, union with GOD:

233. 'Among all those gifts, of water, food, kine, 'land, clothes, *tila*, gold, clarified butter, and the rest, a 'gift of spiritual knowledge is consequently the most 'important;

234. 'And for whatever purpose a man bestows any 'gift, for a similar purpose he shall receive, with due 'honor, a similar reward.

235. 'Both he, who respectfully bestows a present, 'and he who respectfully accepts it, shall go to a seat 'of bliss; but, if they act otherwise, to a region of 'horror.

236. 'Let not a man be proud of his rigorous devo-'tion; let him not, having sacrificed, utter a falsehood; 'let him not, though injured, insult a priest; having 'made a donation, let him never proclaim it:

237. 'By falsehood, the sacrifice becomes vain; by 'pride, the merit of devotion is lost; by insulting 'priests, life is diminished; and by proclaiming a 'largess, its fruit is destroyed.

238. 'Giving no pain to any creature, let him collect 'virtue by degrees, for the sake of acquiring a compa-'nion to the next world, as the white ant by degrees 'builds his nest;

239. 'For, in his passage to the next world, neither 'his father, nor his mother, nor his wife, nor his son, 'nor his kinsmen, will remain in his company: his 'virtue alone will adhere to him.

240. 'Single is each man born; single he dies; sin-'gle he receives the reward of his good, and single the 'punishment of his evil deeds:

241. 'When he leaves his corpse, like a log or a 'lump of clay, on the ground, his kindred retire with 'averted faces; but his virtue accompanies his soul.

242. 'Continually, therefore, by degrees, let him 'collect virtue, for the sake of securing an inseparable 'companion; since with virtue for his guide, he will 'traverse a gloom, how hard to be traversed!

243. 'A man, habitually virtuous, whose offences 'have been expiated by devotion, is instantly conveyed 'after death to the higher world, with a radiant form 'and a body of ethereal substance.

244. He, who seeks to preserve an exalted rank, 'must constantly form connexions with the highest 'and best families, but avoid the worst and the 'meanest;

245. 'Since a priest who connects himself with the 'best and highest of men, avoiding the lowest and worst, 'attains eminence; but sinks, by an opposite conduct, 'to the class of the servile.

246. 'He, who perseveres in good actions, in sub-'duing his passions, in bestowing largesses, in gentle-'ness of manners, who bears hardships patiently, who 'associates not with the malignant, who gives pain to 'no sentient being, obtains final beatitude.

247. 'Wood, water, roots, fruit, and food placed be-'fore him without his request, he may accept from all 'men; honey also, and protection from danger.

248. 'Gold, or other alms, voluntarily brought and 'presented, but unasked and unpromised, BRAHMA' con-'sidered as receivable even from a sinner:

249. 'Of him, who shall disdain to accept such alms, 'neither will the manes eat the funeral oblations for 'fifteen years, nor will the fire convey the burnt sacri-'fice to the gods.

250. 'A bed, houses, blades of *kuṣa*, perfumes, water, 'flowers, jewels, butter-milk, ground rice, fish, new milk, 'flesh-meat, and green vegetables, let him not proudly 'reject.

251. 'When he wishes to relieve his natural parents 'or spiritual father, his wife or others, whom he is bound

'to maintain, or when he is preparing to honor deities 'or guests, he may receive gifts from any person, but 'must not gratify himself with such presents:

252. 'If his parents, however, be dead, or if he live 'without them in his own house, let him, when he seeks 'nourishment for himself, receive presents invariably 'from good men alone.

253. 'A labourer in tillage, a family friend, a herds-'man, a slave, a barber, a poor stranger offering his 'humble duty, are men of the servile class, who may 'eat the food of their superiors:

254. 'As the nature of the poor stranger is, as the 'work is, which he desires to perform, and as he may 'show most respect *to the master of the house*, even thus 'let him offer his service;

255. 'For he, who describes himself to worthy men, 'in a manner contrary to truth, is the most sinful wretch 'in this world: he is the worst of thieves, a stealer of 'minds.

256. 'All things have their sense ascertained by 'speech; in speech they have their basis; and from 'speech they proceed: consequently, a falsifier of speech 'falsifies every thing.

257. 'When he has paid, as the law directs, his debts 'to the sages, to the manes, and to the gods, *by reading the scripture, begetting a son, and performing regular sacrifices*, he may resign all to his son *of mature age*, and reside in his family-house, with no employ-'ment, but that of an umpire.

258. 'Alone, in some solitary place, let him con-'stantly meditate on the divine nature of the soul, for 'by such meditation he will attain happiness.

259. 'Thus has been declared the mode, by which a 'Bráhman, who keeps house, must continually subsist, 'together with the rule of devotion ordained for a pupil 'returned from his preceptor; a laudable rule, which 'increases the best of *the three* qualities.

260. 'A priest who lives always by these rules, who 'knows the ordinances of the *Veda*, who is freed from 'the bondage of sin, shall be absorbed in the divine 'essence.

CHAP. V.

On Diet, Purification, and Women.

---

1. The sages, having heard those laws delivered for 'the conduct of house-keepers, thus addressed the high-'minded Bhrigu, who proceeded *in a former birth* 'from the genius of fire.

2. 'How, Lord, can death prevail over *Bráhmans*, 'who know the scriptural ordinances, and perform their 'duties as they have been declared?'

3. 'Then he, whose disposition was perfect virtue, 'even Bhrigu, the son of Manu, thus answered the 'great *Rishis*: 'Hear, from what sin proceeds the in-'clination of death, to destroy the chief of the twice-'born:

4. 'Through a neglect of reading the *Veda*, through 'a desertion of approved usages, through supine remiss-'ness *in performing holy rites*, and through various 'offences in diet, *the genius of* death becomes eager to 'destroy them.

5. 'Garlic, onions, leeks, and mushrooms (which no

'twice-born man must eat), and all vegetables raised 'in dung.

6. 'Red gums or resins, exuding from trees, and 'juices from wounded stems, the fruit *sélu,* and the 'thickened milk of a cow within ten days after her 'calving, a priest must avoid with great care.

7. 'Rice-pudding boiled with *tila,* frumenty, rice-'milk, and baked bread, which have not been first offer-'ed to some deity, flesh-meat also, the food of gods, and 'clarified butter, which have not first been touched, 'while holy texts were recited,

8. 'Fresh milk from a cow, whose ten days are not 'passed, the milk of a camel, or any quadruped with a 'hoof not cloven, that of an ewe, and that of a cow in 'heat, or whose calf is dead or absent from her,

9. 'That of any forest-beast, except the buffalo, the 'milk of a woman, and anything naturally sweet but 'acidulated, must all be carefully shunned :

10. 'But among such acids, butter-milk may be swal-'lowed, and every preparation of butter-milk, and all 'acids extracted from pure flowers, roots, or fruit *not 'cut with iron* .

11. 'Let every twice-born man avoid carnivorous 'birds, and such as live in towns, and quadrupeds with 'uncloven hoofs, except those allowed by the *Veda,* and 'the bird called *tittibha ;*

12. 'The sparrow, the water-bird *plava,* the pheni-'copteros, the *chakraváka,* the breed of the town-cock, 'the *sárasa,* the *rajjuvála,* the woodpecker, and the par-'rot, male and female ;

13. 'Birds, that strike with their beaks, web-footed 'birds, the *kóyashti,* those, who wound with strong

'talons, and those, who dive to devour fish; let him 'avoid meat kept at a slaughter-house, and dried meat,

14. 'The heron, the raven, the *c'hanjana*, all amphibious fish-eaters, tame hogs, and fish of every sort, *but* '*those expressly permitted.*

15. 'He, who eats the flesh of any animal, is called 'the eater of that animal itself; and a fish-eater is an 'eater of all flesh; from fish, therefore, he must diligently abstain:

16. 'Yet the two fish, called *pát'hína* and *róhita*, may 'be eaten *by the guests*, when offered at a repast in honor of the gods or the manes; and so may the *rájíva*, 'the *sinhatunda*, and the *saṣalka* of every species.

17. 'Let him not eat the flesh of any solitary animals, nor of unknown beasts or birds, though by general words declared eatable, nor of any creature with 'five claws;

18. 'The hedgehog and porcupine, the lizard *gódhá*, 'the *gandaka*, the tortoise, and the *rabbit or* hare, wise 'legislators declare lawful food among five-toed animals; and all quadrupeds, camels excepted, which have 'but one row of teeth.

19. 'The twice-born man, who has intentionally 'eaten a mushroom, the flesh of a tame hog, or a 'town-cock, a leek, or an onion, or garlic, is degraded 'immediately;

20. 'But having undesignedly tasted either of those 'six things, he must perform the penance *sántapana*, 'or the *chándráyana*, which anchorets practise; for 'other things he must fast a whole day.

21. 'One of those harsh penances, called *prájápatya*, 'the twice-born man must perform annually, to purify 'him from the unknown taint of illicit food; but he

'must do particular penance for such food intentionally 'eaten.

22. 'Beasts and birds of excellent sorts may be 'slain by *Bráhmans* for sacrifice, or for the sustenance 'of those, whom they are bound to support; since 'AGASTYA did this of old.

23. 'No doubt, in the primeval sacrifices by holy 'men, and in oblations by those of the priestly and mi-'litary tribes, the flesh of such beasts and birds, as may 'be legally eaten, was presented to the deities.

24. 'That, which may be eaten or drunk, *when fresh*, 'without blame, may be swallowed, if touched with oil, 'though it has been kept a whole night; and so may 'the remains of clarified butter:

25. 'And every mess prepared with barley or wheat, 'or with dressed milk, may be eaten by the twice-born, 'although not sprinkled with oil.

26. 'Thus has the food, allowed or forbidden to a 'twice-born man, been comprehensively mentioned: I 'will now propound the *special* rules for eating and for 'avoiding flesh-meat.

27. 'He should taste meat, which has been hallowed 'for a sacrifice with appropriated texts, and, *once only*, 'when a priest shall desire him, and when he is per-'forming a legal act, or in danger of losing life.

28. 'For the sustenance of the vital spirit, BRAHMA' 'created all this *animal and vegetable system*; and all, 'that is moveable or immoveable, that spirit devours.

29. 'Things fixed are eaten by creatures with loco-'motion; toothless animals, by animals with teeth; 'those without hands, by those to whom hands were 'given; and the timid, by the bold.

30. 'He, who eats *according to law*, commits no sin, 'even though every day he tastes the flesh of such animals, who may lawfully be tasted; since both animals, who may be eaten, and those who eat them, 'were equally created by BRAHMA'.

31. 'It is delivered as a rule of the gods, that meat 'must be swallowed only for the purpose of sacrifice; 'but it is a rule of gigantic demons, that it may be 'swallowed for any other purpose.

32. 'No sin is committed by him, who, having honored the deities and the manes, eats flesh-meat, 'which he has bought, or which he has himself acquired, or which has been given him by another.

33. 'Let no twice-born man, who knows the law, 'and is not in urgent distress, eat flesh without observing this rule; for he, unable to save himself, will be 'devoured in the next world by those animals, whose 'flesh he has thus illegally swallowed.

34. 'The sin of him, who kills deer for gain, is not so 'heinous, with respect to *the punishment in* another life, 'as that of him, who eats flesh-meat in vain, *or not previously offered as a sacrifice:*

35. 'But the man, who, engaged *in holy rites* according to law, refuses to eat it, shall sink in another world, 'for twenty-one births, to the state of a beast.

36. 'Never let a priest eat the flesh of cattle unhallowed with *mantras*, but let him eat it, observing the 'primeval rule, when it has been hallowed with those 'texts of the *Veda*.

37. 'Should he have an earnest desire to taste flesh-meat, he may gratify his fancy by forming the image 'of some beast with clarified butter thickened, or he 'may form it with dough; but never let him indulge a 'wish to kill any beast in vain:

38. 'As many hairs as grow on the beast, so many 'similar deaths shall the slayer of it, for his own satis-'faction in this world, endure in the next from birth to 'birth.

39. 'By the self-existing in person were beasts creat-'ed for sacrifice; and the sacrifice *was ordained* for the 'increase of this universe: the slaughterer, therefore, of 'beasts for sacrifice is in truth no slaughterer.

40. 'Gramineous plants, cattle, timber-trees, amphi-'bious animals, and birds, which have been destroyed 'for the purpose of sacrifice, attain in the next world 'exalted births.

41. 'On a solemn offering to a guest, at a sacrifice, 'and in holy rites to the manes or to the gods, but on 'those occasions only, may cattle be slain: this law 'MANU enacted.

42. 'The twice-born man, who, knowing the mean-'ing and principles of the *Veda*, slays cattle on the oc-'casions mentioned, conveys both himself and those 'cattle to the summit of beatitude.

43. 'Let no twice-born man, whose mind is improv-'ed by learning, hurt animals without the sanction of 'scripture, even though in pressing distress, whether he 'live in his own house, or in that of his preceptor, or 'in a forest.

44. 'That hurt, which the scripture ordains, and 'which is done in this world of moveable and immove-'able creatures, he must consider as no hurt at all; 'since law shone forth from *the light of* the scripture.

45. 'He, who injures animals, that are not injurious, 'from a wish to give himself pleasure, adds nothing to 'his own happiness, living or dead;

46. 'While he, who gives no creature willingly the

'pain of confinement or death, but seeks the good of 'all *sentient beings*, enjoys bliss without end.

47. 'He, who injures no animated creature, shall attain without hardship whatever he thinks of, whatever 'he strives for, whatever he fixes his mind on.

48. 'Flesh-meat cannot be procured without injury 'to animals, and the slaughter of animals obstructs the 'path to beatitude; from flesh-meat, therefore, let man 'abstain:

49. 'Attentively, considering the formation of bodies, 'and the death or confinement of embodied spirits, let 'him abstain from eating flesh-meat of any kind.

50. 'The man, who forsakes not the law, and eats 'not flesh-meat, like a blood-thirsty demon, shall attain 'good will in this world, and shall not be afflicted with 'maladies.

51. 'He, who consents to the death of an animal; 'he, who kills it; he, who dissects it; he, who buys it; 'he, who sells it; he, who dresses it; he, who serves it 'up; and he, who makes it his food; these are eight 'principals in the slaughter:

52. 'Not a mortal exists more sinful than he, who, 'without an oblation to the manes or the gods, desires 'to enlarge his own flesh with the flesh of another creature.

53. 'The man, who performs annually, for a hundred 'years, an *aswamédha*, or *sacrifice of a horse*, and the 'man, who abstains from flesh-meat, enjoy for their 'virtue an equal reward.

54. 'By subsisting on pure fruit and on roots, and 'by eating such grains as are eaten by hermits, a man 'reaps not so high a reward, as by carefully abstaining 'from animal food.

55. ' "Me he *(mân sa)* will devour in the next world, ' whose flesh I eat in this life;" *thus should a flesh eater* ' *speak, and* thus the learned pronounce the true deri- ' vation of the word *mánsa,* or flesh.

56. ' In lawfully tasting meat, in drinking fermented ' liquor, in caressing women, there is no turpitude; for ' to such enjoyments men are naturally prone: but a ' virtuous abstinence from them produces a signal com- ' pensation.

57. ' Now will I promulgate the rules of purification ' for the dead, and the modes of purifying inanimate ' things, as the law prescribes them for the four classes ' in due order.

58. ' When a child has teethed, and when, after teeth- ' ing, his head has been shorn, and when he has been ' girt with his thread, and when, being full grown, he ' dies, all his kindred are impure: on the birth of a ' child the law is the same.

59. ' By a dead body, the *sapindas* are rendered ' impure in the law for ten days, or until *the fourth* ' *day, when* the bones have been gathered up, or for ' three days, or for one day only, *according to the qua-* ' *lities of the deceased:*

60. ' Now the relation of the *sapindas,* or men con- ' nected by the funeral cake, ceases with the seventh ' person, *or in the sixth degree of ascent or descent,* and ' that of *samánódakas,* or those connected by an equal ' oblation of water, ends only, when their births and fa- ' mily-names are no longer known.

61. ' As this impurity, by reason of a dead kinsman, ' is ordained for *sapindas,* even thus it is ordained on a ' child-birth, for those who seek absolute purity.

62. ' Uncleanness, on account of the dead, is ordain- ' ed for all; but on the birth of a child, for the mother

'and father: impurity, for ten days after the child-'birth, affects the mother only; but the father, having 'bathed, becomes pure.

63. 'A man, having wasted his manhood, is purified 'by bathing; but, after begetting a child on a *para-'púrvá*, he must meditate for three days on his impure 'state.

64. 'In one day and night, added to nights three 'times three, the *sapindas* are purified after touching 'the corpse; but the *samánódakas*, in three days.

65. 'A pupil in theology, having performed the ce-'remony of burning his deceased preceptor, becomes 'pure in ten nights: he is equal, in that case, to the '*sapindas*, who carry out the dead.

66. 'In a number of nights, equal to the number of 'months from conception, a woman is purified on a mis-'carriage; and a woman in her courses is rendered 'pure by bathing, when her effusion of blood has quite 'stopped.

67. 'For deceased male children, whose heads have 'not been shorn, purity is legally obtained in one night; 'but for those, on whom that ceremony has been per-'formed, a purification of three nights is required.

68. 'A dead child under the age of two years, let 'his kinsmen carry out having decked him *with flowers*, '*and bury him* in pure ground, without collecting his 'bones *at a future time*.

69. 'Let no ceremony with fire be performed for 'him, nor that of sprinkling water; but his kindred, 'having left him like a piece of wood in the forest, 'shall be unclean for three days.

70. 'For a child under the age of three years, the ce-

'remony with water shall not be performed by his kindred; but, if his teeth be completely grown, or a 'name have been given him, they may perform it, or 'not, *at their option.*

71. 'A fellow student in theology being dead, three 'days of impurity are ordained; and, on the birth of a '*samánódaka,* purification is required for three nights.

72. 'The relations or *bethrothed but* unmarried damsels, are in three days made pure; and, in as many, 'are their paternal kinsmen purified *after their mar-'riage:*

73. 'Let them eat vegetable food without factitious, '*that is, only with native,* salt; let them bathe for three 'days at intervals; let them taste no flesh-meat; and 'let them sleep apart on the ground.

74. 'This rule, which ordains impurity by reason of 'the dead, relates to the case of one dying near his kinsmen; but, in the case of one dying at a distance, the 'following rule must be observed by those, who share 'the same cake, and by those, who share only the same 'water:

75. 'The man, who hears that a kinsman is dead in 'a distant country, becomes unclean, if ten days after 'the death have not passed, for the remainder of those 'ten days only;

76. 'But, if the ten days have elapsed, he is impure 'for three nights, and, if a year have expired, he is purified merely by touching water.

77. 'If, after the lapse of ten days, he know the 'death of a kinsman, or the birth of a male child, he 'must purify himself by bathing together with his 'clothes.

78. 'Should a child, whose teeth are not grown, or

'should a *samánódaka*, die in a distant region, the kinsman, having bathed with his apparel, becomes immediately pure.

79. 'If, during the ten days, another death or another birth intervene, a *Bráhman* remains impure, only 'till those ten days have elapsed.

80. 'A spiritual teacher being dead, the sages declare his pupil impure for three days; but for a day 'and a night, if the son or wife of the teacher be deceased: such is the sacred ordinance.

81. 'For a reader of the whole *Veda*, who dwells in 'the same house, a man is unclean three nights; but 'for a maternal uncle, a pupil, an officiating priest, and 'a distant kinsman, only one night winged *with two* '*days*.

82. 'On the death of a military king, in whose dominion he lives, *his impurity lasts* while the sun or the 'stars give light; but *it lasts* a whole day, on the death 'of a priest, who has not read the whole *Veda*, or of a 'spiritual guide, who has read only part of it, with its '*Angas*.

83. 'A man of the sacerdotal class becomes pure in 'ten days; of the warlike, in twelve; of the commercial, 'in fifteen;* of the servile, in a month.

84. 'Let no man prolong the days of impurity; 'let him not intermit the ceremonies to be performed 'with holy fires: while he performs those rites, even 'though he be a *sapinda*, he is not impure.

85. 'He, who has touched a *Chandála*, a woman in 'her courses, an outcast for deadly sin, a new-born 'child, a corpse, or one who has touched a corpse, is 'made pure by bathing.

* See Note on Book V. verse 83.

86. 'If, having sprinkled his mouth with water, and 'been long intent on his devotion, he see an unclean 'person, let him repeat, as well as he is able, the solar 'texts of the *Veda,* and those, which confer purity.

87. 'Should a *Bráhman* touch a human bone moist 'with oil, he is purified by bathing; if it be not oily, 'by stroking a cow, or by looking at the sun, having 'sprinkled his mouth duly with water.

88. 'A student in theology shall not perform the 'ceremony of pouring water at obsequies, until he 'have completed his course of religious acts; but if, 'after the completion of them, he thus make an offer-'ing of water, he becomes pure in three nights.

89. 'For those, who discharge not their prescribed 'duties, for those, whose fathers were of a lower class 'than their mothers, for those, who wear a dress of re-'ligion unauthorized by the *Veda,* and for those, who '*illegally* kill themselves, the ceremony of giving fune-'ral water is forbidden by law;

90. 'And for women imitating such heretics, as wear 'an unlawful dress, and for such women as live at their 'own pleasure, or have caused an abortion, or have 'stricken their husbands, or have drunk any spirituous 'liquor.

91. 'A student violates not the rules of his order, 'by carrying out, when dead, his own instructor in the '*Vedas,* who invested him with his holy cord, or his 'teacher of particular chapters, or his reverend ex-'pounder of their meaning, or his father, or his mother,

92. 'Let men carry out a dead *Súdra* by the south-'ern gate of the town; but the twice-born, in due order, 'by the western, northern, and eastern gates.

93. 'No taint of impurity can light on kings or stu-'dents in theology, *while employed in discharging their*

'*several duties,* nor on those who have actually begun a 'sacrifice; for the first are then placed on the seat of 'INDRA, and the others are always equally pure with 'the celestial spirit.

94. 'To a king, on the throne of magnanimity, the 'law ascribes instant purification, because his throne 'was raised for the protection of his people and the 'supply of their nourishment:

95. 'It is the same with *the kinsmen of* those, who 'die in battle, after the king has been slain, or have 'been killed by lightning, or legally by the king him-'self, or in defence of a cow, or of a priest; and with 'all those, whom the king wishes to be pure.

96. 'The corporeal frame of a king is composed of 'particles from SO'MA, AGNI, SU'RYA, PAVANA, INDRA, 'KUVE'RA, VARUNA, and YAMA, the eight guardian 'deities of the world:

97. 'By those guardians of men in substance is the 'king pervaded, and he cannot by law be impure; since 'by those tutelar gods are the purity and impurity of 'mortals both caused and removed.

98. 'By a soldier, discharging the duties of his class, 'and slain in the field with brandished weapons, the 'highest sacrifice is, in that instant, complete; and so 'is his purification: this law is fixed.

99. 'A priest, having performed funeral rites, is pu-'rified by touching water; a soldier, by touching his 'horse or elephant, or his arms; a husbandman, by 'touching his goad, or the halter of his cattle; a servant, 'by touching his staff.

100. 'This mode of purifying *sapindas,* O chief of 'the twice-born, has been fully declared to you! learn 'now the purification required on the death of kinsmen 'less intimately connected.

101. 'A *Bráhman*, having carried out a dead *Bráhman*, though not a *sapinda*, with the affection of a 'kinsman, or any of those nearly related to him by his 'mother, becomes pure in three days;

102. 'But, if he taste the food offered by their *sapindas*, he is purified in ten days; and in one day, if he 'neither partake of their food, nor dwell in the same 'house.

103. 'If he voluntarily follow a corpse, whether of a 'paternal kinsman or of another, and afterwards bathe 'with his apparel, he is made pure by touching fire and 'tasting clarified butter.

104. 'Let no kinsman, whilst any of his own class 'are at hand, cause a deceased *Bráhman* to be carried 'out by a *Súdra*; since the funeral rite, polluted by the 'touch of a servile man, obstructs his passage to heaven.

105. 'Sacred learning, austere devotion, fire, holy 'aliment, earth, the mind, water, smearing with cow-'dung, air, prescribed acts of religion, the sun, and time, 'are purifiers of imbodied spirits;

106 'But of all pure things, purity in acquiring 'wealth, is pronounced the most excellent: since he, 'who gains wealth with clean hands, is truly pure; not 'he, who is purified merely with earth and water.

107. 'By forgiveness of injuries, the learned are pu-'rified; by liberality, those who have neglected their 'duty; by pious meditation, those who have secret 'faults; by devout austerity, those who best know the '*Veda*.

108. 'By water and earth is purified what ought to 'be made pure; a river, by its current; a woman, 'whose thoughts have been impure, by her monthly 'discharge, and the chief of twice-born men, by fixing 'his mind wholly on GOD.

109. 'Bodies are cleansed by water; the mind is 'purified by truth; the vital spirit, by theology and 'devotion; the understanding, by clear knowledge.

110. 'Thus have you heard me declare the precise 'rules for purifying animal bodies: hear now the modes 'of restoring purity to various inanimate things.

111. 'Of brilliant metals, of gems, and of every 'thing made with stone, the purification ordained by 'the wise, is with ashes, water, and earth.

112. 'A golden vessel, not smeared, is cleansed with 'water only; and every thing produced in water *as* '*coral, shells, or pearls*, and every stony substance, and 'a silver vessel not enchased.

113. 'From a junction of water and fire arose gold 'and silver; and they two, therefore, are best purified 'by the elements, whence they sprang.

114. 'Vessels of copper, iron, brass, pewter, tin and 'lead, may be fitly cleansed with ashes, with acids, or 'with water.

115. 'The purification ordained for all sorts of li-'quids, is by stirring them with *kuṣa*-grass; for cloths 'folded, by sprinkling them with hallowed water; for 'wooden utensils, by planing them.

116. 'For the sacrificial pots to hold clarified but-'ter and juice of the moon-plant, by rubbing them 'with the hand, and washing them, at the time of the 'sacrifice:

117. 'Implements to wash the rice, to contain the 'oblations, to cast them into the fire, to collect, win-'now, and prepare the grain, must be purified with 'water made hot.

118. 'The purification by sprinkling is ordained for

'grain and cloths in large quantities; but to purify 'them in small parcels, *which a man may easily carry,* 'they must be washed.

119. 'Leathern utensils, and such as are made with 'cane, must generally be purified in the same manner 'with cloths; green vegetables, roots, and fruit, in the 'same manner with grain;

120. 'Silk and woollen stuff, with saline earths; 'blankets from *Nepála,* with pounded *arishtas,* or *nimba* 'fruit; vests and long drawers, with the fruit of the '*Vilva*; mantles of *kshumá,* with white mustard-seeds.

121. 'Utensils made of shells or of horn, of bones 'or of ivory, must be cleansed by him, who knows the 'law, as mantles of *kshumá* are purified, with the ad- 'dition of cows' urine or of water.

122. 'Grass, firewood, and straw, are purified by 'sprinkling them with water; a house, by rubbing, 'brushing, and smearing with cow-dung; an earthern 'pot, by a second burning:

123. 'But an earthern pot, which has been touched 'with any spirituous liquor, with urine, with ordure, 'with spittle, with pus, or with blood, cannot, even by 'another burning, be rendered pure.

124. 'Land is cleansed by five modes; by sweeping, 'by smearing with cow-dung, by sprinkling with cows' 'urine, by scraping, or by letting a cow pass a day and 'a night on it.

125. 'A thing nibbled by a bird, smelt at by a cow, 'shaken with a foot, sneezed on, or defiled by lice, is 'purified byearth scattered over it.

126. 'As long as the scent or moisture, caused by 'any impurity, remains on the thing soiled, so long must

'earth and water be repeatedly used in all purifications 'of things inanimate.

127. 'The gods declared three pure things peculiar 'to *Bráhmans;* what has been defiled without their 'knowledge; what, in cases of doubt, they sprinkle with 'water; and what they commend with their speech.

128. 'Waters are pure, as far as a cow goes to quench 'her thirst in them, if they flow over clean earth, and 'are sullied by no impurity, but have a good scent, 'colour, and taste.

129. 'The hand of an artist *employed in his art* is 'always pure; so is every vendible commodity, when 'exposed to sale; and that food is always clean, which 'a student in theology has begged and received: such 'is the sacred rule.

130. 'The mouth of a woman is constantly pure; a 'bird is pure on the fall of fruit, which he has pecked; 'a sucking animal, on the flowing of the milk; a dog, 'on his catching the deer:

131. 'The flesh of a wild beast slain by dogs, MANU 'pronounces pure; and that of an animal slain by other 'carnivorous creatures, or by men of the mixed class, 'who subsist by hunting.

132. 'All the cavities above the navel are pure, and 'all below it, unclean; so are all excretions, that fall 'from the body.

133. 'Gnats, clear drops from the mouth of a speak'er, a shadow, a cow, a horse, sun-beams, dust, earth, 'air, and fire, must all be considered as clean, even when 'they touch *an unclean thing.*

134. 'For the cleansing of vessels, which have held 'ordure or urine, earth and water must be used, as long 'as they are needful; and the same for cleansing the 'twelve corporeal impurities.

135. 'Oily exudations, seminal fluids, blood, dan-'druff, urine, feces, ear-wax, nail-parings, phlegm, tears, 'concretions on the eyes, and sweat, are the twelve im-'purities of the human frame.

136. 'By the man, who desires purity, one piece of 'earth *together with water* must be used for the conduit 'of urine, three for that of the feces; so, ten for one 'hand, *that is, the left*; then seven for both: *but, if ne-'cessary, more must be used.*

137. 'Such is the purification of married men; that 'of students must be double; that of hermits, triple; 'that of men wholly recluse, quadruple.

138. 'Let each man sprinkle the cavities of his body, 'and taste water in due form, when he has discharged 'urine or feces; when he is going to read the *Veda*; 'and, invariably, before he takes his food:

139. 'First, let him thrice taste water; then twice 'let him wipe his mouth, if he *be of a twice-born class, 'and* desire corporeal purity; but a woman or servile 'man may once respectively make that ablution.

140. '*Súdras*, engaged in religious duties, must 'perform each month the ceremony of shaving their 'heads; their food must be the orts of *Bráhmans*; 'and their mode of purification, the same with that of 'a *Vaisya*.

141. 'Such drops of water, as fall from the mouth 'or any part of the body, render it not unclean; nor 'hairs of the beard, that enter the mouth; nor what 'adheres awhile to the teeth.

142. 'Drops, which trickle on the feet of a man 'holding water for others, are held equal to waters 'flowing over pure earth: by them he is not defiled.

143. 'He, who carries in any manner an inanimate

'burden, and is touched by any thing impure, is cleans'ed by making an ablution, without laying his burden 'down.

144. 'Having vomited or been purged, let him 'bathe and taste clarified butter, but, if he have eaten 'already, let him only perform an ablution: for him, 'who has been connected with a woman, bathing is or'dained by law.

145. 'Having slumbered, having sneezed, having 'eaten, having spitten, having told untruths, having 'drunk water, and going to read sacred books, let him, 'though pure, wash his mouth.

146. 'This perfect system of rules for purifying men 'of all classes, and for cleansing inanimate things, has 'been declared to you: hear now the laws concerning 'women.

147. 'By a girl, or by a young woman, or by a wo'man advanced in years, nothing must be done, even 'in her own dwelling place, according to her mere plea'sure:

148. 'In childhood must a female be dependent on 'her father; in youth, on her husband; her lord being 'dead, on her sons; *if she have no sons, on the near 'kinsmen of her husband; if he left no kinsmen, on those 'of her father; if she have no paternal kinsmen, on the 'sovereign:* a woman must never seek independence.

149. 'Never let her wish to separate herself from 'her father, her husband, or her sons; for, by a separa'tion from them, she exposes both families to contempt.

150. 'She must always live with a cheerful temper, 'with good management in the affairs of the house, 'with great care of the household furniture, and with a 'frugal hand in all her expences.

151. 'Him, to whom her father has given her, or her 'brother with the paternal assent, let her obsequiously 'honor, while he lives; and, when he dies, let her never 'neglect him.

152. 'The recitation of holy texts, and the sacrifice 'ordained by the lord of creatures, are used in marriages 'for the sake of procuring good fortune to brides; but 'the first gift, *or troth plighted,* by the husband, is the 'primary cause *and origin* of marital dominion.

153. 'When the husband has performed the nuptial 'rites with texts from the *Veda,* he gives bliss con'tinually to his wife here below, both in season and out 'of season; and he will give her happiness in the next 'world.

154. 'Though inobservant of approved usages, or 'enamoured of another woman, or devoid of good quali'ties, yet a husband must constantly be revered as a 'god by a virtuous wife.

155. 'No sacrifice is allowed to women apart from 'their husbands, no religious rite, no fasting; as far only 'as a wife honors her lord, so far she is exalted in 'heaven.

156. 'A faithful wife, who wishes to attain in heaven 'the mansion of her husband, must do nothing unkind 'to him, be he living or dead:

157. 'Let her emaciate her body, by living volun'tarily on pure flowers, roots, and fruit; but let her not, 'when her lord is deceased, even pronounce the name 'of another man.

158. 'Let her continue till death forgiving all injuries, 'performing harsh duties, avoiding every sensual plea'sure, and cheerfully practising the incomparable rules 'of virtue, which have been followed by such women, 'as were devoted to one only husband.

159. 'Many thousands of *Bráhmans*, having avoided 'sensuality from their early youth, and having left no 'issue in their families, have ascended, *nevertheless*, to 'heaven;

160. 'And, like those abstemious men, a virtuous 'wife ascends to heaven, though she have no child, if, 'after the decease of her lord, she devote herself to pious 'austerity:

161. 'But a widow, who, from a wish to bear chil-'dren, slights her deceased husband *by marrying again*, 'brings disgrace on herself here below, and shall be ex-'cluded from the seat of her lord.

162. 'Issue, begotten on a woman by any other '*than her husband*, is here declared to be no progeny 'of hers; no more than a child, begotten on the 'wife of another man, *belongs to the begetter:* nor is 'a second husband allowed, in any part of this code, to 'a virtuous woman.

163. 'She, who neglects her former *(púrva)* lord, 'though of a lower class, and takes another *(para)* of 'a higher, becomes despicable in this world, and is 'called *parapúrvá, one who had a different husband* '*before.*

164. 'A married woman, who violates the duty, 'which she owes to her lord, brings infamy on herself 'in this life, and, *in the next*, shall enter the womb of a 'shakal, or be afflicted with *elephantiasis and other* 'diseases, which punish crimes;

165. 'While she, who slights not her lord, but keeps 'her mind, speech, and body, devoted to him, attains 'his heavenly mansion, and by good men is called '*sádhwí*, or *virtuous*.

166. 'Yes; by this course of life it is, that a woman, 'whose mind, speech, and body are kept in subjection,

'acquires high renown in this world, and, in the next, 'the same abode with her husband.

167. 'A twice-born man, versed in sacred ordi'nances, must burn, with hallowed fire and fit imple'ments of sacrifice, his wife dying before him, if she 'was of his own class, and lived by these rules:

168. 'Having thus kindled sacred fires, and perform'ed funeral rites to his wife, who died before him, he 'may again marry, and again light the nuptial fire.

169. 'Let him not cease to perform day by day, ac'cording to the preceding rules, the five great sacra'ments; and, having taken a lawful consort, let him 'dwell in his house during the second period of his 'life.

CHAP. VI.

On Devotion; or on the Third and Fourth Orders.

---

1. 'HAVING thus remained in the order of a house'keeper, as the law ordains, let the twice-born man, 'who had before completed his studentship, dwell in a 'forest, his faith being firm and his organs wholly sub'dued.

2. 'When the father of a family, perceives his mus'cles become flaccid and his hair grey, and sees the child 'of his child, let him then seek refuge in a forest:

3. 'Abandoning all food eaten in towns, and all his 'household utensils, let him repair to the lonely wood, 'committing the care of his wife to her sons, or accom'panied by her, *if she choose to attend him.*

4. 'Let him take up his consecrated fire, and all his

'domestic implements of making oblations to it, and, 'departing from the town to the forest, let him dwell 'in it with complete power over his organs *of sense and 'of action.*

5. 'With many sorts of pure food, such as holy sages 'used to eat, with green herbs, roots, and fruit, let him 'perform the five great sacraments before mentioned, 'introducing them with due ceremonies.

6. 'Let him wear a black antelope's hide, or a ves'ture of bark; let him bathe evening and morning; 'let him suffer the hairs of his head, his beard, and his 'nails to grow continually.

7. 'From such food, as himself may eat, let him, to 'the utmost of his power, make offerings and give alms; 'and with presents of water, roots, and fruit, let him 'honor those who visit his hermitage.

8. 'Let him be constantly engaged in reading the '*Veda*; patient of all extremities, universally benevo'lent, with a mind intent on the Supreme Being; a 'perpetual giver, but no receiver of gifts; with tender 'affection for all animated bodies.

9. 'Let him, as the law directs, make oblations on 'the hearth with three sacred fires; not omitting in 'due time the ceremonies to be performed at the con'junction and opposition of the moon.

10. 'Let him also perform the sacrifice ordained in 'honor of the lunar constellations, make the prescribed 'offering of new grain, and solemnize holy rites every 'four months, and at the winter and summer solstices.

11. 'With pure grains, the food of ancient sages, 'growing in the vernal and autumnal seasons, and 'brought home by himself, let him severally make, as 'the law ordains, the oblations of cakes and boiled 'grains;

12. 'And, having presented to the gods, that purest 'oblation, which the wild woods produced, let him eat 'what remains, together with some native salt, which 'himself collected.

13. 'Let him eat green herbs, flowers, roots, and 'fruit, that grow on earth or in water, and the produc- 'tions of pure trees, and oils formed in fruit.

14. 'Honey and flesh-meat he must avoid, and all 'sorts of mushrooms, the plant *bhústrina*, that named '*sigruka*, and the fruit of the *sleshmátaka*.

15. 'In the month *A'swina* let him cast away the 'food of sages, which he before had laid up, and his 'vesture, then become old, and his herbs, roots, and 'fruit.

16. 'Let him not eat the produce of ploughed land, 'though abandoned by any man, *who owns it*, nor fruit 'and roots produced in a town, even though hunger op- 'press him.

17. 'He may eat what is mellowed by fire, and he 'may eat what is ripened by time; and either let him 'break hard fruits with a stone, or let his teeth serve as 'a pestle.

18. 'Either let him pluck enough for a day, or let 'him gather enough for a month; or let him collect 'enough for six months, or lay up enough for a year.

19. 'Having procured food, as he is able, he may eat 'it at eve or in the morning; or he may take only every 'fourth, or every eighth, such regular meal;

20. 'Or, by the rules of the lunar penance, he may 'eat a mouthful less each day of the bright, and a 'mouthful more each day of the dark fortnight; or he 'may eat only once, at the close of each fortnight, a 'mess of boiled grains:

21. 'Or he may constantly live on flowers and roots, 'and on fruit matured by time, which has fallen spontaneously, strictly observing the laws ordained for hermits.

22. 'Let him slide backwards and forwards on the 'ground; or let him stand a whole day on tiptoe; or 'let him continue in motion rising and sitting alternate-'ly; but at sunrise, at noon, and at sunset, let him go 'to the waters and bathe.

23. 'In the hot season, let him sit exposed to five 'fires, *four blazing around him with the sun above*; in 'the rains, let him stand uncovered, *without even a mantle*, where the clouds pour *the heaviest* showers; in the 'cold season, let him wear humid vesture; and let him 'increase by degrees the austerity of his devotion:

24. 'Performing his ablution at the three *Savanas*, 'let him give satisfaction to the manes and to the gods; 'and, enduring harsher and harsher mortifications, let 'him dry up his bodily frame.

25. 'Then, having reposited his holy fires, as the 'law directs, in his mind, let him live without external 'fire, without a mansion, wholly silent, feeding on roots 'and fruit;

26. 'Not solicitous for the means of gratification, 'chaste as a student, sleeping on the bare earth, in the 'haunts of pious hermits, without one selfish affection, 'dwelling at the roots of trees.

27. 'From devout *Bráhmans* let him receive alms to 'support life, or from other house-keepers of twice-born 'classes, who dwell in the forest:

28. 'Or the hermit may bring food from a town, 'having received it in a basket of leaves, in his naked 'hand, or in a potsherd: and then let him swallow 'eight mouthfuls.

29. 'These and other rules must a *Bráhman*, who 'retires to the woods, diligently practise; and, for the 'purpose of uniting his soul with the Divine Spirit, let 'him study the various *Upanishads* of scripture, or '*chapters on the essence and attributes of God*,

30. 'Which have been studied with reverence by an'chorites versed in theology, and by house-keepers, who 'dwelt afterwards in forests, for the sake of increasing 'their sublime knowledge and devotion, and for the pu'rification of their bodies.

31. 'Or, *if he has any incurable disease*, let him ad'vance in a straight path, towards the invincible *north 'eastern* point, feeding on water and air, till his mortal 'frame totally decay, and his soul become united with 'the Supreme.

32. 'A *Bráhman*, having shuffled off his body by 'any of those modes, which great sages practised, and 'becoming void of sorrow and fear, rises to exaltation 'in the divine essence.

33. 'Having thus performed religious acts in a forest 'during the third portion of his life, let him become a '*Sannyási* for the fourth portion of it, abandoning all 'sensual affections, *and wholly reposing in the Supreme 'Spirit*:

34. 'The man, who has passed from order to order, 'has made oblations to fire *on his respective changes of 'state*, and has kept his members in subjection, but, tired 'with *so long a course of giving* alms and *making* offer'ings, thus reposes himself entirely on God, shall be 'raised after death to glory.

35. 'When he has paid his three debts *to the sages, 'the manes, and the gods*, let him apply his mind to final 'beatitude; but low shall He fall, who presumes to seek 'beatitude, without having discharged those debts:

36. 'After he has read the *Vedas* in the form prescribed by law, has legally begotton a son, and has performed sacrifices to the best of his power, he *has paid his three debts, and* may then apply his heart to eternal bliss;

37. 'But if a *Bráhman* have not read the *Veda*, if he have not begotten a son, and if he have not performed sacrifices, yet shall aim at final beatitude, he shall sink to a place of degradation.

38. 'Having performed the sacrifice of PRAJA'PATI, accompanied with a gift of all his wealth, *and* having reposited in his mind the sacrificial fires, a *Bráhman* may proceed from his house, *that is, from the second order, or he may proceed even from the first,* to the condition of a *Sannyási*.

39. 'Higher worlds are illuminated with the glory of that man, who passes from his house into the fourth order, giving exemption from fear to all animated beings, and pronouncing the *mystic words of* the *Veda:*

40. 'To the *Bráhman,* by whom not even the smallest dread has been occasioned by sentient creatures, there can be no dread from any quarter whatever, when he obtains a release from his mortal body.

41. 'Departing from his house, taking with him pure implements, *his water-pot and staff,* keeping silence, unallured by desire of the objects near him, let him enter into the fourth order.

42. 'Alone let him constantly dwell, for the sake of his own felicity, observing the happiness of a solitary man, who neither forsakes nor is forsaken, let him live without a companion.

43. 'Let him have no culinary fire, no domicile; let him, *when very hungry,* go to the town for food; let

'him patiently bear disease; let his mind be firm; let 'him study to know God, and fix his attention on God 'alone.

44. 'An earthen water-pot, the roots of large trees, 'coarse vesture, total solitude, equanimity toward all 'creatures, these are the characteristics of a *Bráhman* 'set free.

45. 'Let him not wish for death; let him not wish 'for life; let him expect his appointed time, as a hired 'servant expects his wages.

46. 'Let him advance his foot purified by looking 'down, *lest he touch any thing impure;* let him drink 'water purified by straining with a cloth, *lest he hurt* '*some insect;* let him, *if he choose to speak,* utter words 'purified by truth; let him by all means keep his heart 'purified.

47. 'Let him bear a reproachful speech with patience; 'let him speak reproachfully to no man; let him not, 'on account of this *frail and feverish* body, engage in 'hostility with any one living.

48. 'With an angry man let him not in his turn be 'angry; abused, let him speak mildly; nor let him utter 'a word relating to vain illusory things and confined 'within seven gates, *the five organs of sense, the heart* '*and the intellect; or this world, with three above and* '*three below it.*

49. 'Delighted with meditating on the Supreme 'Spirit, sitting fixed in such meditation, without need- 'ing any thing earthly, without one sensual desire, 'without any companion but his own soul, let him live 'in this world seeking the bliss of the next.

50. 'Neither by explaining omens and prodigies, nor 'by skill in astrology and palmistry, nor by casuistry

'and expositions of holy texts, let him at any time gain 'his daily support.

51. 'Let him not go near a house frequented by hermits, or priests, or birds, or dogs, or other beggars.

52. 'His hair, nails, and beard being clipped, bearing with him a dish, a staff, and a water-pot, his whole 'mind being fixed on GOD, let him wander about continually, without giving pain to *animal or vegetable* 'beings.

53. 'His dishes must have no fracture, nor must 'they be made of bright metals: the purification ordained for them must be with water alone, like that 'of the vessels for a sacrifice.

54. 'A gourd, a wooden bowl, an earthen dish, or a 'basket made of reeds, has MANU, son of the Self-existing, declared fit vessels to receive the food of *Bráhmans* devoted to GOD.

55. 'Only once a day let him demand food; let him 'not habituate him to eat much at a time; for an anchorite, habituated to eat much, becomes inclined to 'sensual gratifications.

56. 'At the time when the smoke of kitchen fires 'has ceased, when the pestle lies motionless, when the 'burning charcoal is extinguished, when people have 'eaten, and when dishes are removed, *that is, late in the* '*day*, let the *Sannyási* always beg food.

57. 'For missing it, let him not be sorrowful; nor 'for gaining it, let him be glad; let him care only for 'a sufficiency to support life, but let him not be anxious about his utensils.

58. 'Let him constantly disdain to receive food after 'humble reverence; since, by receiving it in conse-

'quence of an humble salutation, a *Sannyási*, though 'free, becomes a captive.

59. 'By eating little and by sitting in solitary places, 'let him restrain those organs, which are naturally hur-'ried away by sensual desires.

60. 'By the coercion of his members, by the absence 'of hate and affection, and by giving no pain to sen-'tient creatures, he becomes fit for immortality.

61. 'Let him reflect on the transmigrations of men 'caused by their sinful deeds, on their downfall into a 'region of darkness, and their torments in the mansion 'of YAMA;

62. 'On their separation from those, whom they love, 'and their union with those, whom they hate, on their 'strength overpowered by old age, and their bodies 'racked with disease;

63. 'On their agonizing departure from this cor-'poreal frame, their formation again in the womb, and 'the glidings of this vital spirit through ten thousand 'millions of uterine passages;

64. 'On the misery attached to embodied spirits 'from a violation of their duties, and the unperishable 'bliss attached to them from their abundant perform-'ance of all duties, religious and civil.

65. 'Let him reflect also, with exclusive application 'of mind, on the subtle indivisible essence of the Su-'preme Spirit, and its complete existence in all beings, 'whether extremely high or extremely low.

66. 'Equal-minded towards all creatures, in what 'order soever *he may have been* placed, let him fully 'discharge his duty, though he bear not the visible 'marks of his order: the visible mark, *or mere name,*

'of his order, is by no means an effective discharge of 'his duty;

67. 'As, although the fruit of the tree *kataka* purify water, yet a man cannot purify water by merely 'pronouncing the name of that fruit: *he must throw 'it, when pounded, into the jar.*

68. 'For the sake of preserving minute animals by 'night and by day, let him walk, though with pain to 'his own body, perpetually looking on the ground.

69. 'Let a *Sannyási*, by way of expiation for *the 'death of* those creatures, which he may have destroy-'ed unknowingly by day or by night, make six sup-'pressions of his breath, having duly bathed:

70. 'Even three suppressions of breath, made ac-'cording to the divine rule, accompanied with the tri-'verbal phrase *(bhur bhuvah swah)* and the triliteral 'syllable *(óm)*, may be considered as the highest devo-'tion of a *Bráhman;*

71. 'For as the dross and impurities of metallic ores 'are consumed by fire, thus are the sinful acts of the 'human organs consumed by suppressions of the breath, '*while the mystic words, and the measures of the* gáyatrì '*are revolved in the mind.*

72. 'Let him thus, by such suppressions of breath, 'burn away his offences; by reflecting intensely on the 'steps of ascent to beatitude, *let him destroy sin;* by 'coercing his members, let him restrain all sensual at-'tachments; by meditating on *the intimate union of 'his own soul and* the divine essence, let him extin-'guish all qualities repugnant to the nature of GOD.

73. 'Let him observe, with extreme application of 'mind, the progress of this internal spirit through va-'rious bodies, high and low; *a progress* hard to be dis-'cerned by men with unimproved intellects.

74. 'He, who fully understands the perpetual omnipresence of GOD, can be led no more captive by criminal acts; but he, who possesses not that sublime 'knowledge, shall wander again through the world.

75. 'By injuring nothing animated, by subduing all 'sensual habits, by devout rites ordained in the *Veda*, 'and by rigorous mortifications, men obtain, even in 'this life, the state of beatitude.

76. 'A mansion with bones for its rafters and beams; 'with nerves and tendons, for cords; with muscles and 'blood, for mortar; with skin, for its outward covering; filled with no sweet perfume, but loaded with 'feces and urine;

77. 'A mansion infested by age and by sorrow, the 'seat of malady, harassed with pains, haunted with the 'quality of darkness, and incapable of standing long; 'such a mansion of the vital soul let its occupier always 'cheerfully quit:

78. 'As a tree leaves the bank of a river, *when it falls in*, or as a bird leaves the branch of a tree *at his pleasure*, thus he, who leaves his body *by necessity or by legal choice*, is delivered from the ravening shark, '*or crocodile*, of the world.

79. 'Letting his good acts descend (by the law of 'the *Veda*,) to those, who love him, and his evil deeds, 'to those, who hate him, he may attain, through devout meditation, the eternal spirit.

80. 'When, having well considered the nature and 'consequence of sin, he becomes averse from all sensual 'delights, he then attains bliss in this world; bliss, 'which shall endure after death.

81. 'Thus having gradually abandoned all earthly 'attachments, and indifferent to all pairs of opposite

'things, *as honor and dishonor, and the like,* he remains 'absorbed in the divine essence.

82. 'All, that has now been declared, is obtained by 'pious meditations; but no man, who is ignorant of 'the Supreme Spirit, can gather the fruit of mere ce-'remonial acts.

83. 'Let him constantly study that part of the *Veda,* 'which relates to sacrifice; that, which treats of sub-'ordinate deities; that, which reveals the nature of 'the Supreme GOD; and whatever is declared in the '*Upanishads.*

84. 'This holy scripture is a sure refuge even for 'those, who understand not its meaning, and of course 'for those, who understand it; this *Veda* is a sure re-'source for those, who seek bliss above; this *is a sure* '*resource* for those, who seek bliss eternal.

85. 'That *Bráhman,* who becomes a *Sannyásí* by this 'discipline, *announced* in due order, shakes off sin here 'below, and reaches the Most High.

86. 'This *general* law has been revealed to you for 'anchorites with subdued minds: now learn the parti-'cular discipline of those who become recluses accord-'ing to the *Veda,* that is, *of anchorites in the first of* '*the four degrees.*

87. 'The student, the married man, the hermit, and 'the anchorite, are the offspring, though in four orders, 'of married men keeping house;

88. 'And all, or even any, of those orders, assumed 'in their turn, according to the sacred ordinances, lead 'the *Bráhman,* who acts by the preceding rules, to the 'highest mansion:

89. 'But of all those, the house-keeper, observing 'the regulations of the *Sruti* and *Smriti,* may be called 'the chief; since he supports the three *other orders.*

90. 'As all rivers, female and male, run to their de-'termined place in the sea, thus men of all *other* orders, 'repair to their fixed place in the mansion of the house-'keeper.

91. 'By *Bráhmans*, placed in these four orders, a 'ten-fold system of duties must ever be sedulously 'practised :

92. 'Content, returning good for evil, resistance to 'sensual appetites, abstinence from illicit gain, purifica-'tion, coercion of the organs, knowledge of scripture, 'knowledge of the Supreme Spirit, veracity, and free-'dom from wrath, form their ten-fold system of duties.

93. 'Such *Bráhmans*, as attentively read the ten pre-'cepts of duty, and after reading, carefully practise 'them, attain the most exalted condition.

94. 'A *Bráhman* having practised, with organs un-'der command, this ten-fold system of duty, having 'heard the *Upanishads* explained, as the law directs, and 'who has discharged his three debts, may become an 'anchorite, *in the house of his son*, according to the *Veda* ;

95. 'And, having abandoned all ceremonial acts, 'having expiated all his offences, having obtained a 'command over his organs, and having perfectly under-'stood the scripture, he may live at his ease, while the 'household affairs are conducted by his son.

96. 'When he thus has relinquished all forms, is in-'tent on his own occupation, and free from every other 'desire, when, by devoting himself to GOD, he has effac-'ed sin, he then attains the supreme path of glory.

97, 'This four-fold regulation for the sacerdotal class, 'has thus been made known to you ; a just regulation, 'producing endless fruit after death : next, learn the 'duty of kings, *or the military class*.

CHAP. VII.

On Government, and Public Law; or on the Military Class.

1. 'I WILL fully declare the duty of kings; *and show* 'how a ruler of men should conduct himself, in what 'manner he was framed, and how his ultimate reward '*may be attained by him.*

2. 'By a man of the military class, who has received 'in due form the investiture which the *Veda* prescribes, 'great care must be used to maintain the whole *assem*-'*blage of laws.*

3. 'Since, if the world had no king, it would quake 'on all sides through fear, the ruler of this *universe*, 'therefore, created a king, for the maintenance of this 'system, both religious and civil,

4. 'Forming him of eternal particles drawn from the 'substance of INDRA, PAVANA, YAMA, SU'RYA, of AGNI 'and VARUNA, of CHANDRA and KUVE'RA:

5. 'And since a king was composed of particles drawn 'from those chief guardian deities, he consequently sur-'passes all mortals in glory.

6. 'Like the sun, he burns eyes and hearts; nor can 'any human creature on earth even gaze on him.

7. 'He *is* fire and air; he, both sun and moon; he, 'the god of criminal justice; he, the genius of wealth; 'he the regent of waters; he, the lord of the firmament.

8. 'A king, even though a child, must not be treat-'ed lightly, from an idea that he is a mere mortal; no;

'he is a powerful divinity, who appears in a human 'shape.

9. 'Fire burns only one person, who carelessly goes 'too near it; but the fire of a king in wrath burns a 'whole family, with all their cattle and goods.

10. 'Fully considering the business before him, his 'own force, and the place, and the time, he assumes in 'succession all sorts of forms, for the sake of advancing 'justice.

11. 'He, sure, must be the perfect essence of majesty, 'by whose favor Abundance rises on her lotos, in whose 'valour dwells conquest; in whose anger, death.

12. 'He, who shews hatred of the king, through de-'lusion of mind, will certainly perish; for speedily will 'the king apply his heart to that man's perdition.

13. 'Let the king prepare a just compensation for 'the good, and a just punishment for the bad: the rule 'of strict justice let him never transgress.

14. 'For his use BRAHMA' formed in the beginning 'of time the genius of punishment, with a body of pure 'light, his own son, even abstract criminal justice, the 'protector of all created things:

15. 'Through fear of that genius, all sentient beings, 'whether fixed or locomotive, are fitted for natural en-'joyments and swerve not from duty.

16. 'When the king, therefore, has fully considered 'place and time, and his own strength, and the divine 'ordinance, let him justly inflict punishment on all 'those, who act unjustly.

17. 'Punishment is an active ruler; he is the true 'manager of public affairs; he is the dispenser of laws;

'and wise men call him the sponsor of all the four orders for the discharge of their several duties.

18. 'Punishment governs all mankind; punishment 'alone preserves them; punishment wakes, while their 'guards are asleep; the wise consider punishment as 'the perfection of justice.

19. 'When rightly and considerately inflicted, it 'makes all the people happy; but, inflicted without full 'consideration, it wholly destroys them all.

20. 'If the king were not, without indolence, to pun-'ish the guilty, the stronger would roast the weaker, 'like fish, on a spit; (*or, according to one reading*, the 'stronger would oppress the weaker, like fish in their 'element;)

21. 'The crow would peck the consecrated offering 'of rice; the dog would lick the clarified butter; owner-'ship would remain with none; the lowest would over 'set the highest.

22. 'The whole race of men is kept in order by 'punishment; for a guiltless man is hard to be found: 'through fear of punishment, indeed, this universe is 'enabled to enjoy its blessings;

23. 'Deities and demons, heavenly songsters and 'cruel giants, birds and serpents, are made capable, by 'just correction, of their several enjoyments.

24. 'All classes would become corrupt; all barriers 'would be destroyed, there would be total confusion 'among men, if punishment either were not infflicted, 'or were inflicted unduly:

25. 'But where punishment, with a black hue and a 'red eye, advances to destroy sin, there, if the judge 'discern well, the people are undisturbed.

26. 'Holy sages consider as a fit dispenser of criminal justice, that king, who invariably speaks truth, 'who duly considers all cases, who understands the sacred books, who knows the distinctions of virtue, pleasure, and riches;

27. 'Such a king, if he justly inflict legal punishments, greatly increases those three means of happiness; but punishment itself shall destroy a king, who 'is crafty, voluptuous, and wrathful:

28. 'Criminal justice, the bright essence of majesty, 'and hard to be supported by men with unimproved 'minds, eradicates a king, who swerves from his duty, 'together with all his race:

29. 'Punishment shall overtake his castles, his territories, his peopled land, with all fixed and moveable 'things, that exist on it: even the gods and the sages, '*who lose their oblations*, will be afflicted and ascend to 'the sky.

30. 'Just punishment cannot be inflicted by an ignorant and covetous king, who has no wise and virtuous 'assistant, whose understanding has not been improved, 'and whose heart is addicted to sensuality:

31. 'By a king, wholly pure, faithful to his promise, observant of his scriptures, with good assistants 'and sound understanding, may punishment be justly 'inflicted.

32. 'Let him in his own domains act with justice, 'chastise foreign foes with rigour, behave without duplicity to his affectionate friends, and with lenity to '*Bráhmans*.

33. 'Of a king, thus disposed, even though he subsist by gleaning, *or, be his treasure ever so small*, the 'fame is far spread in the world, like a drop of oil in 'water;

20

34. 'But of a king with a contrary disposition, with 'passions unsubdued, *be his riches ever so great,* the 'fame is contracted in the world, like clarified butter 'in the same element.

35. 'A king was created as the protector of all those 'classes and orders, who, from the first to the last, dis- 'charge their several duties;

36. '*And* all, that must be done by him, for the pro- 'tection of his people, with the assistance of good mi- 'nisters, I will declare to you, as the law directs, in 'due order.

37. 'Let the king, having risen at early dawn, res- 'pectfully attend to *Bráhmans,* learned in the three '*Vedas,* and in the science of ethics; and by their de- 'cision let him abide.

38. 'Constantly must he show respect to *Bráhmans,* 'who have grown old, *both in years and in piety,* who 'know the scriptures, who *in body and mind* are pure; 'for he, who honors the aged, will perpetually be ho- 'nored even by cruel demons:

39. 'From them, though he may have acquired mo- 'dest behavior *by his own good sense and by study,* let 'him continually learn habits of modesty and compo- 'sure; since a king, whose demeanor is humble and 'composed, never perishes.

40. 'While, through want of such humble virtue, 'many kings have perished with all their possessions, 'and, through virtue united with modesty, even her- 'mits have obtained kingdoms.

41. 'Through want of that virtuous humility VE'NA 'was utterly ruined, and so was the great king NA- 'HUSHA, and SUDA'SA and YAVANA, *(or, by a different* '*reading,* and SUDA'MAN, the son of PIYAVANA) and 'SUMAC'HA, and NIMI;

42. 'But, by virtues with humble behavior, PRIT'HU 'and MANU acquired sovereignty; KUVE'RA, wealth in-'exhaustible; and VISWA'MITRA, son of GA'DHI, the 'rank of a priest, *though born in the military class.*

43. 'From those, who know the three *Vedas,* let him 'learn the triple doctrine comprised in them, together 'with the primeval science of criminal justice and sound 'policy, the system of logic and metaphysics, and sub-'lime theological truth: from the people he must learn 'the theory of *agriculture, commerce, and other* practi-'cal arts.

44. 'Day and night must he strenuously exert him-'self to gain complete victory over his own organs; 'since that king alone, whose organs are completely 'subdued, can keep his people firm to their duty.

45. 'With extreme care let him shun eighteen vices, 'ten proceeding from love of pleasure, eight springing 'from wrath, and all ending in misery;

46. 'Since a king, addicted to vices arising from love 'of pleasure, must lose both his wealth and his virtue, 'and, addicted to vices arising from anger, he may lose 'his life *from the public resentment.*

47. 'Hunting, gaming, sleeping by day, censuring 'rivals, excess with women, intoxication, singing, in-'strumental music, dancing, and useless travel, are the 'ten-fold set of vices produced by love of pleasure:

48. 'Tale bearing, violence, insidious wounding, envy, 'detraction, unjust seizure of property, reviling, and 'open assault are in like manner the eight-fold set of 'vices, to which anger gives birth.

49. 'A selfish inclination, which all wise men know 'to be the root of those two sets, let him suppress with 'diligence: both sets of vices are constantly produced 'by it.

50. 'Drinking, dice, women, and hunting, let him 'consider as the four most pernicious in the set, which 'love of pleasure occasions:

51. 'Battery, defamation, and injury to property, let 'him always consider as the three most heinous in the 'set, which arises from wrath:

52. '*And* in this seven-fold assemblage of vices, too 'frequently prevailing in all kingdoms, let an enlighten-'ed prince consider the first, and so forth in order, as 'the most abominable in each set.

53. 'On a comparison between death and vice, the 'learned pronounce vice the more dreadful; since, after 'death, a vicious man sinks to regions lower and lower, 'while a man, free from vice, reaches heaven.

54. 'The king must appoint seven or eight ministers, 'who must be sworn *by touching a sacred image and 'the like;* men, whose ancestors were servants of 'kings; who are versed in the holy books; who 'are personally brave; who are skilled in the use of 'weapons; and whose lineage is noble.

55. 'Even an act easy in itself is hard sometimes to 'be performed by a single man, especially if he have 'no assistant near: how much harder *must it be to per-'form alone the business of* a kingdom with great re-'venues!

56. 'Let him perpetually consult with those minis-'ters on peace and war, on his forces, on his revenues, 'on the protection of his people, and on the means of 'bestowing aptly the wealth which he has acquired:

57. 'Having ascertained the several opinions of his 'counsellors, *first* apart and *then* collectively, let him 'do what is most beneficial for him in public affairs.

58. 'To one learned *Bráhman*, distinguished among

'them all, let the king impart his momentous counsel, 'relating to six *principal* articles.

59. 'To him, with full confidence, let him intrust all 'transactions; and with him, having taken his final 'resolution, let him begin all his measures.

60. 'He must likewise appoint other officers; men 'of integrity, well informed, steady, habituated to gain 'wealth, by honorable means, and tried by experience.

61. 'As many officers as the due performance of his 'business requires, not slothful men, *but active*, able, 'and well instructed, so many, and no more, let him 'appoint.

62. 'Among those let him employ the brave, the 'skilful, the well-born, and the honest, in his mines *of* '*gold or gems*, and in other similar works *for amassing* '*wealth*; but the pusillanimous, in the recesses of his 'palace.

63. 'Let him likewise appoint an ambassador versed 'in all the *Śástras*, who understands hints, external 'signs, and actions, *whose hand and heart are* pure, 'whose abilities are great, and whose birth was illus- 'trious:

64. 'That royal ambassador is applauded most, who 'is generally beloved, pure within and without, dexter- 'ous in business, and endued with an excellent memo- 'ry; who knows countries and times, is handsome, in- 'trepid, and eloquent.

65. 'The forces of the realm must be immediately 'regulated by the commander in chief; the actual in- 'fliction of punishment, by the officers of criminal jus- 'tice; the treasury and the country, by the king him- 'self; peace and war, by ambassadors.

66. 'For it is the ambassador alone who unites, who

'alone disjoins the united; that is, he transacts the 'business, by which kingdoms are at variance or in 'amity.

67. In the transaction of affairs let the ambassador 'comprehend the visible signs and hints, and discover 'the acts, of the foreign king, by the signs, hints, and 'acts of his confidential servants, and the measures, 'which that king wishes to take, by *the character and* '*conduct of* his ministers.

68. 'Thus, having learned completely *from his am*'*bassador* all the designs of the foreign prince, let the 'king so apply his vigilant care, that he bring no evil 'on himself.

69. 'Let him fix his abode in a district containing 'open champaigns; abounding with grain; inhabited 'chiefly by the virtuous; not infected with maladies; 'beautiful to the sight; surrounded by submissive '*mountaineers, foresters, or other* neighbours; a country, 'in which the subjects may live at ease.

70. 'There let him reside in a capital, having, by 'way of a fortress, a desert *rather more than twenty* '*miles round it,* or a fortress of earth, a fortress of water, 'or of trees, a fortress of armed men, or a fortress of 'mountains.

71. 'With all possible care let him secure a fortress 'of mountains; for, among those just mentioned, a for'tress of mountains has many transcendent properties.

72. 'In the three first of them live wild beasts, ver'min, and aquatic animals; in the three last, apes, men, 'and gods, in order as they are named:

73. 'As enemies hurt them not in the shelter of 'their several abodes, thus foes hurt not a king, who 'has taken refuge in his *durga,* or *place of difficult ac*'*cess.*

74. 'One bowman, placed on a wall, is a match in 'war for a hundred enemies; and a hundred, for ten 'thousand; therefore is a fort recommended.

75. 'Let that fort be supplied with weapons, with 'money, with grain, with beasts, with *Bráhmans*, with 'artificers, with engines, with grass, and with water.

76. 'In the centre of it let him raise his own palace, 'well finished in all its parts, completely defended, ha-'bitable in every season, brilliant *with white stucco*, sur-'rounded with water and trees:

77. 'Having prepared it for his mansion, let him 'choose a consort of the same class with himself, en-'dued with all the bodily marks of excellence, born of 'an exalted race, captivating his heart, adorned with 'beauty and the best qualities.

78. 'He must appoint also a domestic priest, and re-'tain a performer of sacrifices, who may solemnize the 'religious rites of his family, and those performed with 'three sacred fires.

79. 'Let the king make sacrifices, accompanied with 'gifts of many different kinds; and, for the full dis-'charge of his duty, let him give the *Bráhmans* both '*legal* enjoyments and *moderate* wealth.

80. 'His annual revenue he may receive from his 'whole dominion through his collectors; but let him 'in this world observe the divine ordinances; let him 'act as a father to his people.

81. 'Here and there he must appoint many sorts of 'intelligent supervisors, who may inspect all the acts of 'the officers engaged in his business.

82. 'To *Bráhmans* returned from the mansions of 'their preceptors, let him show due respect; for that is

'called a precious unperishable gem, deposited by kings 'with the sacerdotal class:

83. 'It is a gem, which neither thieves or foes take 'away; which never perishes: kings must, therefore, 'deposit with *Bráhmans* that indestructible jewel *of res-'pectful presents.*

84. 'An oblation in the mouth, *or hand*, of a *Bráh-'man*, is far better than offerings to holy fire: it never 'drops; it never dries; it is never consumed.

85. 'A gift, to one not a *Bráhman*, produces fruit of 'a middle standard; to one who calls himself a *Bráh-'man*, double; to a well-read *Bráhman*, a hundred 'thousand-fold; to one who has read all the *Vedas*, 'infinite.

86. 'Of a gift made with faith in the *Śástra*, to a 'person highly deserving it, the giver shall indubitably 'gain the fruit after death, be the present small or 'great.

87. 'A KING, while he protects his people, being de-'fied by an enemy of equal, greater, or less force, must 'by no means turn his face from battle, but must re-'member the duty of his military class:

88. 'Never to recede from combat, to protect the 'people, and to honor the priests, is the highest duty of 'kings and ensures their felicity.

89. 'Those rulers of the earth, who, desirous of de-'feating each other, exert their utmost strength in bat-'tle, without ever averting their faces, ascend after 'death directly to heaven.

90. 'Let no man, engaged in combat, smite his foe 'with *sharp* weapons concealed *in wood*, nor with arrows 'mischievously barbed, nor with poisoned arrows, nor 'with darts blazing with fire;

91. ' Nor let him *in a car or on horseback* strike his ' enemy alighted on the ground ; nor an effeminate ' man ; nor one, *who sues for life* with closed palms ; ' nor one, whose hair is loose *and obstructs his sight* ; ' nor one, who sits down *fatigued* ; nor one, who says ' " I am thy *captive* ;"

92. ' Nor one, who sleeps ; nor one, who has lost his ' coat of mail ; nor one, who is naked ; nor one, who ' is disarmed ; nor one, who is a spectator, but not a ' combatant ; nor one, who is fighting with another ' man :

93. ' Calling to mind the duty of honorable men, ' let him never slay one, who has broken his weapon ; ' nor one, who is afflicted *with private sorrow* ; nor ' one, who has been grievously wounded ; nor one, who ' is terrified ; nor one, who turns his back.

94. ' The soldier, indeed, who, fearing and turning ' his back, happens to be slain by his foes in an engage- ' ment, shall take upon himself all the sin of his com- ' mander, whatever it be ;

95. ' And the commander shall take to himself *the ' fruit of* all the good conduct, which the soldier, who ' turns his back and is killed, had previously stored up ' for a future life.

96. ' Cars, horses, elephants, umbrellas, habiliments, ' *except the jewels which may adorn them*, grain, cattle, ' women, all sorts of liquids and metals, except gold ' and silver, are the lawful prizes of the man who takes ' them in war ;

97. ' But of those prizes, the captors must lay the ' most valuable before the king ; such is the rule in the ' *Veda* concerning them ; and the king should distri- ' bute among the whole army what has not been sepa- ' rately taken.

98. 'Thus has been declared the blameless primeval 'law for military men; from this law a king must 'never depart, when he attacks his foes in battle.

99. 'What he has not gained *from his foe*, let him 'strive to gain; what he has acquired, let him pre- 'serve with care; what he preserves, let him augment; 'and what he has augmented, let him bestow on the de- 'serving.

100. 'This is the four-fold rule, which he must con- 'sider as the sure means of attaining the great object 'of man, *happiness;* and let him practise it fully with- 'out intermission, without indolence:

101. 'What he has not gained, let him strive to gain 'by military strength; what he has acquired, let him 'preserve by careful inspection; what he has preserv- 'ed, let him augment by legal modes of increase; and 'what he has augmented, let him dispense with just li- 'berality.

102. 'Let his troops be constantly exercised; his 'prowess, constantly displayed; what he ought to se- 'cure, constantly secured; and the weakness of his foe, 'constantly investigated.

103. 'By a king, whose forces are always ready for 'action, the whole world may be kept in awe; let him 'then, by a force always ready, make all creatures liv- 'ing his own.

104. 'Let him act on all occasions without guile, and 'never with insincerity; but, keeping himself ever on 'his guard, let him discover the fraud intended by his 'foe.

105. 'Let not his enemy discern his vulnerable part, 'but the vulnerable part of his enemy let him well dis- 'cern: like a tortoise, let him draw in his members

'*under the shell of concealment*, and diligently let him 'repair any breach that may be made in it.

106. 'Like a heron, let him muse on gaining ad-'vantages; like a lion, let him put forth his strength; 'like a wolf, let him creep towards his prey; like a hare, 'let him double to secure his retreat.

107. 'When he thus has prepared himself for con-'quest, let him reduce all opposers to submission by 'negotiation and three other expedients, *namely, pre-'sents, division, and force of arms:*

108. 'If they cannot be restrained by the three first 'methods, then let him, firmly but gradually, bring 'them to subjection by military force.

109. 'Among those four modes of obtaining success, 'the wise prefer negotiation and war for the exaltation 'of kingdoms.

110. 'As a husbandman plucks up weeds and pre-'serves his corn, thus let a king destroy his opponents 'and secure his people.

111. 'That king, who, through weakness of intellect, 'rashly oppresses his people, will, together with his 'family, be deprived both of kingdom and life:

112. 'As, by the loss of bodily sustenance, the lives 'of animated beings are destroyed, thus, by the distress 'of kingdoms, are destroyed even the lives of kings.

113. 'For the sake of protecting his dominions, let 'the king perpetually observe the following rules; for, 'by protecting his dominions, he will increase his own 'happiness.

114. 'Let him place, as the protectors of his realm, 'a company of guards, commanded by an approved offi-

'cer, over two, three, five, or a hundred districts, *ac-'cording to their extent.*

115. 'Let him appoint a lord of one town with its 'district, a lord of ten towns, a lord of twenty, a lord of 'a hundred, and a lord of a thousand.

116. 'Let the lord of one town certify of his own ac-'cord to the lord of ten towns any *robberies, tumults, or 'other* evils, which arise in his district, *and which he 'cannot suppress*; and the lord of ten, to the lord of 'twenty:

117. 'Then let the lord of twenty towns notify them 'to the lord of a hundred; and let the lord of a hundred 'transmit the information himself to the lord of a thou-'sand townships.

118. 'Such food, drink, wood, and other articles, as 'by law should be given each day to the king by the 'inhabitants of the township, let the lord of one town 'receive *as his perquisite:*

119. 'Let the lord of ten towns enjoy the produce 'of two plough-lands, *or as much ground as can be tilled 'with two ploughs, each drawn by six bulls;* the lord of 'twenty, that of ten* plough-lands; the lord of a hun-'dred, that of a village or small town; the lord of a 'thousand, that of a large town.

120. 'The affairs of those *townships*, either jointly 'or separately transacted, let another minister of the 'king inspect; who should be well affected, and by no 'means remiss.

121. 'In every large town or city, let him appoint one 'superintendent of all affairs, elevated in rank, formi-'dable in power, distinguished as a planet among stars:

* See Note on Book VII. verse 119.

122. 'Let that governor from time to time survey all 'the rest in person, and, by means of his emissaries, 'let him perfectly know their conduct in their several 'districts.

123. 'Since the servants of the king, whom he has 'appointed guardians of districts, are generally knaves, 'who seize what belongs to other men, from such knaves 'let him defend his people:

124. 'Of such evil-minded servants, as wring wealth 'from subjects attending them on business, let the king 'confiscate all the possessions, and banish them from 'his realm.

125. 'For women, employed in the service of the 'king, and for his whole set of menial servants, let him 'daily provide a maintenance, in proportion to their 'station and to their work:

126. 'One *pana* of copper must be given *each day* 'as wages to the lowest servant, with two cloths *for* '*apparel* every half-year, and a *dróna* of grain every 'month; to the highest *must be given wages in the ratio* '*of* six *to one*.

127. 'Having ascertained the rates of purchase and 'sale, *the length of* the way, the expenses of food and of 'condiments, the charges of securing the goods carried, 'and the net profits of trade, let the king oblige traders 'to pay taxes *on their saleable commodities*:

128. 'After full consideration, let a king so levy 'those taxes continually in his dominions, that both he 'and the merchant may receive a just compensation for 'their several acts.

129. 'As the leech, the suckling calf, and the bee, 'take their natural food by little and little, thus must 'a king draw from his dominions an annual revenue.'

130. 'Of cattle, of gems, of gold and silver, *added* '*each year to the capital stock,* a fiftieth part may be 'taken by the king; of grain, an eighth part, a sixth or 'a twelfth, *according to the difference of the soil, and the* '*labour necessary to cultivate it.*

131. 'He may also take a sixth part of the clear an-'nual increase of trees, flesh-meat, honey, clarified but-'ter, perfumes, medical substances, liquids, flowers, 'roots, and fruit,

132. 'Of gathered leaves, potherbs, grass, utensils 'made with leather or cane, earthen pots, and all things 'made of stone.

133. 'A king, even though dying *with want,* must 'not receive any tax from a *Bráhman* learned in the '*Vedas,* nor suffer such a *Bráhman,* residing in his ter-'ritories, to be afflicted with hunger.

134. 'Of that king, in whose dominion a learned '*Bráhman* is afflicted with hunger, the whole kingdom 'will in a short time be afflicted with famine.

135. 'The king, having ascertained his knowledge 'of scripture and good morals, must allot him a suit-'able maintenance, and protect him on all sides, as a 'father protects his own son:

136. 'By that religious duty, which such a *Bráhman* 'performs each day, under the full protection of the 'sovereign, the life, wealth, and dominions of his pro-'tector shall be greatly increased.

137. 'Let the king order a mere trifle to be paid, in 'the name of the annual tax, by the meaner inhabitants 'of his realm, who subsist by petty traffic:

138. 'By low handicraftsmen, artificers, and servile 'men, who support themselves by labour, the king may 'cause work to be done for a day in each month.

139. 'Let him not cut up his own root *by taking* 'no revenue, nor the root of other men by excess of 'covetousness; for, by cutting up his own root *and* '*theirs*, he makes both himself and them wretched.

140. 'Let him, considering the *diversity of* cases, be '*occasionally* sharp and *occasionally* mild, since a king, 'duly sharp and mild, becomes universally approved.

141. 'When tired of overlooking the affairs of men, 'let him assign the station *of such an inspector* to a 'principal minister, who well knows his duty, who is 'eminently learned, whose passions are subdued, and 'whose birth is exalted.

142. 'Thus must he protect his people, discharging, 'with great exertion and without langour, all those du-'ties, which the law requires him to perform.

143. 'That monarch, whose subjects are carried from 'his kingdom by ruffians, while they call aloud for pro-'tection, and he barely looks on them with his minis-'ters, is a dead, and not a living king.

144. 'The highest duty of a military man is the de-'fence of his people, and the king who receives the 'consideration just mentioned, is bound to discharge 'that duty.

145. 'Having risen in the last watch of the night, 'his body being pure, and his mind attentive, having 'made oblations to fire, and shown due respect to the 'priests, let him enter his hall *decently* splendid:

146. 'Standing there, let him gratify his subjects, 'before he dismiss them, *with kind looks and words*; 'and, having dismissed them all, let him take secret 'council with his principal ministers:

147. 'Ascending up the back of a mountain, or

'going privately to a terrace, a bower, a forest, or a 'lonely place, without listeners, let him consult with 'them unobserved.

148. 'That prince, of whose weighty secrets all assemblies of men are ignorant, shall attain dominion 'over the whole earth, though *at first* he possess no 'treasure.

149. 'At the time of consultation, let him remove 'the stupid, the dumb, the blind, and the deaf, talking 'birds, decrepit old men, women, and infidels, the 'diseased and the maimed;

150. 'Since those, who are disgraced *in this life by 'reason of sins formerly committed,* are apt to betray se'cret council; so are talking birds; and so above all 'are women: them he must, for that reason, diligently 'remove.

151. 'At noon or at midnight, when his fatigues 'have ceased, and his cares are dispersed, let him deli'berate, with those ministers or alone, on virtue, lawful 'pleasure, and wealth;

152. 'On the means of reconciling the acquisition of 'them, when they oppose each other; on bestowing his 'daughters in marriage, and on preserving his sons *from 'evil by the best education*;

153. 'On sending ambassadors and messengers; on 'the probable events of his measures; on the behaviour '*of his women* in the private apartment; and on the 'acts even of his own emissaries.

154. 'On the whole eight-fold business of kings, *re'lating to the revenue, to their expenses, to the good or 'bad conduct of their ministers, to legislation in dubious 'cases, to civil and criminal justice, and to expiations 'for crimes,* let him reflect with the greatest attention; 'on his five sorts of spies, *or active and artful youths, de-*

'*graded anchorets, distressed husbandmen, decayed mer-*
'*chants, and fictitious penitents, whom he must pay and*
'*see privately*; on the good will or enmity of his neigh-
'bours, and on the state of the circumjacent countries.

155. 'On the conduct of that foreign prince, who has 'moderate strength *equal to one ordinary foe, but no* '*match for two*; on the designs of him, who is willing 'and able to be a conqueror; on the condition of him, 'who is pacific, *but a match even for the former unallied*; 'and on that of his *natural* enemy, let him sedulously 'meditate:

156. 'Those *four powers,* who, in one word, are the 'root or *principal strength* of the countries round him, 'added to eight others, *who are called the* branches, *and* '*are as many degrees of allies and opponents variously* '*distinguished,* are declared to be twelve chief objects '*of the royal consideration*;

157. 'And five other heads, namely, their ministers, 'their territories, their strong holds, their treasuries, 'and their armies, being applied to each *of those twelve,* 'there are in all, *together with them,* seventy-two *foreign* 'objects *to be carefully investigated.*

158. 'Let the king consider as hostile to him, the 'power immediately beyond him, and the favorer of 'that power; as amicable, the power next beyond his '*natural* foe; and as neutral, the powers beyond that '*circle*:

159. 'All those *powers* let him render subservient to 'his interest by mild measures and the other *three* ex-'pedients *before mentioned,* either separate or united, 'but principally by valor and policy *in arms and nego-*'*tiation.*

160 'Let him constantly deliberate on the six mea-'sures of a military prince, *namely,* waging war, and 'making peace or alliance, marching to battle, and sit-

'ting encamped, distributing his forces, and seeking the 'protection of a more powerful monarch:

161. 'Having considered the posture of affairs, let 'him occasionally apply to it the measure of sitting 'inactive, or of marching to action, of peace, or of war, 'of dividing his force, or of seeking protection.

162. 'A king must know, that there are two sorts 'of alliance and war; two, of remaining encamped, and 'of marching; *two, likewise, of dividing his army,* and 'two of obtaining protection from another power.

163. 'The two sorts of alliance, attended with pre-'sent and future advantages, are held to be those, when 'he acts in conjuntion with his ally, and when he acts 'apart from him.

164. 'War is declared to be of two sorts; when it 'is waged for an injury to himself, and when it is wag-'ed for an injury to his ally, with a view to harass the 'enemy both in season and out of season.

165. 'Marching is of two sorts, when destructive 'acts are done at his own pleasure by himself apart, or 'when his ally attends him.

166. 'The two sorts of sitting encamped are, *first,* 'when he has been gradually weakened by the Divine 'Power, or by the operation of past sins, and, *secondly,* 'when, to favor his ally, he remains in his camp.

167. 'A detachment commanded by the king in per-'son, and a detachment commanded by a general officer, 'for the purpose of carrying some important point, are 'declared by those, who well know the six measures, 'to be the two modes of dividing his army.

168. 'The two modes of seeking protection, that his 'powerful support may be proclaimed in all countries,

'are, *first,* when he wishes to be secure from apprehended injury, and, *next,* when his enemies actually assail him.

169. 'When the king knows with certainty, that at some future time his force will be greatly augmented, and when, at the time present, he sustains little injury, let him then have recourse to peaceful measures;

170. 'But, when he sees all his subjects considerably firm in strength, and feels himself highly exalted in power, let him protect his dominions by war.

171. 'When he perfectly knows his own troops to be cheerful and well supplied, and those of his enemy quite the reverse, let him eagerly march against his foes;

172. 'But, when he finds himself weak in beasts of burden and in troops, let him then sit quiet in camp, using great attention, and pacifying his enemy by degrees.

173. 'When a king sees his foes stronger in all respects than himself, let him detach a part of his army, *to keep the enemy amused,* and secure his own safety *in an inaccessible place;*

174. 'But, when he is in all places assailable by the hostile troops, let him speedily seek the protection of a just and powerful monarch.

175. 'Him, who can keep in subjection both his own subjects and his foes, let him constantly soothe by all sorts of attentive respect, as he would honor his father, *natural or spiritual:*

'176. 'But if, even in that situation, he find such protection a cause of evil, let him alone, though weak, wage vigorous war without fear.

177. 'By all these expedients let a politic prince act 'with such wisdom, that neither allies, neutral powers, 'nor foes, may gain over him any great advantage.

178. 'Perfectly let him consider the state of his 'kingdom, both *actually* present and *probably* future, 'with the good and bad parts of all his actions:

179. 'That king shall never be overcome by his 'enemies, who foresees the good and evil to ensue from 'his measures; who, on present occasions, takes his 'resolution with prudent speed, and who weighs the 'various events of his past conduct.

180. 'Let him so arrange all his affairs, that no ally, 'neutral prince, or enemy, may obtain any advantage 'over him: this, in a few words, is the sum of political 'wisdom.

181. 'When the king begins his march against the 'domains of his foe, let him gradually advance, in the 'following manner, against the hostile metropolis.

182. 'Let him set out on his expedition in the fine 'month *Márgasírsha*, or about the month of *Phálguna* 'and *Chaitra*, according to *the number of* his forces, *that* '*he may find autumnal or vernal crops in the country* '*invaded by him*:

183. 'Even in other seasons, when he has a clear 'prospect of victory, and when any disaster has befal- 'len his foe, let him advance *with the greater part of* '*his army*.

184. 'Having made a due arrangement of affairs in 'his own dominions, and a disposition fit for his en- 'terprize, having provided all things necessary for his 'continuance in the foreign realm, and having seen all 'his spies dispatched with propriety,

185. 'Having secured the three sorts of ways, *over*

'*water, on plains, and through forests,* and placed his 'six-fold army, *elephants, cavalry, cars, infantry, officers,* and *attendants,* in complete military form, let 'him proceed by fit journeys toward the metropolis of 'his enemy :

186. 'Let him be much on his guard against every 'secret friend in the service of the hostile prince, and 'against emissaries, who go and return ; for in such 'friends he may find very dangerous foes.

187. 'On his march let him form his troops, either 'like a staff, *or in an even column* ; like a wain, *or in* '*a wedge with the apex foremost* ; like a boar, *or in a* '*rhomb with the van and rear narrow and the centre* '*broad* ; like a *Macara* or *sea-monster, that is, in a* '*double triangle with apices joined* ; like a needle, *or in* '*a long line* ; or like the bird of VISHNU, *that is, in a* '*rhomboid with the wings far extended* :

188. 'From whatever side he apprehends danger, to 'that side let him extend his troops ; and let him al-'ways conceal himself in the midst of a squadron form-'ed like a lotos-flower,

189. 'Let him cause his generals and the chief com-'mander *under himself,* to act in all quarters ; and from 'whatever side he perceives a design of attacking him, 'to that side let him turn his front.

190. 'On all sides let him station troops of soldiers, 'in whom he confides, distinguished by known *colours* '*and other* marks ; who are excellent both in sustain-'ing a charge and in charging, who are fearless and in-'capable of desertion.

191. 'Let him at his pleasure order a few men to 'engage in a close phalanx, or a large number of war-'riors in loose ranks ; and, having formed them in *a* '*long line like* a needle, or in *three divisions like* a thun-'derbolt, let him give orders for battle.

192. 'On a plain, let him fight with his armed cars 'and horses; on watery places, with manned boats and 'elephants; on ground full of trees and shrubs, with 'bows; on cleared ground, with swords and targets, 'and *other* weapons.

193. 'Men born in *Kurukshêtra*, near *Indraprast'ah* 'in *Matsya*, or *Viráta*, in *Panchála*, or *Kányakubja*, and 'in *Súrasêna*, in the district of *Mat'hurà*, let him cause 'to engage in the van; and men, *born in other coun-'tries*, who are tall and light.

194. 'Let him, when he has formed his troops in ar-'ray, encourage them *with short animated speeches;* and 'then, let him try them completely: let him know, 'likewise, how his men severally exert themselves, 'while they charge the foe.

195. 'If he block up his enemy, let him sit encamp-'ed, and lay waste the hostile country; let him conti-'nually spoil the grass, water, and wood of the adverse 'prince.

196. Pools, wells, and trenches let him destroy, let 'him harass the foe *by day*, and alarm him by night.

197. 'Let him secretly bring over to his party all 'such *leaders* as he can safely bring over; let him be 'informed of all that his enemies are doing; and, when 'a fortunate moment is offered by heaven, let him give 'battle, pushing on to conquest and abandoning fear.

198. 'Yet he should be more sedulous to reduce his 'enemy by negotiation, by well applied gifts, and by 'creating divisions, using either all or some of those 'methods, than by hazarding at any time a decisive 'action.

199. 'Since victory or defeat are not surely foreseen 'on either side, when two armies engage in the field;

'let the king then, *if other expedients prevail,* avoid a 'pitched battle:

200. 'But, should there be no means of applying the 'three *before-mentioned* expedients, let him, after due 'preparation, fight so valiantly, that his enemy may be 'totally routed.

201. 'Having conquered a country, let him respect 'the deities *adored in it* and their virtuous priests; let 'him also distribute largesses *to the people,* and cause a 'full exemption from terror to be loudly proclaimed.

202. 'When he has perfectly ascertained the conduct 'and intention of all the vanquished, let him fix in that 'country *a prince of* the royal race, and give him pre-'cise instructions.

203. 'Let him establish the laws *of the conquered 'nation* as declared *in their books;* and let him gratify 'the new prince with gems *and other precious gifts.*

204. 'The seizure of desirable property, though it 'cause hatred, and the donation of it, though it cause 'love, may be laudable or blameable on different occa-'sions:

205. 'All this *conduct of human affairs* is considered 'as dependent on acts ascribed to the deity, and on acts 'ascribed to men; now the operations of the deity 'cannot be known by any intenseness of thought, but 'those of men may be clearly discovered.

206. 'Or the victor, considering an ally, territory, 'and wealth as the triple fruit of conquest, may form 'an alliance with the vanquished prince, and proceed in 'union with him, using diligent circumspection.

207. 'He should pay due attention to the prince, 'who supported his cause, and to any other prince in

'the circumjacent region, who checked that supporter, 'so that, both from a well-wisher and from an opponent, 'he may secure the fruit of his expedition.

208. 'By gaining wealth and territory a king acquires 'not so great an increase of strength, as by obtaining a 'firm ally, who, though weak, may hereafter be power- 'ful.

209. 'That ally, though feeble, is highly estimable, 'who knows the whole extent of his duties, who grate- 'fully remembers benefits, whose people are satisfied, '*or, who has a gentle nature*, who loves his friend, and 'perseveres in his good resolutions.

210. 'Him have the sages declared an enemy hard 'to be subdued, who is eminently learned, of a noble 'race, personally brave, dexterous in management, li- 'beral, grateful, and firm.

211. 'Good-nature, knowledge of mankind, valor, 'benignity of heart, and incessant liberality, are the as- 'semblage of virtues, which adorn a neutral prince, '*whose amity must be courted.*

212. 'Even a salubrious and fertile country, where 'cattle continually increase, let a king abandon without 'hesitation for the sake of preserving himself:

213. 'Against misfortune, let him preserve his 'wealth; at the expence of his wealth, let him preserve 'his wife; but let him at all events preserve himself, 'even at the hazard of his wife and his riches.

214. 'A wise prince, who finds every sort of cala- 'mity rushing violently upon him, should have recourse 'to all just expedients, united or separate:

215. 'Let him consider the business to be expedited, 'the expedients collectively, and himself who must ap-

'ply them; and, taking refuge completely in those 'three, let him strenuously labor for his own prosperity.

216. 'Having consulted with his ministers, in the 'manner before prescribed, on all this *mass of public 'affairs*; having used exercise *becoming a warrior*, 'and having bathed *after it*, let the king enter at noon 'his private apartment for the purpose of taking food.

217. 'There let him eat lawful aliment, prepared by 'servants attached to his person, who know the differ-'ence of times and are incapable of perfidy, after it has 'been proved innocent *by certain experiments*, and hal-'lowed by texts of the *Veda* repulsive of poison.

218. 'Together with all his food let him swallow 'such medical substances as resist venom; and let him 'constantly wear with attention such gems, as are 'known to repel it.

219. 'Let his females, well tried and attentive, their 'dress and ornaments having been examined, *lest some 'weapon should be concealed in them*, do him humble ser-'vice with fans, water, and perfumes:

220. 'Thus let him take diligent care, when he goes 'out in a carriage or on horseback, when he lies down 'to rest, when he sits, when he takes food, when he 'bathes, anoints his body *with odorous essences*, and 'puts on all his habiliments.

221. 'After eating, let him divert himself with his 'women in the recesses of his palace; and, having idled 'a reasonable time, let him again think of public 'affairs:

222. 'When he has dressed himself completely, let 'him once more review his armed men, with all their 'elephants, horses, and cars, their accoutrements, and 'weapons.

223. 'At sunset, having performed his religious 'duty, let him privately, but well armed, in his interior 'apartment, hear what has been done by his reporters 'and emissaries:

224. 'Then, having dismissed those informers, and 'returning to another secret chamber, let him go, at- 'tended by women, to the inmost recess of his mansion 'for the sake of his evening meal;

225. 'There, having a second time eaten a little, and 'having been recreated with musical strains, let him 'take rest early, and rise refreshed from his labour.

226. 'THIS perfect system of rules let a king, free 'from illness, observe; but, when really afflicted with 'disease, he may intrust all these affairs to his officers.'

CHAP. VIII.

On Judicature; and on Law, Private and Criminal.

---

1. 'A KING, desirous of inspecting judicial proceed- 'ings, must enter his court of justice, composed and 'sedate in his demeanour, together with *Bráhmans* and 'counsellors, who know how to give him advice:

2. 'There, either sitting or standing, holding forth 'his right arm, without ostentation in his dress and or- 'naments, let him examine the affairs of litigant par- 'ties.

3. 'Each day let him decide causes, one after ano- 'ther, under the eighteen *principal* titles of law, by 'arguments and rules drawn from local usages, and 'from written codes:

4. 'Of those *titles*, the first is debt, on loans for con-'sumption; *the second*, deposits, and loans for use; *the* '*third*, sale without ownership; *the fourth*, concerns 'among partners; *the fifth*, subtraction of what has been 'given;

5. '*The sixth*, non-payment of wages or hire; *the se-*'*venth*, non-performance of agreements; *the eighth*, res-'cission of sale and purchase; *the ninth*, disputes be-'tween master and servant;

6. '*The tenth*, contests on boundaries; *the eleventh* '*and twelfth*, assault and slander; *the thirteenth*, lar-'ceny; *the fourteenth*, robbery and other violence; *the* '*fifteenth*, adultery;

7. '*The sixteenth*, altercation between man and wife, 'and their several duties; *the seventeenth*, the law of in-'heritance; *the eighteenth*, gaming with dice and with 'living creatures: these eighteen titles of law are settled 'as the ground-work of all judicial procedure in this 'world.

8. 'Among men, who contend for the most part on 'the titles just mentioned, *and on a few miscellaneous* '*heads not comprised under them*, let the king decide 'causes justly, observing primeval law;

9. 'But, when he cannot inspect such affairs in per-'son, let him appoint, for the inspection of them, a '*Bráhman* of eminent learning:

10. 'Let that chief judge, accompanied by three as-'sessors, fully consider all causes brought before the 'king; and, having entered the court-room, let him sit 'or stand, *but not move backwards and forwards*.

11. 'In whatever country three *Bráhmans*, particu-'larly skilled in the three several *Vedas*, sit together 'with the very learned *Bráhman*, appointed by the

'king, the wise call that *assembly* the court of BRAHMA' '*with four faces*.

12. 'When justice, having been wounded by iniquity, approaches the court, and the judges extract not 'the dart, they also shall be wounded by it.

13. 'Either the court must not be entered *by judges*, '*parties, and witnesses*, or law and truth must be openly declared: that man is criminal, who either says nothing, or says what is false or unjust.

14. 'Where justice is destroyed by iniquity, and 'truth by false evidence, the judges, who basely look 'on *without giving redress*, shall also be destroyed.

15. 'Justice being destroyed, will destroy; being 'preserved, will preserve: it must never, therefore, be 'violated. "Beware, *O judge*, lest justice, being overturned, overturn *both* us and thyself."

16. 'The divine form of justice is represented as '*Vrisha*, or *a bull*, and the gods consider him, who violates justice, as a *Vrishala*, or one who slays a bull: 'let the king, therefore, and his judges beware of violating justice.

17. 'The only firm friend, who follows men even 'after death, is justice: all others are extinct with the 'body.

18. 'Of injustice *in decisions*, one quarter falls on the 'party in the cause; one quarter, on his witnesses; one 'quarter, on all the judges; and one quarter on the king;

19. 'But where he, who deserves condemnation, 'shall be condemned, the king is guiltless, and the 'judges free from blame: an evil deed shall recoil on 'him, who committed it.

20. 'A *Bráhman* supported only by his class, and

'one barely reputed a *Bráhman*, but without performing any sacerdotal acts, may, at the king's pleasure, interpret the law to him: *so may the two middle classes*; but a *Súdra*, in no cases whatever.

21. 'Of that king, who stupidly looks on, while a *Súdra* decides causes, the kingdom itself shall be embarrassed, like a cow in deep mire.

22. 'The whole territory, which is inhabited by a number of *Súdras*, overwhelmed with atheists, and deprived of *Bráhmans*, must speedily perish afflicted with dearth and disease.

23. 'Let the king *or his judge*, having seated himself on the bench, his body properly clothed and his mind attentively fixed, begin with doing reverence to the deities, who guard the world; and then let him enter on the trial of causes.

24. 'Understanding what is expedient or inexpedient, but considering only what is law or not law, let him examine all disputes between parties, in the order of their several classes.

25. 'By external signs let him see through the thoughts of men; by their voice, colour, countenance, limbs, eyes, and action:

26. 'From the limbs, the look, the motion of the body, the gesticulation, the speech, the changes of the eye and the face, are discovered the internal workings of the mind.

27. 'The property of a student and of an infant, whether by descent or otherwise, let the king hold in his custody, until the owner shall have ended his studentship, or until his infancy shall have ceased *in his sixteenth year*.

28. 'Equal care must be taken of barren women, of

'women without sons, *whose husbands have married* '*other wives,* of women without kindred, or whose 'husbands are in distant places, of widows true to 'their lords, and of women afflicted with illness.

29. 'Such kinsmen, as, *by any pretence,* appropriate 'the fortunes of women during their lives, a just king 'must punish with the severity due to thieves.

30. 'Three years let the king detain the property 'of which no owner appears, *after a distinct procla-* '*mation:* the owner, appearing within the three years, 'may take it; but, after that term, the king may 'confiscate it.

31. 'He, who says "This is mine," must be duly 'examined; and if, *before he inspect it,* he declare its 'form, number, and other circumstances, the owner 'must have his property;

32. 'But if he show not at what place and time it 'was lost, and specify not its colour, shape, and dimen- 'sions, he ought to be amerced.

33. 'The king may take a sixth part of the property 'so detained by him, or a tenth, or a twelfth, remem- 'bering the duty of good kings.

34. 'Property lost *by one man,* and found *by ano-* '*ther,* let the king secure, by committing it to the care 'of trustworthy men; and those, whom he shall con- 'vict of stealing it, let him cause to be trampled on by 'an elephant.

35. 'From the man, who shall say with truth, "This 'property, which has been kept, belongs to me," the 'king may take a sixth or twelfth part, *for having se-* '*cured it;*

36. 'But he, who shall say so falsely, may be fined 'either an eighth part of his own property, or else in

'some small proportion to the value of the goods falsely claimed, a just calculation having been made.

37. 'A learned *Bráhman*, having found a treasure 'formerly hidden, may take it without any deduction; 'since he is the lord of all;

38. 'But of a treasure anciently reposited under 'ground, which *any other subject or* the king has dis'covered, the king may lay up half in his treasury, hav'ing given half to the *Bráhmans*.

39. 'Of old hoards, and precious minerals in the 'earth, the king is entitled to half by reason of his ge'neral protection, and because he is the lord paramount 'of the soil.

40. 'To men of all classes, the king must restore 'their property, which robbers have seized; since a 'king, who takes it for himself, incurs the guilt of a 'robber.

41. 'A king, who knows the revealed law, must en'quire into the particular laws of classes, the laws *or* '*usages* of districts, the customs of traders, and the 'rules of certain families, and establish their peculiar 'laws, *if they be not repugnant to the law of* GOD;

42. 'Since all men, who mind their own customary 'ways of proceeding, and are fixed in the discharge of 'their several duties, become united by affection with 'the people at large, even though they dwell far as'under.

43. 'Neither the king himself nor his officers must 'ever promote litigation; nor ever neglect a law-suit 'instituted by others.

44. 'As a hunter traces the lair of a *wounded* beast 'by the drops of blood; thus let a king investigate the 'true point of justice by deliberate arguments:

45. 'Let him fully consider the nature of truth, the 'state of the case, and his own person; and next, the 'witnesses, the place, the mode, and the time; firmly 'adhering to all the rules of practice:

46. 'What has been practised by good men and by 'virtuous *Bráhmans,* if it be not inconsistent with the 'legal customs of provinces or districts, of classes and 'families, let him establish.

47. 'When a creditor sues before him for the reco- 'very of his right from a debtor, let him cause the 'debtor to pay what the creditor shall prove due.

48. 'By whatever lawful means a creditor may have 'gotten possession of his own property, let the king 'ratify such payment by the debtor, though obtained 'even by compulsory means.

49. 'By the mediation of friends, by suit in court, 'by artful management, or by distress, a creditor may 'recover the property lent; and, fifthly, by legal 'force.

50. 'That creditor, who recovers his right from his 'debtor, must not be rebuked by the king for retaking 'his own property.

51. 'In a suit for a debt, which the defendant de- 'nies, let him award payment to the creditor of what, 'by good evidence, he shall prove due, and exact a 'small fine, *according to the circumstance of the debtor.*

52. 'On the denial of a debt, which the defendant 'has in court been required to pay, the plaintiff must 'call a witness who was present at the place of the 'loan, or produce other evidence, *as a note and the like.*

53. 'The plaintiff, who calls a witness not present 'at the place, *where the contract was made,* or, having 'knowingly called him, disclaims him as his witness;

'or who perceives not, that he asserts confused and 'contradictory facts;

54. 'Or who, having stated what he designs to 'prove, varies afterwards from his case; or who, being 'questioned on a fact, which he had before admitted, 'refuses to acknowledge that very fact;

55. 'Or who has conversed with the witnesses in 'a place unfit for such conversation; or who declines 'answering a question properly put; or who departs 'from the court;

56. 'Or who, being ordered to speak, stands mute; 'or who proves not what he has alleged; or who 'knows not what is capable or incapable of proof; *such 'a plaintiff* shall fail in that suit.

57. 'Him who has said "I have witnesses," and, 'being told to produce them, produces them not, the 'judge must on this account declare non-suited.

58. 'If the plaintiff delay to put in his plaint, he 'may, *according to the nature of the case,* be corporally 'punished or justly amerced; and, if the defendant 'plead not within three fortnights, he is by law con'demned.

59. 'In the double of that sum, which the defendant 'falsely denies, or on which the complainant falsely 'declares, shall those two men, wilfully offending 'against justice, be fined by the king.

60. 'When a man has been brought into court by 'a suitor for property, and, being called on to answer, 'denies the debt, the cause should be decided by the '*Bráhman* who represents the king, having heard 'three witnesses *at least.*

61. 'What sort of witnesses must be produced by 'creditors *and others* on the trial of causes, I will com-

'prehensively declare; and in what manner those wit-'nesses must give true evidence.

62. 'Married house-keepers, men with male issue, 'inhabitants of the same district, either of the military, 'the commercial, or the servile class, are competent, 'when called by the party, to give their evidence; not 'any persons indiscriminately, except in *such* cases of 'urgency *as will soon be mentioned*.

63. 'Just and sensible men of all the *four* classes 'may be witnesses on trials; men, who know their 'whole duty, and are free from covetousness: but men 'of an opposite character the judge must reject.

64. 'Those must not be admitted who have a pecu-'niary interest; nor familiar friends; nor menial ser-'vants; nor enemies; nor men formerly perjured; nor 'persons grievously diseased; nor those, who have 'committed heinous offences.

65. 'The king cannot be made a witness; nor *cooks*, '*and the like* mean artificers; nor public dancers and 'singers; nor a priest of deep learning in scripture; 'nor a student in theology; nor an anchoret secluded 'from all worldly connexions;

66. 'Nor one wholly dependent; nor one ot bad 'fame; nor one, who follows a cruel occupation; nor 'one, who acts openly against the law; nor a decrepit 'old man; nor a child; nor one man only, *unless he be* '*distinguished for virtue*; nor a wretch of the lowest 'mixed class; nor one, who has lost the organs of sense;

67. 'Nor one extremely grieved; nor one intoxi-'cated; nor a madman; nor one tormented with hunger 'or thirst; nor one oppressed by fatigue; nor one ex-'cited by lust; nor one inflamed by wrath; nor one 'who has been convicted of theft.

68. 'Women should regularly be witnesses for

'women; twice-born men, for men alike twice-born; 'good servants and mechanics, for servants and mechanics; and those of the lowest race, for those of 'the lowest;

69. 'But any person whatever, who has positive 'knowledge *of transactions* in the private apartments of 'a house, or in a forest, or at a time of death, may 'give evidence between the parties:

70. 'On failure *of witnesses duly qualified,* evidence 'may *in such cases* be given by a woman, by a child, or 'by an aged man, by a pupil, by a kinsman, by a slave, 'or by a hired servant;

71. 'Yet of children, of old men, and of the diseased, who are all apt to speak untruly, the judge must 'consider the testimony as weak; and *much more,* that 'of men with disordered minds:

72. 'In all cases of violence, of theft and adultery, 'of defamation and assault, he must not examine too 'strictly the competence of witnesses.

73. 'If there be contradictory evidence, let the king 'decide by the plurality of credible witnesses; if 'equality in number, by superiority in virtue; if parity 'in virtue, by the testimony of such twice-born men, as 'have best performed public duties.

74. 'Evidence of what has been seen, or of what 'has been heard, *as slander and the like,* given by 'those who saw or heard it, is admissible; and a 'witness, who speaks truth in those cases, neither deviates from virtue nor loses his wealth:

75. 'But a witness, who knowingly says any thing, 'before an assembly of good men, different from what 'he had seen or heard, shall fall headlong, after death, 'into a region of horror, and be debarred from heaven.

76. 'When a man sees or hears any thing, without 'being then called upon to attest it, yet, if he be '*afterwards* examined as a witness, he must declare it, 'exactly as *it was* seen, *and* as *it was* heard.

77. 'One man, untainted with covetousness *and* '*other vices,* may *in some cases* be the sole witness, and 'will have more weight than many women, because 'female understandings are apt to waver; or than 'many other men, who have been tarnished with crimes.

78. 'What witnesses declare naturally, *or without* '*bias,* must be received on trials; but what they im-'properly say, from some unnatural bent, is inapplica-'ble to the purposes of justice.

79. 'The witnesses being assembled in the middle 'of the court-room, in the presence of the plaintiff and 'the defendant, let the judge examine them, after 'having addressed them *all together* in the following 'manner:

80. '"What ye know to have been transacted in the 'matter before us, between the parties reciprocally, 'declare at large and with truth; for your evidence in 'this cause is required."

81. 'A witness, who gives testimony with truth, 'shall attain exalted seats of beatitude above, and the 'highest fame here below: such testimony is revered 'by BRAHMA' himself;

82. 'The witness who speaks falsely, shall be fast 'bound *under water,* in the *snaky* cords of VARUNA, 'and be wholly deprived of power *to escape torment* 'during a hundred transmigrations: let mankind, there-'fore, give no false testimony.

83. 'By truth is a witness cleared from sin; by truth

'is justice advanced: truth must, therefore, be spoken 'by witnesses of every class.

84. 'The soul itself is its own witness; the soul it-'self is its own refuge; offend not thy conscious soul, 'the supreme internal witness of men!

85. 'The sinful have said in their hearts: "None 'sees us." Yes; the gods distinctly see them; and 'so does the spirit within their breasts.

86. 'The guardian deities of the firmament, of the 'earth, of the waters, of the human heart, of the moon, 'of the sun, and of fire, of punishment after death, of 'the winds, of night, of both twilights, and of justice, 'perfectly know the state of all spirits clothed with 'bodies.

87. 'In the forenoon let the judge, being purified, 'severally call on the twice-born, being purified also, to 'declare the truth, in the presence of *some image, a 'symbol* of the divinity, and of *Bráhmans,* while the 'witnesses turn their faces either to the north or to 'the east.

88. 'To a *Bráhman* he must begin with saying, '"Declare;" to a *Kshatriya,* with saying, "Declare 'the truth;" to a *Vaisya,* with *comparing perjury to the 'crime of stealing* kine, grain, or gold; to a *Súdra,* 'with comparing it *in some or all of the following sen-'tences,* to every crime *that men can commit.*

89. '"Whatever places of torture have been pre-'pared for the slayer of a priest, for the murderer of a 'woman or of a child, for the injurer of a friend, and 'for an ungrateful man, those places are ordained for a 'witness who gives false evidence.

90. '"The fruit of every virtuous act, which thou 'hast done, O good man, since thy birth, shall depart

'from thee to dogs, if thou deviate in speech from the 'truth.

91. '" O friend to virtue, that supreme spirit, which 'thou believest one and the same with thyself, resides 'in thy bosom perpetually, and is an all-knowing in'spector of thy goodness or of thy wickedness.

92. '" If thou beest not at variance, *by speaking 'falsely*, with YAMA, or the subduer of all: with VAI'VASWATA, or the punisher, with that great divinity who 'dwells in thy breast, go not *on a pilgrimage* to the 'river *Gangá*, nor to the plains of KURU, *for thou hast 'no need of expiation.*

93. '" Naked and shorn, tormented with hunger 'and thirst, and deprived of sight, shall the man, who 'gives false evidence, go with a potsherd to beg food 'at the door of his enemy.

94. '" Headlong, in utter darkness, shall the impi'ous wretch tumble into hell, who, being interrogated 'in a judicial inquiry, answers one question falsely.

95. '" He, who in a court of justice gives an imper'fect account of any transaction, or asserts a fact of 'which he was no eye-witness, shall receive pain *instead 'of pleasure*, and resemble a man, who eats fish *with 'eagerness* and swallows the sharp bones.

96. '" The gods are acquainted with no better mor'tal in this world, than the man, of whom the intel'ligent spirit, which pervades his body, has no distrust, 'when he prepares to give evidence.

97. '" Hear, honest man, from a just enumeration 'in order, how many kinsmen, in evidence of different 'sorts, a false witness kills, *or incurs the guilt of killing:*

98. '" He kills five by false testimony concerning 'cattle in general; he kills ten by false testimony con-

'cerning kine; he kills a hundred by false evidence 'concerning horses; and a thousand by false evidence 'concerning the human race:

99. '"By speaking falsely in a cause concerning 'gold, he kills the born and the unborn; by speaking 'falsely concerning land, he kills every thing *animated*; 'beware then of speaking falsely in a cause concern-'ing land!

100. '"The sages have held false evidence concern-'ing water, and the possession or enjoyment of women, 'equal to false evidence concerning land; and it is 'equally criminal in causes concerning *pearls and other* 'precious things formed in water, and concerning all 'things made of stone.

101. '"Marking well all the murders which are 'comprehended in the crime of perjury, declare thou 'the whole truth with precision, as *it was* heard, *and* as '*it was* seen by thee."

102. '*Bráhmans,* who tend herds of cattle, who 'trade, who practise mechanical arts, who profess 'dancing and singing, who are hired servants or usurers, 'let the judge exhort and examine as if they were '*Súdras.*

103. 'In some cases, a giver of false evidence from 'a pious motive, even though he know the truth, shall 'not lose a seat in heaven: such evidence wise men call 'the speech of the gods.

104. 'Whenever the death of a man, *who had not* '*been a grievous offender,* either of the servile, the 'commercial, the military, or the sacerdotal class, 'would be occasioned by true evidence, *from the known* '*rigour of the king, even though the fault arose from* '*inadvertence or error,* falsehood may be spoken: it 'is even preferable to truth.

105. 'Such *witnesses* must offer, as oblations to 'SARASWATI', cakes of rice and milk addressed to the 'goddess of speech; and thus will they fully expiate 'that venial sin of benevolent falsehood:

106. 'Or such a *witness* may pour clarified butter 'into the holy fire, according to the sacred rule, hal- 'lowing it with the texts called *kúshmándá*, or with 'those which relate to VARUNA, beginning with *ud*; or 'with the three texts appropriated to the watergods.

107. 'A man who labours not under illness, yet 'comes not to give evidence in cases of loans and the 'like, within three fornights *after due summons*, shall 'take upon himself the whole debt, and pay a tenth 'part of it as a fine *to the king*.

108. 'The witness, who has given evidence, and to 'whom, within seven days after, *misfortune* happens '*from* disease, fire, or the death of a kinsman, shall be 'condemned to pay the debt and a fine.

109. 'In cases, where no witness can be had, be- 'tween two parties opposing each other, the judge 'may acquire a knowledge of the truth by the oath 'of the parties; *or* if he cannot *otherwise* perfectly as- 'certain it.

110. 'By the *seven* great *Rishis*, and by the deities 'themselves, have oaths been taken, for the purpose 'of judicial proof; and even VASISHT'HA, *being accused* '*by* VISWA'MITRA *of murder*, took an oath before the '*king* SUDA'MAN, son of PIYAVANA.

111. 'Let no man of sense take an oath in vain, '*that is, not in a court of justice*, on a trifling occasion; 'for the man, who takes an oath in vain, shall be 'punished in this life and in the next:

112. 'To women, however, at a time of dalliance, 'or on a proposal of marriage, in the case of grass or

'fruit eaten by a cow, of wood taken for a sacrifice, or 'of a promise made for the preservation of a *Bráhman*, 'it is no deadly sin to take a light oath.

113. 'Let the judge cause a priest to swear by his 'veracity; a soldier, by his horse, or elephant, and his 'weapons; a merchant, by his kine, grain, and gold; 'a mechanic, or servile man, by *imprecating on his 'own head, if he speak falsely,* all possible crimes;

114. 'Or, *on great occasions,* let him cause the party 'to hold fire, or to dive under water, or severally to 'touch the heads of his children and wife:

115. 'He, whom the blazing fire burns not, whom 'the water soon forces not up, or who meets with no 'speedy misfortune, must be held veracious in his tes-'timony on oath.

116. 'Of the sage VATSA, whom his younger *half-'brother* formerly attacked, *as the son of a servile woman,* 'the fire, which pervades the world, burned not even a 'hair, by reason of his perfect veracity.

117. 'Whenever false evidence has been given in 'any suit, the king must reverse the judgment; and 'whatever has been done, must be considered as undone.

118. 'Evidence, given from covetousness, from dis-'traction of mind, from terror, from friendship, from 'lust, from wrath, from ignorance, and from inatten-'tion, must be held invalid.

119. 'The distinctions of punishment for a false wit-'ness, from either of those motives, I will propound 'fully and in order:

120. 'If he speak falsely through covetousness, he 'shall be fined a thousand *panas;* if through distrac-'tion of mind, *two hundred and fifty,* or the lowest

'amercement ; if through terror, two mean amerce-'ments ; if through friendship, four times the lowest ;

121. 'If through lust, ten times the lowest amerce-'ment ; if through wrath, three times the next, *or* '*middlemost ;* if through ignorance, two hundred com-'plete ; if through inattention, a hundred only.

122. 'Learned men have specified these punish-'ments, *which were* ordained by sage legislators for 'perjured witnesses, with a view to prevent a failure of 'justice and to restrain iniquity.

123. 'Let a just prince banish men of the three *lower* 'classes, if they give false evidence, having first levied 'the fine ; but a *Bráhman* let him only banish.

124. 'Manu, son of the Self-existent, has named ten 'places of punishment, which are appropriated to the 'three *lower* classes ; but a *Bráhman* must depart from 'the realm unhurt *in any one of them :*

125. 'The part of generation, the belly, the tongue, 'the two hands, and, fifthly, the two feet, the eye, the 'nose, both ears, the property, and, *in a capital case,* 'the whole body.

126. 'Let the king, having considered and ascertained 'the frequency of a similar offence, the place and time, 'the ability of the criminal *to pay or suffer,* and the 'crime itself, cause punishment to fall on those alone, 'who deserve it.

127. 'Unjust punishment destroys reputation during 'life, and fame after death ; it even obstructs, in the 'next life, the path to heaven : unjust punishment, 'therefore, let the king by all means avoid.

128. 'A king, who inflicts punishment on such as 'deserve it not, and inflicts no punishment on such as 'deserve it, brings infamy on himself, while he lives, 'and shall sink, when he dies, to a region of torment.

129. 'First, let him punish by gentle admonition; 'afterwards, by harsh reproof; thirdly, by deprivation 'of property; after that, by corporal pain:

130. 'But, when even by corporal punishment he 'cannot restrain such offenders, let him apply to them 'all the four modes with rigor.

131. 'Those names of copper, silver, and gold weights, 'which are commonly used among men, for the purpose 'of worldly business, I will now comprehensively 'explain.

132. 'The very small mote, which may be discerned 'in a sun-beam passing through a lattice, is the least 'visible quantity, and men call it a *trasarénu:*

133. 'Eight of those *trasarénus* are supposed equal 'in weight to one minute poppy-seed; three of those 'seeds are equal to one black mustard-seed; and three 'of those last, to a white mustard-seed:

134. 'Six white mustard-seeds are equal to a middle-'sized barley-corn; three such barley-corns to one '*raktiká*, or seed of the *Gunjà;* five *raktikás* of gold are 'one *másha*, and sixteen such *máshas*, one *suvarna;*

135. 'Four *suvarnas* make a *pala;* ten *palas*, a *dha-'rana;* but two *raktikas* of silver, weighed together, 'are considered as one *máshaka;*

136. 'Sixteen of those *máshakas* are a silver *dharana*, 'or *purána;* but a *karsha*, or eighty *kartikás* of copper, 'is called a *pana* or *kárshápana*.

137. 'Ten *dharanas* of silver are known by the name 'of a *satamána;* and the weight of four *suvarnas* has 'also the appellation of a *nishka*.

138. 'Now two hundred and fifty *panas* are declared 'to be the first *or lowest* amercement; five hundred of

'them are considered as the mean; and a thousand, as 'the highest.

139. 'A debt being admitted by the defendant, he 'must pay five in the hundred, *as a fine to the king*; 'but, if it be denied *and proved*, twice as much: this 'law was enacted by MANU.

140. 'A lender of money may take, in addition to 'his capital, the interest allowed by VASISHTHA, *that is*, 'an eightieth part of a hundred, *or one and a quarter*, 'by the month, *if he have a pledge*;

141. 'Or, *if he have no pledge*, he may take two in 'the hundred *by the month*, remembering the duty of 'good men: for, by *thus* taking two in the hundred, he 'becomes not a sinner for gain.

142. 'He may thus take *in proportion to the risk, and* 'in the direct order of the classes, two in the hundred '*from a priest*, three *from a soldier*, four *from a mer-'chant*, and five *from a mechanic or servile man*, but 'never more, as interest by the month.

143. 'If he take a beneficial pledge, *or a pledge to* '*be used for his profit*, he must have no other interest 'on the loan; nor, after a great length of time, *or when* '*the profits have amounted to the debt*, can he give or sell 'such a pledge, *though he may assign it in pledge to* '*another*.

144. 'A pledge *to be kept only* must not be used by 'force, *that is, against consent:* the pawnee so using it 'must give up his whole interest, or must satisfy the 'pawnor, *if it be spoiled or worn out*, by paying him the 'original price of it; otherwise, he commits a theft of 'the pawn.

145. 'Neither a pledge *without limit*, nor a deposit, 'are lost to the owner by lapse of time: they are both

'recoverable, though they have long remained *with the* '*bailee.*

146. 'A milch cow, a camel, a riding-horse, *a bull or* '*other beast,* which has been sent to be tamed for la-'bour, and other things used with friendly assent, are 'not lost *by length of time to the owner.*

147. '*In general,* whatever chattel the owner sees en-'joyed by others for ten years, while, though present, 'he says nothing, that chattel he shall not recover:

148. 'If he be neither an idiot, nor an infant under 'the full age of fifteen years, and if the chattel be 'adversely possessed in a place where he may see it, his 'property in it is extinct by law, and the adverse 'possessor shall keep it.

149. 'A pledge, a boundary of land, the property of 'an infant, a deposit either open or in a chest sealed, 'female slaves, the wealth of a king, and of a learned '*Bráhman,* are not lost in consequence af adverse 'enjoyment.

150. 'The fool, who secretly uses a pledge without, '*though not against,* the assent of the owner, shall give 'up half of his interest, as a compensation for such 'use.

151. 'Interest on money, received at once, *not month* '*by month, or day by day, as it ought,* must never be 'more than enough to double the debt, *that is, more* '*than the amount of the principal paid at the same* '*time:* on grain, on fruit, on wool or hair, on beasts 'of burden, *lent to be paid in the same kind of equal* '*value,* it must not be more than enough to make the 'debt quintuple.

152. 'Stipulated interest beyond the legal rate, and 'different from the *preceding* rule, is invalid; and the

'wise call it an usurious way *of lending:* the lender 'is entitled *at most* to five in the hundred.

153. 'Let no lender *for a month, or for two or three* '*months, at a certain interest,* receive *such* interest 'beyond the year; nor any interest, which is unap-'proved; nor interest upon interest *by previous agree-*'*ment;* nor monthly interest exceeding in time the 'amount of the principal; nor interest exacted from a 'debtor, *as the price of the risk, when there is no public* '*danger or distress;* nor immoderate profits from a 'pledge to be used by way of interest.

154. 'He, who cannot pay the debt *at the fixed* '*time,* and wishes to renew the contract, may renew it 'in writing, *with the creditor's assent,* if he pay all the 'interest then due;

155. 'But if, *by some unavoidable accident,* he can-'not pay the whole interest, he may insert *as principal* 'in the renewed contract so much of the interest ac-'crued as he ought to pay.

156. 'A lender at interest on *the risk of* safe carri-'age, who has agreed on the place and time, shall not 'receive such interest, if *by accident* the goods are not 'carried to the place, or within the time:

157. 'Whatever interest, *or price of the risk,* shall 'be settled *between the parties,* by men well acquainted 'with sea-voyages or journies by land, with times and 'with places, such interest shall have legal force.

158. 'The man, who becomes surety for the appear-'ance of a debtor in this world, and produces him not, 'shall pay the debt out of his own property;

159. 'But money, due by a surety, or idly promised '*to musicians and actresses,* or lost at play, or due for 'spirituous liquors, or what remains unpaid of a fine or

'toll, the son *of the surety or debtor* shall not *in general* 'be obliged to pay:

160. 'Such is the rule in cases of a surety for ap-'pearance *or good behaviour*; but, if a surety for pay-'ment should die, the judge may compel even his 'heirs to discharge the debt.

161. 'On what account then is it, that, after the 'death of a surety other than for payment, the cre-'ditor may *in one case* demand the debt *of the heir*, 'all the affairs of the deceased being known and 'proved?

162. 'If the surety had received money from the 'debtor, and had enough to pay the debt, the son of 'him, who so received it, shall discharge the debt out 'of his *inherited* property: this is a sacred ordinance.

163. 'A contract made by a person intoxicated or 'insane, or grievously disordered, or wholly dependent, 'by an infant or a decrepit old man, or *in the name of* '*another* by a person without authority, is utterly null.

164. 'That plaint can have no effect, though it may 'be supported by evidence, which contains a cause of 'action inconsistent with positive law or with settled 'usage.

165. 'When the judge discovers a fraudulent pledge 'or sale, a fraudulent gift and acceptance, or in what-'ever other case he detects fraud, let him annul the 'whole transaction.

166. 'If the debtor be dead, and if the money bor-'rowed was expended for the use of his family, it must 'be paid by that family, divided or undivided, out of 'their own estate.

167. 'Should even a slave make a contract *in the* '*name of his absent master* for the behoof of the family,

'that master, whether in his own country or abroad, 'shall not rescind it.

168. 'What is given by force *to a man who cannot* '*accept it legally*, what is by force enjoyed, by force 'caused to be written, and all other things done by 'force *or against free consent*, MANU has pronounced 'void.

169. 'Three are troubled by means of others, *name*-'*ly*, witnesses, sureties, and inspectors of causes, and 'four collect wealth slowly, *with benefit to others*, a '*Bráhman*, a money-lender, a merchant, and a king.

170. 'Let no king, how indigent soever, take any 'thing which ought not to be taken; nor let him, how 'wealthy soever, decline taking that which he ought to 'take, be it ever so small:

171. 'By taking what ought not to be taken, and by 'refusing what ought to be received, the king betrays 'his own weakness, and is lost both in this world and 'in the next;

172. 'But by taking his due, by administering jus-'tice, and by protecting the weak, the king augments 'his own force, and is exalted in the next world and 'in this.

173. 'Therefore, let the king, like YAMA, resigning 'what may be pleasing or unpleasing to himself, live 'by the strict rules of YAMA, his anger being repressed, 'and his organs kept in subjection.

174. 'That evil-minded king, who, through infatua-'tion, decides causes with injustice, his enemies, *through* '*the disaffection of his people*, quickly reduce to a state of 'dependence;

175. 'But him, who subduing both lust and wrath,

'examines causes with justice, his people naturally seek, 'as rivers the ocean.

176. 'The debtor, who complains before the king, 'that his creditor has recovered the debt by his own 'legal act, *as before-mentioned*, shall be compelled by 'the king to pay a quarter of the sum *as a fine*, and the 'creditor shall be left in possession of his own.

177. 'Even by personal labour shall the debtor pay 'what is adjudged, if he be of the same class with the 'creditor, or of a lower; but a debtor of a higher 'class must pay it *according to his income* by little and 'little.

178. 'By this system of rules let the king decide, 'with equal justice, all disputes between men opposing 'each other, having ascertained the truth by evidence 'or the oaths of the parties.

179. 'A sensible man should make a deposit with 'some person of high birth, and of good morals, well 'acquainted with law, habitually veracious, having a 'large family, wealthy and venerable.

180. 'Whatever thing, and in whatever manner, a 'person shall deposit in the hands of another, the same 'thing, and in the same manner, ought to be received 'back by the owner: as the delivery *was*, so *must be* 'the receipt.

181. 'He, who restores not to the depositor, on his 'request, what has been deposited, may first be tried 'by the judge *in the following manner*, the depositor 'himself being absent.

182. 'On failure of witnesses, let the judge actually 'deposit gold, *or precious things*, with the defendant, by 'the artful contrivance of spies, who have passed the 'age of childhood, and whose persons are engaging:

183. 'Should the defendant restore that deposit in 'the manner and shape, in which it was bailed *by the 'spies*, there is nothing in his hands, for which others 'can justly accuse him;

184. 'But if he restore not the gold, or *precious 'things*, as he ought, to those emissaries, let him be 'apprehended and compelled to pay the value of both 'deposits: this is a settled rule.

185. 'A deposit, whether sealed up or not, should 'never be re-delivered, while the depositor is alive, to 'his heir apparent or presumptive: both sorts of de-'posits, indeed, are extinct, *or cannot be demanded by 'the heir*, if the depositor die, *in that case*; but not, 'unless he die, *for, should the heir apparent keep them, 'the depositor himself may sue the bailee*:

186. 'But, if a depositary by his own free act shall 'deliver a deposit to the heir of a deceased bailor, 'he must not be harassed *with claims of a similar kind*, 'either by the king, or by that heir:

187. 'And, *if similar claims be made*, the king must 'decide the questions after friendly admonition, *without 'having recourse to artifice*; for, the honest disposition 'of the man being proved, the judge must proceed with 'mildness.

188. 'Such is the mode of ascertaining the right in 'all these cases of a deposit: in the case of a deposit 'sealed up, the bailee shall incur no censure *on the re-'delivery*, unless he have *altered the seal or* taken out 'something.

189. 'If a deposit be seized by thieves, *or destroyed 'by vermin*, or washed away by water, or consumed 'by fire, the bailee shall not be obliged to make it 'good, unless he took part of it for himself.

190. 'The defendant, who denies a deposit, and the

'plaintiff, who asserts it, let the king try by all sorts 'of expedients, and by the modes of ordeal prescribed 'in the *Veda*.

191. 'He who restores not a thing really deposited, 'and he, who demands what he never bailed, shall both, '*for a second offence*, be punished as thieves, *if gold, 'pearls or the like be demanded*; or, *in the case of a 'trifling demand*, shall pay a fine equal to the value of 'the thing claimed :

192. '*For the first offence*, the king should compel 'a fraudulent depositary, without any distinction be-'tween a deposit under seal or open, to pay a fine equal 'to its value.

193. 'That man, who, by false pretences, gets into 'his hands the goods of another, shall, together with 'his accomplices, be punished by various degrees of '*whipping or mutilation, or even by* death.

194. '*Regularly*, a deposit should be produced, the same in kind and quantity as it was bailed, by the same and to the same person, by whom and from whom it was received, and before the same company, '*who were witnesses to the deposit:* he who produces it in a different manner, ought to be fined ;

195. 'But a thing, privately deposited, should be privately restored by and to the person, by and from 'whom it was received : as the bailment *was*, so *should be* the delivery, *according to a rule in the* Veda.

196. 'Thus let the king decide causes concerning a 'deposit, or a friendly loan for use, without showing 'rigour to the depositary.

197. 'Him, who sells the property of another man, 'without the assent of the owner, the judge shall not 'admit as a competent witness, but shall treat as a 'thief, who pretends that he has committed no theft :

198. 'If, indeed, he be a near kinsman of the 'owner, he shall be fined six hundred *panas;* but, if 'he be neither his kinsman nor a claimant under him, 'he commits an offence equal to larceny.

199. 'A gift or sale, thus made by any other than 'the true owner, must, by a settled rule, be considered, 'in judicial proceedings, as not made.

200. 'Where occupation *for a time* shall be proved, 'but no sort of title shall appear, *the sale cannot be 'supported:* title, not occupation, is essential to its 'support*; and* this rule *also* is fixed.

201. 'He, who has received a chattel, by purchase 'in open market, *before a number of men,* justly ac-'quires the absolute property, by having paid the price 'of it, *if he can produce the vendor;*

202. 'But, if the vendor be not producible, and that 'vendee prove the public sale, the latter must be dis-'missed by the king without punishment; and the 'former owner, who lost the chattel, may take it back '*on paying the vendee half its value.*

203. 'One commodity, mixed with another, shall 'never be sold as *unmixed;* nor a bad commodity *as 'good;* nor less *than agreed on;* nor any thing kept at 'a distance or concealed, *lest some defect in it should be 'discovered.*

204. 'If, after one damsel has been shown, another 'be offered to the bridegroom, *who had purchased leave 'to marry her from her next kinsman,* he may become 'the husband of both for the same price: this law 'MANU ordained.

205. 'The kinsman, who gives a damsel in mar-'riage, having first openly told her blemishes, whether 'she be insane, or disordered with elephantiasis, or

'defiled by connexion with a man, shall suffer no 'punishment.

206. 'If an officiating priest, actually engaged in 'a sacrifice, abandon his work, a share only, in pro-'portion to his work done, shall be given to him by 'his partners in the business, *out of their common pay*:

207. 'But, if he discontinue his work *without fraud*, 'after the time of giving the sacrificial fees, he may 'take his full share, and cause what remains to be per-'formed by another priest.

208. 'Where, on the performance of solemn rites, 'a specific fee is ordained for each part of them, shall 'he alone, who performs that part, receive the fee, or 'shall all the priests take the perquisites jointly?

209. '*At some holy rites*, let the reader of the *Ya-'jurveda* take the car, and the *Brahmá*, or superin-'tending priest, the horse; or, *on another occasion*, 'let the reader of the *Rigveda* take the horse, and the 'chanter of the *Sámaveda* receive the carriage, in 'which the purchased materials of the sacrifice had 'been brought.

210. '*A hundred cows being distributable among six-'teen priests*, the four chief, *or first set*, are entitled to '*near* half, *or forty-eight*; the next four, to half of that 'number; the third set, to a third part of it; and the 'fourth set, to a quarter:

211. 'According to this rule, *or in proportion to the 'work*, must allotments of shares be given to men here 'below, who, *though* in conjunction, perform their seve-'ral parts of the business.

212. 'Should money or goods be given, *or promised 'as a gift*, by one man to another, who asks it for some 'religious act, the gift shall be void, if that act be not 'afterwards performed:

213. 'If the money be delivered, and the receiver, 'through pride or avarice, refuse *in that case* to return 'it, he shall be fined one *suverna* by the king, as a pun- 'ishment for his theft.

214. 'Such, as here declared, is the rule ordained for 'withdrawing what has been given : I will, next, 'propound the law for non-payment of wages.

215. 'That hired servant or workman, who, not from 'any disorder but from indolence, fails to perform his 'work according to his agreement, shall be fined eight '*raktikás*, and his wages or hire shall not be paid.

216. 'But, if he be really ill, and, when restored to 'health, shall perform his work according to his original 'bargain, he shall receive his pay even for a very long 'time :

217. 'Yet, whether he be sick or well, if the work 'stipulated be not performed *by another for him or by 'himself*, his whole wages are forfeited, though the work 'want but a little of being complete.

218. 'This is the general rule concerning work un- 'dertaken for wages or hire : next, I will fully declare 'the law concerning such men as break their promises.

219. 'The man, among the traders and other inha- 'bitants of a town or district, who breaks a promise 'through avarice, though he had taken an oath to per- 'form it, let the king banish from his realm :

220. 'Or, *according to circumstances*, let the judge, 'having arrested the promise-breaker, condemn him to 'pay six *nishkas*, or four *suvernas*, or one *satamána* of 'silver, *of all three if he deserve such a fine*.

221. 'Among all citizens, and in all classes, let a 'just king observe this rule for imposing fines on men, 'who shall break their engagements.

222. 'A man, who has bought or sold any thing in 'this world, *that has a fixed price, and is not perishable,* '*as land or metals,* and wishes to rescind the contract, 'may give or take back such a thing within ten days;

223. 'But, after ten days, he shall neither give nor 'take it back: the giver or the taker, *except by consent,* 'shall be fined by the king six hundred *panas.*

224. 'The king himself shall take a fine of ninety-'six *panas* from him, who gives a blemished girl *in* '*marriage for a reward,* without avowing her blemish;

225. 'But the man, who, through malignity, says 'of a damsel, that she is no virgin, shall be fined a 'hundred *panas,* if he cannot prove her defilement.

226. 'The holy nuptial texts are applied solely to 'virgins, and no where on earth to girls, who have lost 'their virginity; since those women are *in general* ex-'cluded from legal ceremonies:

227. 'The nuptial texts are a certain rule in regard 'to wedlock, and the bridal contract is known by the 'learned to be complete *and irrevocable* on the seventh 'step *of the married pair, hand in hand, after those texts* '*have been pronounced.*

228. 'By this law, in all business whatever here 'below, must the judge confine, within the path of 'rectitude, a person inclined to rescind his contract of 'sale and purchase.

229. 'I now will decide exactly, according to prin-'ciples of law the contests usually arising from the 'fault of such as own herds of cattle, and of such as are 'hired to keep them.

230. 'By day the blame falls on the herdsman; by 'night on the owner, *if the cattle be fed and kept* in

'his own house; but, if the place of their food and 'custody be different, the keeper incurs the blame.

231. 'That hired servant, whose wages are paid 'with milk, may, with the assent of the owner, milk 'the best cow out of ten: such are the wages of herds-'men, unless they be paid in a different mode.

232. 'The herdsman himself shall make good the 'loss of a beast, which through his want of due care 'has strayed, has been destroyed by reptiles, or killed 'by dogs, or has died by falling into a pit;

233. 'But he shall not be compelled to make it 'good, when robbers have carried it away, if, after fresh 'proclamation and pursuit, he give notice to his master 'in a proper place and season.

234. 'When cattle die, let him carry to his master 'their ears, their hides, their tails, the skin below their 'navels, their tendons, and the liquor exuding from 'their foreheads: let him also point out their limbs.

235. 'A flock of goats or of sheep being attacked 'by wolves, and the keeper not going *to repel the* '*attack*, he shall be responsible for every one of them, 'which a wolf shall violently kill;

236. 'But, if any one of them, while they graze 'together near a wood, and the shepherd keeps them 'in order, shall be suddenly killed by a wolf spring-'ing on it, he shall not in that case be responsible.

237. 'On all sides of a village or small town, let a 'space be left for pasture, in breadth either four 'hundred cubits, or three casts of a large stick; and 'thrice that space round a city or considerable town:

238. 'Within that pasture ground, if cattle do any 'damage to grain in a field uninclosed with a hedge, 'the king shall not punish the herdsman.

239. 'Let the owner of the field enclose it with a 'hedge *of thorny plants,* over which a camel could not 'look; and let him stop every gap, through which a 'dog or a boar could thrust his head.

240. 'Should cattle, attended by a herdsman, do 'mischief near a highway, in an enclosed field or near 'the village, he shall be fined a hundred *panas;* but 'against cattle which have no keeper, let the owner of 'the field secure it.

241. 'In other fields, the *owner of* cattle *doing mis'chief* shall be fined one *pana* and a quarter; but, in 'all places, the *value of the damaged* grain must be 'paid: such is the fixed rule concerning a husband'man.

242. 'For damage by a cow before ten days have 'passed since her calving, by bulls kept for impreg'nation, and by cattle consecrated to the deity, whether 'attended or unattended, MANU has ordained no fine.

243. 'If land be injured, by the fault of the farmer 'himself, *as if he fails to sow it in due time,* he shall 'be fined ten times as much as the *king's* share *of the 'crop, that might otherwise have been raised;* but only 'five times as much, if it was the fault of his servants 'without his knowledge.

244. 'These rules let a just prince observe in all 'cases of transgression by masters, their cattle, and 'their herdsmen.

245. 'If a contest arise between two villages, *or 'landholders,* concerning a boundary, let the king, *or his 'judge* ascertain the limits in the month of *Jyaisht'ha,* 'when the landmarks are seen more distinctly.

246. '*When boundaries first are established,* let strong 'trees be planted on them, *Vatas, Pippalas Paláṣas, 'Sálmalis, Sálas* or *Tálas;* or such trees (*like the* Udum'bara *or* Vajradru) as abound in milk;

247. 'Or clustering shrubs, or *Venus* of different 'sorts, or *Samí*-trees, and creepers, or *Saras*, and 'clumps of *kubjanas:* and mounds of earth should be 'raised on them, so that the landmark may not easily 'perish :

248. 'Lakes and wells, pools and streams, ought 'also to be made on the common limits, and temples 'dedicated to the gods.

249. 'The persons concerned, reflecting on the per- 'petual trespasses committed by men here below 'through ignorance of boundaries, should cause other 'landmarks to be concealed *under ground:*

250. 'Large pieces of stone, bones, tails of cows, 'bran, ashes, potsherds, dried cow-dung, bricks and 'tiles, charcoal, pebbles, and sand,

251. 'And substances of all sorts, which the earth 'corrodes not even in a long time, should be placed *in* '*jars* not appearing *above ground* on the common 'boundary.

252. 'By such marks, or by the course of a stream, 'and long continued possession, the judge may ascer- 'tain the limit between the lands of two parties in 'litigation.

553. 'Should there be a doubt, even on the in- 'spection of those marks, recourse must be had, for the 'decision of such a contest, to the declarations of 'witnesses.

254. 'Those witnesses must be examined concerning 'the landmarks, in the presence of all the townsmen or 'villagers, or of both the contending parties :

255. 'What the witnesses, thus assembled and in- 'terrogated, shall positively declare concerning the

'limits, must be recorded in writing, together with all 'their names.

256. 'Let them, putting earth on their heads, wear-'ing chaplets of red flowers and clad in red mantles, be 'sworn by *the reward of* all their several good actions, 'to give correct evidence concerning the metes and 'bounds.

257. 'Veracious witnesses, who give evidence as the 'law requires, are absolved from their sins; but such, 'as give it unjustly, shall each be fined two hundred '*panas*.

258. 'If there be no witnesses, let four men, who 'dwell on all the four sides of the two villages, make a 'decision concerning the boundary, being duly prepared, '*like the witnesses*, in the presence of the king.

259. 'If there be no such neighbours on all sides, nor 'any men, whose ancestors had lived there since the 'villages were built, nor other inhabitants of towns, 'who can give evidence on the limits, the judge must 'examine the following men, who inhabit the woods;

260. 'Hunters, fowlers, herdsmen, fishers, diggers 'for roots, catchers of snakes, gleaners, and other 'foresters:

261. 'According to their declaration, when they 'are duly examined, let the king with precision order 'landmarks to be fixed on the boundary line between 'the two villages.

262. 'As to the bounds of arable fields, wells or 'pools, gardens and houses, the testimony of next 'neighbours on every side must be considered as the 'best means of decision:

263. 'Should the neighbours say any thing untrue,

'when two men dispute about a landmark, the king 'shall make each of those witnesses pay the middlemost 'of the three usual amercements.

264. 'He, who, by means of intimidation, shall pos-'sess himself of a house, a pool, a field, or a garden, 'shall be fined five hundred *panas*; but only two hun-'dred, if he trespassed through ignorance *of the right*.

265. 'If the boundary cannot be *otherwise* ascertained, 'let the king, knowing what is just, *that is, without* '*partiality, and* consulting the future benefit of both 'parties, make a bound-line between their lands: this 'is a settled law.

266. 'Thus has the rule been propounded for deci-'sions concerning landmarks: I, next, will declare the 'law concerning defamatory words.

267. 'A soldier, defaming a priest, shall be fined a 'hundred *panas*; a merchant, *thus offending*, an hundred 'and fifty, or two hundred; but, *for such an offence*, a 'mechanic or servile man shall be whipped.

268. 'A priest shall be fined fifty,* if he slander a 'soldier; twenty-five, if a merchant; and twelve, if he 'slander a man of the servile class.

169. 'For abusing one of the same class, a twice-born 'man shall be fined only twelve; but for ribaldry not to 'be uttered, even that *and every fine* shall be doubled.

270. 'A once-born man, who insults the twice-born 'with gross invectives, ought to have his tongue slit; 'for he sprang from the lowest part *of* BRAHMA':

271. 'If he mention their names and classes with 'contumely, *as if he say* "*Oh* DEVADATTA, *thou refuse* '*of* Bráhmans," an iron style, ten fingers long, shall be 'thrust red hot into his mouth.

* See Note on Book VIII. verse 268.

272. 'Should he, through pride, give instruction to 'priests concerning their duty, let the king order some 'hot oil to be dropped into his mouth and his ear.

273. 'He, who falsely denies, through insolence, the 'sacred knowledge, the country, the class, or the cor-'poreal investiture *of a man equal in rank*, shall be 'compelled to pay a fine of two hundred *panas*.

274. 'If a man call another blind with one eye, or 'lame, or defective in any similar way, he shall pay the 'small fine of one *pana*, even though he speak truth.

275. 'He shall be fined a hundred, who defames his 'mother, his father, his wife, his brother, his son, or 'his preceptor; and he, who gives not his preceptor the 'way.

276. 'For *mutual* abuse by a priest and a soldier, 'this fine must be imposed by a learned king; the 'lowest amercement on the priest, and the middlemost 'on the soldier.

277. 'Such exactly, *as before-mentioned*, must be the 'punishment of a merchant and a mechanic, in respect 'of their several classes, except the slitting of the 'tongue: this is a fixed rule of punishment.

278. 'Thus fully has the law been declared for the 'punishment of defamatory speech: I will, next, pro-'pound the established law concerning assault and 'battery.

279. 'With whatever member a low-born man shall 'assault or hurt a superior, even that member of his 'must be slit, *or cut more or less in proportion to the 'injury*: this is an ordinance of MANU.

280. 'He, who raises his hand or a staff against ano-'ther, shall have his hand cut; and he, who kicks 'another in wrath, shall have an incision made in his 'foot.

281. 'A man of the lowest class, who shall insolently 'place himself on the same seat with one of the highest, 'shall either be banished with a mark on his hinder 'parts, or the king shall cause a gash to be made on 'his buttock:

282. 'Should he spit on him through pride, the 'king shall order both his lips to be gashed; should 'he urine on him, his penis; should he break wind 'against him, his anus.

283. 'If he seize the *Bráhman* by the locks, or by 'the feet, or by the beard, or by the throat, or by the 'scrotum, let the king without hesitation cause incisions 'to be made in his hands.

284. 'If any man scratch the skin *of his equal in* '*class*, or fetch blood *from him*, he shall be fined a 'hundred *panas*; if he wound a muscle, six *nishkas*; 'but, if he break a bone, let him be instantly banished.

285. 'According to the use and value of all great 'trees, must a fine be set for injuring them: this is an 'established rule.

286. 'If a blow, attended with much pain, be given 'either to human creatures or cattle, the king shall 'inflict on the striker a punishment as heavy as the 'presumed suffering.

287. 'In all cases of hurting a limb, wounding, or 'fetching blood, the assailant shall pay the expense of 'a perfect cure; or, *on his failure*, both full damages 'and a fine to the same amount.

288. 'He, who injures the goods of another, whether 'acquainted or unacquainted with the owner of them 'shall give satisfaction to the owner, and pay a fine to 'the king equal to the damage.

289. 'If injury be done to leather or to leathern bags, 'or to utensils made of wood or clay, the fine shall be 'five times their value.

290. 'The wise reckon ten occasions, in regard to 'a carriage, its driver, and its owner, on which the fine 'is remitted ; on other occasions a fine is ordained by 'law :

291. 'The nose-cord or bridle being cut, *by some accident without negligence*, or the yoke being snapped, 'on a sudden overturn, or running against any thing '*without fault*, the axle being broken, or the wheel 'cracked ;

292. 'On the breaking of the thongs, of the halter, 'or of the reins, and when the driver has called aloud 'to make way, *on these occasions* has MANU declared 'that no fine shall be set :

293. 'But, where a carriage has been overturned by 'the unskilfulness of the driver, there, in the case 'of any hurt, the master shall be fined two hundred '*panas*

294. 'If the driver be skilful, *but negligent*, the 'driver alone shall be fined ; and those in the carriage 'shall be fined each a hundred, if the driver be clearly 'unskilful.

295. 'Should a driver, being met in the way by another carriage or by cattle, kill any animal *by his* '*negligence*, a fine shall, without doubt, be imposed *by* '*the following rule* :

296. 'For killing a man, a fine, equal to that for 'theft, shall be instantly set ; half that amount, for 'large brute animals, as for a bull or cow, an elephant, 'a camel, or a horse ;

297. 'For killing very young cattle, the fine shall be

'two hundred *panas*; and fifty, for elegant quadrupeds 'or beautiful birds, as *antelopes, parrots, and the like*;

298. 'For an ass, a goat, or a sheep, the fine must be 'five silver *máshas*; and one *másha*, for killing a dog 'or a boar.

299. 'A wife, a son, a servant, a pupil, and a '*younger* whole brother, may be corrected, when they 'commit faults, with a rope or the small shoot of a 'cane;

300. 'But on the back part only of their bodies, and 'not on a noble part by any means: he who strikes 'them otherwise than by this rule, incurs the guilt, *or* '*shall pay the fine*, of a thief.

301. 'This law of assault and battery has been com'pletely declared: I proceed to declare the rule for the 'settled punishment of theft.

302. 'In restraining thieves and robbers, let the 'king use extreme diligence; since, by restraining 'thieves and robbers, his fame and his domain are 'increased.

303. 'Constantly, no doubt, is that king to be ho'noured, who bestows exemption from fear; since he 'performs, *as it were*, a perpetual sacrifice, giving exemp'tion from fear as a constant sacrificial present.

304. 'A sixth part of *the reward for* virtuous deeds, 'performed by the whole people, belongs to the king, 'who protects them; but, if he protect them not, a 'sixth part of their iniquity lights on him.

305. 'Of *the reward for* what every subject reads in 'the *Veda*, for what he sacrifices, for what he gives in 'charity, for what he performs in worship, the king 'justly takes a sixth part in consequence of protection.

306. 'A king, who acts with justice in defending all 'creatures, and slays only those, who ought to be slain, 'performs, *as it were*, each day a sacrifice with a hundred 'thousand gifts;

307. 'But a king, who gives no such protection, yet 'receives taxes in kind or in value, market duties and 'tolls, the small daily presents for his household, and 'fines for offences, falls directly *on his death* to a region 'of horror.

308. 'That king, who gives no protection, yet takes 'a sixth part of the grain as hisrevenue, wise men have 'considered as a prince, who draws to him the foulness 'of all his people.

309. 'Be it known, that a monarch, who pays no 'regard to the scriptures, who denies a future state, who 'acts with rapacity, who protects not his people, yet 'swallows up their possessions, will sink low indeed '*after death*.

310. 'With great care and by three methods let him 'restrain the unjust; by imprisonment, by confinement 'in fetters, and by various kinds of corporal punish-'ment;

311. 'Since, by restraining the bad, and by encourag-'ing the good, kings are perpetually made pure, as the 'twice-born are purified by sacrificing.

312. 'A king, who seeks benefit to his own soul, must 'always forgive parties litigant, children, old men, and 'sick persons, who inveigh against him:

313. 'He, who forgives persons in pain, when they 'abuse him, shall on that account be exalted in heaven; 'but he, who excuses them not, through the pride of 'dominion, shall for that reason sink into hell.

314. 'The stealer *of gold from a priest* must run

'hastily to the king, with loosened hair, proclaiming 'the theft *and adding*: "Thus have I sinned; punish 'me."

315. 'He must bear on his shoulder a pestle of stone, 'or a club of *chadira*-wood, or a javelin pointed at both 'ends, or an iron mace:

316. 'Whether the king strike him with it, or dis-'miss him unhurt, the thief is then absolved from the 'crime; but the king, if he punish him not, shall incur 'the guilt of the thief.

317. '*The killer of a priest* or destroyer of an embryo, 'casts his guilt on the *willing* eater of his provisions; 'an adulterous wife, on her *negligent* husband; a bad 'scholar and sacrificer, on their *ignorant* preceptor; 'and a thief, on the *forgiving* prince:

318. 'But men, who have committed offences, and 'have received from kings the punishment due to them, 'go pure to heaven, and become as clear as those who 'have done well.

319. 'He, who steals the rope or the water-pot from 'a well, and he, who breaks down a cistern, shall be 'fined a *másha* of gold; and that, *which he has taken or* '*injured*, he must restore to its former condition.

320. 'Corporal punishment shall be inflicted on him, 'who steals more than ten *kumbhas* of grain (a *kumbha* 'is twenty *drónas*, and a *dróna*, two hundred *palas*): 'for less he must be fined eleven times as much, and 'shall pay to the owner the amount of his property.

321. 'So shall corporal punishment be inflicted for 'stealing commodities usually sold by weight, or more 'than a hundred head of cattle, or gold, or silver, or 'costly apparel:

322. 'For stealing more than fifty *palas*, it is enact-

'ed that a hand shall be amputated : for less, the king 'shall set a fine eleven times as much as the value.

323. 'For stealing men of high birth, and women 'above all, and the most precious gems, *as diamonds or* '*rubies,* the thief deserves capital punishment.

324. 'For stealing large beasts, weapons, or me-'dicines, let the king inflict *adequate* punishment, con-'sidering the time and the act.

325. 'For taking kine belonging to priests, and 'boring their nostrils, or for stealing their other cattle, 'the offender shall instantly lose half of one foot.

326. 'For stealing thread, raw cotton, materials to 'make spirituous liquor, cow-dung, molasses, curds, 'milk, butter-milk, water, or grass,

327. 'Large canes, baskets of canes, salt of every 'kind, earthen pots, clay or ashes,

328. 'Fish, birds, oil, or clarified butter, flesh-meat, 'honey, or any thing, *as leather, horn, or ivory,* that 'came from a beast,

329. 'Or other things not precious, or spirituous 'liquors, rice dressed with clarified butter, or other 'messes of boiled rice, the fine must be twice the value 'of the commodity stolen.

330. 'For stealing *as much as a man can carry* of 'flowers, green corn, shrubs, creepers, small trees, or 'other vegetables, enclosed by a hedge, the fine shall be 'five *raktikás* of gold or silver :

331. 'But for corn, pot-herbs, roots, and fruit, un-'enclosed by a fence, the fine is an hundred *panas,* if 'there be no sort of relation *between the taker and the* '*owner* ; or half a hundred, if there be such relation.

332. 'If the taking be violent, and in the sight of 'the owner, it is robbery; if privately in his absence, it 'is only theft; and *it is considered as theft*, when a 'man, having received any thing, refuses to give it back.

333. 'On him, who steals the before-mentioned 'things, when they are prepared for use, let the king 'set the lowest amercement *of the three*; and *the same* 'on him, who steals only fire from the temple.

334. 'With whatever limb a thief commits the offence 'by any means in this world, *as if he break a wall with* '*his hand or his foot*, even that limb shall the king 'amputate, for the prevention of a similar crime.

335. 'Neither a father, nor a preceptor, nor a friend, 'nor a mother, nor a wife, nor a son, nor a domestic 'priest, must be left unpunished by the king, if they 'adhere not with firmness to their duty.

336. 'Where another man of lower birth would be 'fined one *pana*, the king shall be fined a thousand, *and* '*he shall give the fine to the priests, or cast it into the* '*river*: this is a sacred rule.

337. 'But the fine of a *Súdra* for theft shall be 'eight-fold; that of a *Vaisya*, sixteen-fold; that of a '*Kshatriya*, two and thirty-fold.

338. 'That of a *Bráhman*, four and sixty-fold; or a 'hundred-fold complete, or even twice four and sixty-'fold; each of them knowing the nature of his offence.

339. 'The taking of roots and fruit from a large tree, '*in a field or a forest* unenclosed, or of wood for a 'sacrificial fire, or of grass to be eaten by cows, Manu 'has pronounced no theft.

340. 'A priest who willingly receives any thing, 'either for sacrificing or for instructing, from the hand

'of a man who had taken what the owner had not 'given, shall be *punished* even as the thief.

341. 'A twice-born man, who is travelling, and 'whose provisions are scanty, shall not be fined, for 'taking only two sugar canes, or two esculent roots, 'from the field of another man.

342. 'He who ties the unbound, or looses the bound, '*cattle of another*, and he, who takes a slave, a horse, or 'a carriage *without permission*, shall be punished as for 'theft.

343. 'A king, who by *enforcing* these laws restrains 'men from committing theft, acquires in this world 'fame, and, in the next, beatitude.

344. 'Let not the king, who ardently desires a seat 'with INDRA, and wishes for glory, which nothing can 'change or diminish, endure for a moment the man, who 'has committed atrocious violence, *as by robbery, arson*, '*or homicide*.

345. 'He, who commits great violence, must be con-'sidered as a more grievous offender than a defamer, a 'thief, or a striker with a staff:

'346. 'That king, who endures a man convicted of 'such atrocity, quickly goes to perdition, and incurs 'public hate.

347. 'Neither on account of friendship, nor for the 'sake of great lucre, shall the king dismiss the per-'petrators of violent acts, who spread terror among all 'creatures.

348. 'The twice-born may take arms, when their 'duty is obstructed by force; and when, in some evil 'time, a disaster has befallen the twice-born classes;

349. 'And in their own defence; and in a war for

'just cause; and in defence of a woman or a priest: he, 'who kills justly, commits no crime.

350. 'Let a man, without hesitation, slay another, '*if he cannot otherwise escape*, who assails him with 'intent to murder, whether young or old, or his pre-'ceptor, or a *Bráhman* deeply versed in the scripture.

351. 'By killing an assassin, who attempts to kill, 'whether in public or in private, no crime is committed 'by the slayer: fury recoils upon fury.

352. 'Men, who commit overt-acts of adulterous in-'clinations for the wives of others, let the king banish 'from his realm, having punished them with such 'bodily marks, as excite aversion;

353. 'Since adultery causes, to the general ruin, a 'mixture of classes among men: thence arises viola-'tion of duties; and thence is the root of felicity quite 'destroyed.

354. 'A man before noted for such an offence, who 'converses in secret with the wife of another, shall pay 'the first of the three usual amercements;

355. 'But a man, not before noted, who thus con-'verses with her for some reasonable cause, shall pay 'no fine; since in him there is no transgression.

356. 'He, who talks with the wife of another man 'at a place of pilgrimage, in a forest or a grove, or at 'the confluence of rivers, incurs the guilt of an adul-'terous inclination:

357. 'To send her flowers or perfumes, to sport and 'jest with her, to touch her apparel and ornaments, to 'sit with her on the same couch, are held adulterous 'acts on his part;

358. 'To touch a married woman on *her breasts or*

'any *other* place, which ought not to be touched, or, 'being touched unbecomingly by her, to bear it complacently, are adulterous acts with mutual assent.

359. 'A man of the servile class, who commits 'actual adultery with the wife of a priest, ought to 'suffer death; the wives, indeed, of all the four classes 'must ever be most especially guarded.

360. 'Mendicants, encomiasts, men, prepared for a 'sacrifice, and *cooks and other* artisans are not prohibited from speaking to married women.

361. 'Let no man converse, after he has been forbidden, with the wives of others; he, who thus converses, *after a husband or father has* forbidden *him*, 'shall pay a fine of one *suvarna*.

362. 'These laws relate not to the wives of public 'dancers or singers, or of such base men, as live by 'intrigues of their wives; men, who either carry 'women to others, or, lying concealed at home, permit 'them to hold a culpable intercourse:

363. 'Yet he, who has a private connexion with such 'women, or with servant-girls kept by one master, or 'with female anchorets *of an heretical religion*, shall be 'compelled to pay a small fine.

364. 'He, who vitiates a damsel without her consent, shall suffer corporal punishment instantly; but 'he, who enjoys a willing damsel, shall not be corporally punished, if his class be the same with hers.

365. 'From a girl, who makes advances to a man 'of a high class, let not the king take the smallest 'fine; but her, who first addresses a low man, let him 'constrain to live in her house well guarded.

366. 'A low man, who makes love to a damsel of 'high birth, ought to be punished corporally; but he,

'who addresses a maid of equal rank, shall give the 'nuptial present *and marry her*, if her father please.

367. 'Of the man, who through insolence forcibly 'contaminates a damsel, let the king instantly order 'two fingers to be amputated, and condemn him to pay 'a fine of six hundred *panas*:

368. 'A man of equal rank, who defiles a consenting 'damsel, shall not have his fingers amputated, but 'shall pay a fine of two hundred *panas*, to restrain him 'from a repetition of his offence.

369. 'A damsel, polluting another damsel, must be 'fined two hundred *panas*, pay the double value of 'her nuptial present, and receive ten lashes with a 'whip;

370. 'But a woman, polluting a damsel, shall have 'her head instantly shaved, and two of her fingers 'chopped off; and shall ride, mounted on an ass, '*through the public street*.

371. 'Should a wife, proud of her family and the 'great qualities of her kinsmen, actually violate the 'duty, which she owes to her lord, let the king con-'demn her to be devoured by dogs in a place much 'frequented;

372. 'And let him place the adulterer on an iron bed 'well heated, under which the executioners shall throw 'logs continually, till the sinful wretch be there burned '*to death*.

373. 'Of a man once convicted, and a year after 'guilty *of the same crime*, the fine must be doubled; *so* '*it must*, if he be connected with the daughter of an 'outcast or with a *Chándálí* women.

374. 'A mechanic or servile man, having an adul-

'terous connexion with a woman of a twice-born class, 'whether guarded at home or unguarded, *shall thus be* '*punished:* if she was unguarded, *he* shall lose the part '*offending*, and his whole substance; if guarded, *and a* '*priestess*, every thing, *even his life*.

375. '*For adultery with a guarded priestess*, a mer'chant shall forfeit all his wealth after imprisonment 'for a year; a soldier shall be fined a thousand *panas*, 'and be shaved with *the* urine *of an ass:*

376. 'But, if a merchant or soldier commit adultery 'with a woman of the sacerdotal class, whom her 'husband guards not at home, the king shall only fine 'the merchant five hundred, and the soldier a thousand:

377. 'Both of them, however, if they commit that 'offence with a priestess *not only* guarded *but eminent* '*for good qualities*, shall be punished like men of the 'servile class, or be burned in a fire of dry grass or 'reeds.

378. 'A *Bráhman*, who carnally knows a guarded 'woman without her free will, must be fined a thou'sand *panas*; but only five hundred if he knew her 'with her free consent.

379. 'Ignominious tonsure is ordained, instead of 'capital punishment, for an adulterer of the priestly 'class, where the punishment of other classes may ex'tend to loss of life.

380. 'Never shall the king slay a *Bráhman*, though 'convicted of all possible crimes; let him banish the 'offender from his realm, but with all his property 'secure, and his body unhurt:

381. 'No greater crime is known on earth than slay'ing a *Bráhman*; and the king, therefore, must not 'even form in his mind an idea of killing a priest

29

382. 'If a merchant converse criminally with a 'guarded woman of the military, or a soldier with one 'of the mercantile class, they both deserve the same 'punishment as in the case of a priestess unguarded:

383. 'But a *Bráhman*, who shall commit adultery 'with a guarded woman of those two classes, must be 'fined a thousand *panas*; and, for the like offence with 'a guarded woman of the servile class, the fine of a 'soldier or a merchant shall be also one thousand.

384. 'For adultery with a woman of the military 'class, if unguarded, the fine of a merchant is five 'hundred; but a soldier, *for the converse of that offence*, 'must be shaved with urine, or pay the fine *just men-'tioned*.

385. 'A priest shall pay five hundred *panas* if he 'connect himself criminally with an unguarded woman 'of the military, commercial, or servile class; and a 'thousand, *for such a connexion with* a woman of a vile '*mixed* breed.

386. 'That king, in whose realm lives no thief, no 'adulterer, no defamer, no man guilty of atrocious 'violence, and no committer of assaults, attains the 'mansion of SAKRA.

387. 'By suppressing those five in his dominion, he 'gains royalty paramount over men of the same kingly 'rank, and spreads his fame through the world.

388. 'The sacrificer, who forsakes the officiating 'priest, and the officiating priest, who abandons the 'sacrificer, each being able to do his work, and guilty of 'no grievous offence, must each be fined a hundred '*panas*.

389. 'A mother, a father, a wife, and a son shall 'not be forsaken: he, who forsakes either of them

'unless guilty of a deadly sin, shall pay six hundred '*panas* as a fine to the king.

390. 'Let not a prince, who seeks the good of his 'own soul, *hastily and alone* pronounce the law, on a 'dispute concerning any legal observance, among 'twice-born men in their several orders;

391. '*But* let him, after giving them due honour according to their merit, and, at first, having soothed 'them by mildness, apprise them of their duty with the 'assistance of *Bráhmans.*

392. 'The priest, who gives an entertainment to 'twenty men of the three first classes, without inviting 'his next neighbour, and his neighbour next but one, if 'both be worthy of an invitation, shall be fined one '*másha* of silver.

393. 'A *Bráhman* of deep learning in the *Veda* who 'invites not another *Bráhman,* both learned and virtuous, to an entertainment *given on some occasion* relating to his wealth, *as the marriage of his child, and 'the like,* shall be made to pay him twice the value of 'the repast, and be fined a *másha* of gold.

394. 'Neither a blind man, nor an idiot, nor a cripple, 'nor a man full seventy years old, nor one who confers 'great benefits on priests of eminent learning, shall be 'compelled by any *king* to pay taxes.

395. 'Let the king always do honour to a learned 'theologian, to a man either sick or grieved, to a little 'child, to an aged or indigent man, to a man of exalted 'birth, and to a man of distinguished virtue.

396. 'Let a washerman wash *the* clothes *of his employers* by little and little, *or piece by piece, and not 'hastily,* on a smooth board of *Sálmali* wood: let 'him never mix *the* clothes *of one person* with *the*

'clothes *of another*, nor suffer any *but the owner* to wear 'them.

397. 'Let a weaver, who has received ten *palas* of 'cotton-thread, give them back increased to eleven *by the 'rice-water and the like used in weaving:* he, who does 'otherwise, shall pay a fine of twelve *panas.*

398. 'As men versed in cases of tolls, and acquaint'ed with all marketable commodities, shall establish 'the price of saleable things, let the king take a twenti'eth part of *the profit on sales at* that price.

399. 'Of the trader, who, through avarice, exports 'commodities, of which the king justly claims the pre'emption, or on which he has laid an embargo, let the 'sovereign confiscate the whole property.

400. 'Any seller or buyer, who *fraudulently* passes 'by the toll-office at *night or* any *other* improper time, 'or who makes a false enumeration *of the articles 'bought,* shall be fined eight times as much as their 'value.

401. 'Let the king establish rules for the sale and 'purchase of all marketable things, having duly con'sidered whence they come, *if imported;* and, *if export'ed,* whither they must be sent; how long they have been 'kept; what may be gained by them; and what has 'been expended on them.

402. 'Once in five nights, or at the close of every 'half month, *according to the nature of the commodities,* 'let the king make a regulation for market prices in 'the presence of those *experienced men:*

403. 'Let all weights and measures be well ascer'tained by him; and once in six months let him re'examine them.

404. 'The toll at a ferry is one *pana* for an empty

'cart; half a *pana*, for a man with a load; a quarter, 'for a beast used in agriculture, or for a woman; and 'an eighth, for an unloaded man.

405. 'Waggons, filled with goods packed up, shall 'pay toll in proportion to their value; but for empty 'vessels and bags, and for *poor* men ill-apparelled, a 'very small toll shall be demanded.

406. 'For a long passage, the freight must be pro-'portioned to places and times; but this must be 'understood of passages up and down rivers: at sea 'there can be no settled freight.

407. 'A woman, who has been two months preg-'nant, a religious beggar, a forester in the third order, 'and *Bráhmans, who are* students in theology, shall not 'be obliged to pay toll for their passage.

408. 'Whatever shall be broken in a boat, by the 'fault of the boatmen, shall be made good by those 'men collectively, each paying his portion.

409. 'This rule, ordained for such as pass rivers in 'boats, relates to the culpable neglect of boatmen on 'the water: in the case of inevitable accident, there can 'be no damages recovered.

410. 'The king should order each man of the mer-'cantile class to practise trade, or money-lending, or 'agriculture and attendance on cattle; and each man of 'the servile class to act in the service of the twice-'born.

411. 'Both him of the military, and him of the com-'mercial class, if distressed for a livelihood, let some 'wealthy *Bráhman* support, obliging them without 'harshness to discharge their several duties.

412. 'A *Bráhman*, who, by his power and through 'avarice, shall cause twice-born men, girt with the

'sacrificial thread, to perform servile acts, *such as washing his feet*, without their consent, shall be fined by 'the king six hundred *panas*;

413. 'But a man of the servile class whether bought 'or unbought, he may compel to perform servile duty; 'because such a man was created by the Self-existent 'for the purpose of serving *Bráhmans*:

414. 'A *Súdra*, though emancipated by his master, 'is not released from a state of servitude; for of a state, 'which is natural to him, by whom can he be divested?

415. 'There are servants of seven sorts; one made 'captive under a standard *or in battle*, one maintained 'in consideration of service, one born of a female slave 'in the house, one sold, or given, or inherited from ancestors, and one enslaved by way of punishment *on his inability to pay a large fine.*

416. 'Three persons, a wife, a son, and a slave, are 'declared by law to have *in general* no wealth exclusively 'their own: the wealth, which they may earn, 'is *regularly* acquired for the man, to whom they 'belong.

417. 'A *Bráhman* may seize without hesitation, *if he be distressed for a subsistence*, the goods of his *Súdra*-'slave; for, as that slave can have no property, his 'master may take his goods.

418. 'With vigilant care should the king exert himself in compelling merchants and mechanics to perform their respective duties; for, when such men 'swerve from their duty, they throw this world into 'confusion.

419. 'Day by day must the king, *though engaged in forensic business*, consider the great objects of public

'measures, and inquire into the state of his carriages, '*elephants, horses, and cars,* his constant revenues and 'necessary expenses, his mines *of precious metals or* '*gems,* and his treasury:

420. 'Thus, bringing to a conclusion all these weighty 'affairs, and removing *from his realm and from himself* 'every taint of sin, a king reaches the supreme path of 'beatitude.'

CHAP. IX.

On the same; and on the Commercial and Servile Classes.

---

1. 'I now will propound the immemorial duties of 'man and woman, who must both remain firm in the 'legal path, whether united or separated.

2. 'Day and night must women be held by their 'protectors in a state of dependence; but in *lawful and* '*innocent* recreations, though rather addicted to them, 'they may be left at their own disposal.

3. 'Their fathers protect them in childhood; their 'husbands protect them in youth; their sons protect 'them in age: a woman is never fit for independence.

4. 'Reprehensible is the father, who gives not his 'daughter in marriage at the proper time; and the 'husband, who approaches not his wife in due season; 'reprehensible also is the son, who protects not his mo-'ther after the death of her lord.

5. 'Women must, above all, be restrained from the 'smallest illicit gratification; for, not being thus res-'trained, they bring sorrow on both families;

6. 'Let husbands consider this as the supreme law 'ordained for all classes; and let them, how weak 'soever, diligently keep their wives under lawful re- 'strictions;

7. 'For he who preserves his wife *from vice*, pre- 'serves his offspring *from suspicion of bastardy*, his 'ancient usages *from neglect*, his family *from disgrace*, 'himself *from anguish*, and his duty *from violation*.

8. 'The husband, after conception by his wife, be- 'comes himself an embryo, and is born a second time 'here below; for which reason the wife is called *jáyá*, 'since by her *(jáyate)* he is born again:

9. 'Now the wife brings forth a son endued with 'similar qualities to those of the father; so that, with 'a view to an excellent offspring, he must vigilantly 'guard his wife.

10. 'No man, indeed, can wholly restrain women by 'violent measures; but by these expedients, they may 'be restrained:

11. 'Let the husband keep his wife employed in the 'collection and expenditure of wealth, in purification 'and female duty, in the preparation of daily food, and 'the superintendence of household utensils.

12. 'By confinement at home, even under affec- 'tionate and observant guardians, they are not secure; 'but those women are truly secure, who are guarded 'by their own good inclinations.

13. 'Drinking *spirituous liquor*, associating with 'evil persons, absence from her husband, rambling 'abroad, unseasonable sleep, and dwelling in the house 'of another, are six faults which bring infamy on a 'married woman:

14. 'Such *women* examine not beauty, nor pay atten-

'tion to age; whether *their lover be* handsome or ugly, 'they think it is enough that he is a man, and pursue 'their pleasures.

15. 'Through their passion for men, their mutable 'temper, their want of settled affection, and their per-'verse nature (let them be guarded in this world 'ever so well), they soon become alienated from their 'husbands.

16. 'Yet should their husbands be diligently care-'ful in guarding them; though they well know the 'disposition, with which the lord of creation formed 'them.

17. 'MANU allotted to such women a love of their 'bed, of their seat, and of ornamn, impure appetites, 'wrath, weak flexibility, desire of mischief, and bad 'conduct.

18. 'Women have no business with the texts of the '*Veda*; thus is the law fully settled: having, therefore, 'no evidence *of law*, and no *knowledge of* expiatory 'texts, sinful women must be as foul as falsehood itself; 'and this is a fixed rule.

19. 'To this effect many texts, which may show their 'true disposition, are chanted in the *Vedas:* hear now 'their expiation for sin.

20 ' "That pure blood, which my mother defiled by 'adulterous desire, frequenting the houses of other men, 'and violating her duty to her lord, that blood may my 'father purify!" Such is the tenor of the holy text, '*which her son, who knows her guilt, must pronounce for* '*her;*

21. '*And* this expiation has been declared for every 'unbecoming thought, which enters her mind, concerning 'infidelity to her husband; since that *is the beginning* '*of* adultery.

22. 'Whatever be the qualities of the man, with 'whom a woman is united by lawful marriage, such 'qualities even she assumes; like a river *united* with 'the sea.

23. 'AKSHAMA'LA', a woman of the lowest birth, 'being thus united to VASISHTHA, and SA'RANGI', being 'united to MANDAPA'LA, were entitled to very high 'honour.

24. 'These, and other females of low birth, have 'attained eminence in this world by the respective 'good qualities of their lords.

25. 'Thus has the law, ever pure, been propounded 'for the civil conduct of men and women: hear, next, 'the laws concerning children, by obedience to which 'may happiness be attained in this and the future life.

26. 'When good women, united with husbands in 'expectation of progeny, eminently fortunate and wor-'thy of reverence, irradiate the houses of their lords, 'between them and goddesses of abundance there is no 'diversity whatever.

27. 'The production of children, the nurture of them, 'when produced, and the daily superintendence of 'domestic affairs are peculiar to the wife:

28. 'From the wife alone proceed offspring, good 'household management, solicitous attention, most ex-'quisite caresses, and that heavenly beatitude which she 'obtains for the manes of ancestors, and for *the husband* 'himself.

29. 'She, who deserts not her lord, but keeps in 'subjection to him her heart, her speech, and her body, 'shall attain his mansion in heaven, and, by the virtuous 'in this world, be called *Sádhwí, or good and faithful*;

30. 'But a wife, by disloyalty to her husband, shall

'incur disgrace in this life, and be born *in the next* from 'the womb of a shakal, or be tormented with horrible 'diseases, which punish vice.

31. 'Learn now that excellent law, universally salutary, which was declared, concerning issue by great 'and good sages formerly born.

32. 'They consider the male issue of a woman as the 'son of the lord; but, on the subject of that lord, 'a difference of opinion is mentioned in the *Veda*; 'some giving that name to the real procreator of the 'child, and others applying it to the married possessor 'of the woman.

33. 'The woman is considered in law as the field, 'and the man as the grain: now vegetable bodies are 'formed by the united operation of the seed and the 'field.

34. 'In some cases the prolific power of the male 'is chiefly distinguished; in others, the receptacle of 'the female: but, when both are equal in dignity, the 'offspring is most highly esteemed:

35. 'In general, as between the male and female 'powers of procreation, the male is held superior; 'since the offspring of all procreant beings is distinguished by marks of the male power.

36. 'Whatever be the quality of seed, scattered in 'a field prepared in due season, a plant of the same 'quality springs in that field, with peculiar visible properties.

37. 'Certainly this earth is called the primeval womb 'of many beings; but the seed exhibits not in its vegetation any properties of the womb.

38. 'On earth here below, even in the same ploughed 'field, seeds of many different forms, having been sown

'by husbandmen in the proper season, vegetate according to their nature:

39. 'Rice-plants, *mature in sixty days, and those, which require transplantation*, mudga, tila, masha, barley, leaks, and sugar-canes, all spring up according to the seeds.

40. 'That one plant should be sown, and another produced, cannot happen: whatever seed may be sown, even that produces its proper stem.

41. Never must it be sown in another man's field by him, who has natural good sense, who has been well instructed, who knows the *Veda* and its *Angas*, who desires long life:

42. 'They who are acquainted with past times, have preserved, on this subject, holy strains chanted by every breeze, *declaring*, that "seed must not be sown in the field of another man."

43. 'As the arrow of that hunter is vain, who shoots it into the wound, which another had made just before in the antelope, thus instantly perishes the seed, which a man throws into the soil of another:

44. 'Sages, who know former times, consider this earth *(Prit'hivi)* as the wife of king PRITHU; and thus they pronounce cultivated land to be the property of him, who cut away the wood, *or who cleared and tilled it*; and the antelope, of the first hunter, who mortally wounded it.

45. 'Then only is a man perfect, when he consists of *three persons united*, his wife, himself, and his son; and thus have learned *Bráhmans* announced this *maxim*: "The husband is even one person with his wife," *for all domestic and religious, not for all civil, purposes*.

46. 'Neither by sale nor desertion can a wife be 'released from her husband: thus we fully acknowledge the law enacted of old by the Lord of creatures.

47. 'Once is the partition of an inheritance made; 'once is a damsel given in marriage; and once does a 'man say "I give:" these three are, by good men, 'done once for all *and irrevocably.*

48. 'As with cows, mares, female camels, slave-'girls, milch buffalos, she-goats, and ewes, it is not 'the owner of the *bull or other* father, who owns the 'offspring, even thus is it with the wives of others.

49. 'They, who have no property in the field, but, 'having grain in their possession, sow it in soil owned 'by another, can receive no advantage whatever from 'the corn, which may be produced:

50. 'Should a bull beget a hundred calves on cows 'not owned by his master, those calves belong solely 'to the proprietors of the cows; and the strength of 'the bull was wasted:

51. 'Thus men, who have no marital property in 'women, but sow in the fields owned by others, may 'raise up fruit to the husbands; but the procreator can 'have no advantage from it.

52. 'Unless there be a special agreement between 'the owners of the land and of the seed, the fruit be-'longs clearly to the land-owners; for the receptacle is 'more important than the seed:

53. 'But the owners of the seed and of the soil may 'be considered in this world as joint owners of the 'crop, which they agree, by special compact in consi-'deration of the seed, to divide between them.

54. 'Whatever man owns a field, if seed, conveyed 'into it by water or wind, should germinate, the plant

'belongs to the land-owner: the mere sower takes not 'the fruit.

55. 'Such is the law concerning the offspring of cows, 'and mares, of female camels, goats, and sheep, of 'slave-girls, hens, and milch buffalos, *unless there be a 'special agreement.*

56. 'Thus has the comparative importance of the soil 'and the seed been declared to you: I will next pro- 'pound the law concerning women, who have no issue '*by their husbands.*

57. 'The wife of an elder brother is considered as 'mother-in law to the younger: and the wife of the 'younger as daughter-in-law to the elder:

58. 'The elder brother, amorously approaching the 'wife of the younger, and the younger, caressing the 'wife of the elder, are both degraded, even though au- 'thorized *by the husband or spiritual guide*, except when 'such wife has no issue.

59. 'On the failure of issue by the husband, *if he be 'of the servile class*, the desired offspring may be pro- 'created, either by his brother or some other *Sapinda*, 'on the wife, who has been duly authorized:

60. 'Sprinkled with clarified butter, silent, in the 'night, let the kinsman thus appointed beget one son, 'but a second by no means, on the widow *or childless 'wife:*

61. 'Some sages, learned in the laws concerning 'women, thinking it possible, that the great object of 'that appointment may not be obtained *by the birth of 'a single son*, are of opinion, that the wife and ap- 'pointed kinsman may legally procreate a second.

62. 'The first object of the appointment being ob-

'tained according to law, both *the brother and the widow* 'must live together like a father and a daughter by 'affinity.

63. 'Either brother, appointed for this purpose, who 'deviates from the strict rule, and acts from carnal 'desire, shall be degraded, as having defiled the bed of 'his daughter-in-law, or of his father.

64. 'By men of twice-born classes no widow, *or* '*childless wife*, must be authorized to conceive by 'any other than her lord; for they, who authorize 'her to conceive by any other, violate the primeval 'law.

65. 'Such a commission *to a brother or other near* '*kinsman* is no where mentioned in the nuptial texts 'of the *Veda;* nor is the marriage of a widow even 'named in the laws concerning marriage.

66. 'This practice, fit only for cattle, is reprehended 'by learned *Bráhmans;* yet it is declared to have been 'the practice even of men, while VENA had sovereign 'power:

67. 'He, possessing the whole earth, and *thence only* '*called* the chief of sage monarchs, gave rise to a con-'fusion of classes, when his intellect became weak 'through lust.

68. 'Since his time the virtuous disapprove of that 'man, who, through delusion of mind, directs a widow '*to receive the caresses of another* for the sake of pro-'geny.

69. 'The damsel, *indeed,* whose husband shall die 'after troth verbally plighted, *but before consummation,* 'his brother shall take in marriage according to this 'rule:

70. 'Having espoused her in due form of law, she

'being clad in a white robe, and pure in her moral 'conduct, let him approach her once in each proper 'season, and until issue *be had*.

71. 'Let no man of sense, who has once given his 'daughter to a suitor, give her again to another; for 'he, who gives away his daughter, whom he had before 'given, incurs the guilt and fine of speaking falsely in 'a cause concerning mankind.

72. 'Even though a man have married a young 'woman in legal form, yet he may abandon her, if he 'find her blemished, afflicted with disease, or previously 'deflowered, and given to him with fraud:

73. 'If any man give a faulty damsel in marriage, 'without disclosing her blemish, the husband may 'annul that act of her ill-minded giver.

74. 'Should a man have business abroad, let him 'assure a fit maintenance to his wife, and then reside '*for a time* in a foreign country; since a wife, even 'though virtuous, may be tempted to act amiss, if she 'be distressed by want of subsistence:

75. 'While her husband, having settled her main-'tenance, resides abroad, let her continue firm in re-'ligious austerities; but, if he leave her no support, 'let her subsist by *spinning and other* blameless arts.

76. 'If he live abroad on account of some sacred 'duty, let her wait for him eight years; if on account 'of knowledge or fame, six; if on account of pleasure, 'three: *after those terms have expired, she must follow 'him.*

77. 'For a whole year let a husband bear with 'his wife, who treats him with aversion; but, after 'a year, let him deprive her of her separate property, 'and cease to cohabit with her.

78. 'She, who neglects her lord, though addicted 'to gaming, fond of spirituous liquors, or diseased, must 'be deserted for three months, and deprived of her 'ornaments and household furniture:

79. 'But she, who is averse from a mad husband, 'or a deadly sinner, or an eunuch, or one without 'manly strength, or one afflicted with such maladies as 'punish crimes, must neither be deserted nor stripped 'of her property,

80. 'A wife, who drinks any spirituous liquors, who 'acts immorally, who shows hatred *to her lord*, who 'is *incurably* diseased, who is mischievous, who wastes 'his property; may at all times be superseded by 'another wife.

81. 'A barren wife may be superseded by another 'in the eighth year: she, whose children are all dead, in 'the tenth; she, who brings forth *only* daughters, in 'the eleventh; she, who speaks unkindly, without 'delay;

82. 'But she, who, though afflicted with illness, is 'beloved and virtuous, must never be disgraced, though 'she may be superseded by another wife with her own 'consent.

83. 'If a wife, legally superseded, shall depart in 'wrath from the house, she must either instantly be 'confined, or abandoned in the presence of the whole 'family:

84. 'But she, who, having been forbidden, addicts 'herself to intoxicating liquor even at jubilees, or 'mixes in crowds at theatres, must be fined six *raktikás* 'of gold.

85. 'When twice-born men take wives, both of their 'own class and others, the precedence, honour, and 'habitation of those wives, must be settled according 'to the order of their classes:

86. 'To all such married men, the wives of the same 'class only (not wives of a different class by any 'means) must perform the duty of personal attend-'ance, and the daily business relating to acts of 'religion;

87. 'For he, who foolishly causes those duties to 'be performed by any other than his wife of the same 'class, when she is near at hand, has been immemori-'ally considered as a mere *Chandála* begotten on a '*Bráhmani*.

88. 'To an excellent and handsome youth of the 'same class, let every man give his daughter in mar-'riage, according to law; even though she have not 'attained her age *of eight years:*

89. '*But* it is better, that the damsel, though mar-'riageable, should stay at home till her death, than 'that he should ever give her in marriage to a bride-'groom void of excellent qualities.

90. 'Three years let a damsel wait, though she be 'marriageable; but, after that term, let her choose for 'herself a bridegroom of equal rank:

91. 'If, not being given in marriage, she choose her 'bridegroom, neither she, nor the youth chosen, com-'mits any offence;

92. 'But a damsel, thus electing her husband, shall 'not carry with her the ornaments, which she received 'from her father, nor those given by her mother or 'brethren: if she carry them away, she commits theft.

93. 'He, who takes to wife a damsel of full age, 'shall not give a nuptial present to her father; since 'the father lost his dominion over her, by detaining 'her at a time, when she might have been a parent.

94. 'A man, aged thirty years, may marry a girl 'of twelve, *if he find one* dear to his heart; or a man

'of twenty-four years, a damsel of eight: but, if *he finish his studentship earlier, and* the duties *of his next order* would otherwise be impeded, let him marry immediately.

95. 'A wife, given by the gods, *who are named in the bridal texts,* let the husband receive and support 'constantly, if she be virtuous, though he married her 'not from inclination: such conduct will please the gods.

96. 'To be mothers, were women created; and to 'be fathers, men; religious rites, therefore are ordained 'in the *Veda*, to be performed *by the husband* together 'with the wife.

97. 'If a nuptial gratuity has actually been given 'to a damsel, and he, who gave it, should die *before marriage*, the damsel shall be married to his brother, 'if she consent;

98. 'But even a man of the servile class ought not 'to receive a gratuity, when he gives his daughter in 'marriage; since a father, who takes a fee *on that occasion*, tacitly sells his daughter.

99. 'Neither ancients nor moderns, who were good 'men, have ever given a damsel in marriage, after she 'had been promised to another man;

100. 'Nor, even in former creations, have we heard '*the virtuous approve* the tacit sale of a daughter for a 'price, under the name of a nuptial gratuity.

101. '"Let mutual fidelity continue to death:" this, 'in few words, may be considered as the supreme law 'between husband and wife.

102. 'Let a man and woman, united by marriage, 'constantly beware, lest, at any time disunited, they 'violate their mutual fidelity.

103. 'Thus has been declared to you the law, 'abounding in the purest affection, for the conduct 'of man and wife; together with the practice of raising up offspring *to a husband of the servile class* on 'failure *of issue by him begotten:* learn now the law of 'inheritance.

104. 'After the death of the father and the mother, 'the brothers being assembled, may divide among 'themselves the paternal *and maternal* estate; but they 'have no power over it, while their parents live, *unless* '*the father choose to distribute it.*

105. 'The eldest brother may take entire possession 'of the patrimony; and the others may live under 'him, as *they lived* under their father, *unless they choose* '*to be separated.*

106. 'By the eldest, at the moment of his birth, 'the father, having begotten a son, discharges his 'debt to his own progenitors; the eldest son, there'fore, ought *before partition* to manage the whole 'patrimony:

107. 'That son alone, by whose birth he discharges 'his debt, and through whom he attains immortality, 'was begotten from a sense of duty: all the rest 'are considered by the wise as begotten from love 'of pleasure.

108. 'Let the father alone support his sons; and 'the first-born, his younger brothers; and let them 'behave to the eldest, according to law, as children '*should behave* to their father.

109. 'The first-born, *if virtuous,* exalts the family, 'or, *if vicious,* destroys it: the first-born is in this 'world the most respectable; and the good never treat 'him with disdain.

110. 'If an elder brother act, as an elder brother

'ought, he is *to be revered* as a mother, as a father; 'and, even if he have not the behaviour of a good elder 'brother, he should be respected as a *maternal uncle,* '*or other* kinsman.

111. 'Either let them thus live together, or, if they 'desire *separately to perform* religious rites, let them 'live apart; since religious duties are multiplied in 'separate houses, their separation is, therefore, legal '*and even laudable.*

112. 'The portion deducted for the eldest is a twen-'tieth part *of the heritage,* with the best of all the 'chattels; for the middlemost, half of that, *or a for-*'*tieth;* for the youngest, a quarter of it, *or an* '*eightieth.*

113. 'The eldest and youngest respectively take 'their just mentioned portions; and, if there be more 'than one between them, each of the intermediate sons 'has the mean portion, *or the fortieth.*

114. 'Of all the goods collected let the first-born *if* '*he be transcendently learned and virtuous,* take the 'best article, whatever is most excellent in its kind, and 'the best of ten *cows or the like:*

115. 'But among brothers equally skilled in per-'forming their several duties, there is no deduction of 'the best in ten, *or the most excellent chattel;* though 'some trifle, as a mark of greater veneration, should 'be given to the first-born.

116. 'If a deduction be thus made, let equal shares 'of the residue be ascertained *and received;* but, if there 'be no deduction, the shares must be distributed in this 'manner:

117. 'Let the eldest have a double share, and the 'next-born, a share and half, *if they clearly surpass the* '*rest in virtue and learning;* the younger sons must

'have each a share: *if all be equal in good qualities,* '*they must all take share and share alike.*

118. 'To the *unmarried* daughters *by the same mo-* '*ther,* let their brothers give portions out of their own 'allotments respectively, *according to the classes of their* '*several mothers:* let each give a fourth part of his own 'distinct share; and they, who refuse to give it, shall 'be degraded.

119. 'Let them never divide *the value of* a single 'goat or sheep, or a single beast with uncloven hoofs: 'a single goat or sheep *remaining after an equal dis-* '*tribution,* belongs to the first-born.

120. 'Should a younger brother, *in the manner be-* '*fore mentioned,* have begotten a son on the wife of his '*deceased* elder brother, the division must then be 'made equally *between that son, who represents the de-* '*ceased, and his natural father;* thus is the law settled.

121. 'The representative is not *so far* wholly sub- 'stituted by law in the place of the *deceased* princi- 'pal, *as to have the portion of an elder son;* and the 'principal became a father in consequence of the pro- 'creation *by his younger brother;* the son, therefore, is 'entitled by law to an equal share, *but not to a double* '*portion.*

122. 'A younger son being born of a first married 'wife, after an elder son had been born of a wife last 'married, *but of a lower class,* it may be a doubt in 'that case, how the division shall be made:

123. 'Let the son, born of the elder wife, take one 'most excellent bull deducted from the inheritance; 'the next excellent bulls are for those, who *were born* '*first, but* are inferior on account of their mothers *who* '*were married last.*

124. 'A son, indeed, who was first born, and brought

'forth by the wife first married, may take, *if learned and virtuous*, one bull and fifteen cows; and the 'other sons may then take, each in right of his 'several mother: such is the fixed rule.

125. 'As between sons, born of wives equal in their 'class *and* without *any other* distinction, there can be 'no seniority in right of the mother; but the seniority 'ordained by law, is according to the birth.

126. 'The right of invoking INDRA by the texts, 'called *swabráhmanyá*, depends on actual priority of 'birth; and of twins also, *if any such be conceived* 'among *different* wives, the eldest is he, who was first 'actually born.

127. 'He, who has no son, may appoint his daugh-'ter in this manner to raise up a son for him, *saying:* '"the male child, who shall be born from her in 'wedlock, shall be mine for the purpose of performing 'my obsequies."

128. 'In this manner DAKSHA himself, lord of created 'beings, anciently appointed all his *fifty* daughters to 'raise up sons to him for the sake of multiplying his 'race:

129. 'He gave ten to DHARMA, thirteen to KASYAPA, 'twenty-seven to SÓMA, king *of Bráhmans and medical plants*, after doing honour to them with an affectionate 'heart.

130. 'The son of a man is even as himself; and as 'the son, such is the daughter *thus appointed:* how 'then, *if he have no son*, can any inherit his property, 'but a daughter, who is closely united with his own 'soul?

131. 'Property, given to the mother on her mar-'riage, is inherited by her *unmarried* daughter; and 'the son of a daughter, *appointed in the manner just*

'*mentioned*, shall inherit the whole estate of her father, 'who leaves no son *by himself begotten*:

132. 'The son, however, of *such* a daughter, who 'succeeds to all the wealth of her father dying without 'a son, must offer two funeral cakes, one to his own 'father, and one to the father of his mother.

133. 'Between a son's son and the son of *such* a 'daughter, there is no difference in law; since their 'father and mother both sprang from the body of the 'same man:

134. 'But, a daughter having been appointed to 'produce a son for her father, and a son, *begotten by* '*himself*, being afterwards born, the division of the 'heritage must in that case be equal; since there is no 'right of primogeniture for a woman.

135. 'Should a daughter, thus appointed to raise up 'a son for her father, die by any accident without 'a son, the husband of that daughter may, without 'hesitation, possess himself of her property.

136. 'By that male child, whom a daughter thus 'appointed, either by an implied intention or a plain 'declaration, shall produce from a husband of an equal 'class, the maternal grandfather becomes in law the 'father of a son: let that son give the funeral cake 'and possess the inheritance.

137. 'By a son, a man obtains victory over all peo-'ple; by a son's son, he enjoys immortality; and, af-'terwards, by the son of that grandson, he reaches the 'solar abode.

138. 'Since the son *(trâyatê)* delivers his father 'from the hell named *put*, he was, therefore, called '*puttra* by BRAHMA' himself:

139. 'Now between the sons of his son and of his

'daughter *thus appointed*, there subsists in this world 'no difference; for even the son of such a daughter 'delivers him in the next, like the son of his son.

140. 'Let the son of such a daughter offer the first 'funeral cake to his mother; the second to her father; 'the third, to her paternal grandfather.

141. 'Of the man, to whom a son has been given, '*according to a subsequent law*, adorned with every 'virtue, that son shall take *a fifth or sixth part of* the 'heritage, though brought from a different family.

142. 'A given son must never claim the family and 'estate of his natural father: the funeral cake follows 'the family and estate; but of him, who has given away 'his son, the funeral oblation is extinct.

143. 'The son of a wife, not authorized to have issue 'by another, and the son begotten, by the brother of 'the husband, on a wife, who has a son then living, 'are both unworthy of the heritage; one being the 'child of an adulterer, and the other produced through 'mere lust.

144. 'Even the son of a wife duly authorized, not 'begotten according to the law *already propounded*, is 'unworthy of the paternal estate; for he was pro-'created by an outcast:

145. 'But the son *legally* begotten on a wife, au-'thorized for the purpose *before mentioned*, may inhe-'rit *in all respects, if he be virtuous and learned*, as 'a son begotten by the husband; since *in that case* the 'seed and the produce belong of right to the owner of 'the field.

146. 'He, who keeps the *fixed and moveable* estate 'of his *deceased* brother, maintains the widow, and 'raises up a son to that brother, must give to that son,

'*at the age of fifteen*, the whole of his brother's *divided* 'property.

147. 'Should a wife, even though legally authorized, 'produce a son by the brother, or any other *sapinda*, 'of her husband, that son, if begotten with *amorous em-'braces, and tokens of* impure desire, the sages proclaim 'base-born and incapable of inheriting.

148. 'This law, *which has preceded*, must be under-'stood of a distribution among sons begotten on women 'of the same class: hear now the law concerning *sons* '*by* several women of different classes.

149. 'If there be four wives of a *Bráhman* in the 'direct order of the classes, and sons are produced 'by them all, this is the rule of partition *among* '*them*:

150. 'The chief servant in husbandry, the bull kept 'for impregnating cows, the riding-horse or carriage, 'the *ring and other* ornaments, and the principal mes-'suage, shall be deducted from the inheritance and 'given to the *Bráhman*-son, together with a larger 'share by way of pre-eminence.

151. 'Let the *Bráhman* take three shares of the 'residue; the son of the *Kshatriyà*-wife, two shares; 'the son of the *Vaisyà*-wife, a share and a half; and 'the son of the *Súdrà*-wife, may take one share.

152. 'Or, *if no deduction be made*, let some person 'learned in the law divide the whole collected estate 'into ten parts, and make a legal distribution by this '*following* rule:

153. 'Let the son of the *Bráhmaní* take four parts; 'the son of the *Kshatriyà* three; let the son of the '*Vaisyà* have two parts; let the son of the *Súdrà* 'take a single part, *if he be virtuous*.

154. 'But whether the *Bráhman* have sons, or have 'no sons, *by wives of the three first classes*, no more 'than a tenth part must be given to the son of a *Sú-'drà*.

155. 'The son of a *Bráhman*, a *Kshatriyá*, or a '*Vaisyá* by a woman of the servile class, shall inhe-'rit no part of the estate, *unless he be virtuous; nor 'jointly with other sons, unless his mother was lawfully 'married:* whatever his father may give him, let that 'be his own.

156. 'All the sons of twice-born men, produced by 'wives of the same class, must divide the heritage 'equally, after the younger brothers have given the 'first-born his deducted allotment.

157. 'For a *Súdra* is ordained a wife of his own 'class, *and* no other: all, produced by her, shall have 'equal shares, though she have a hundred sons.

158. 'Of the twelve sons of men, whom MANU, 'sprung from the Self-existent, has named, six are 'kinsmen and heirs; six, not heirs, *except to their own 'fathers*, but kinsmen.

159. 'The son begotten by a man himself *in law-'ful wedlock*, the son of his wife begotten *in the manner 'before described*, a son given *to him*, a son made *or 'adopted*, a son of concealed birth, *or whose real 'father cannot be known*, and a son rejected *by his natural 'parents*, are the six kinsmen and heirs:

160. 'The son of a young woman *unmarried*, the 'son of a pregnant bride, a son bought, a son by a 'twice-married woman, a son self given, and a son 'by a *Súdrà*, are the six kinsmen, but not heirs *to 'collaterals*.

161. 'Such advantage, as a man would gain, who

'should attempt to pass deep water in a boat made of 'woven reeds, that father obtains, who passes the gloom 'of death, leaving only contemptible sons, *who are the 'eleven, or at least the six last mentioned.*

162. 'If the two heirs of one man be the son of 'his own body and a son of his wife by a kinsman, '*the former of whom was begotten after his recovery 'from an illness thought incurable*, each of the sons, 'exclusively of the other, shall succeed to the whole 'estate of his natural father.

163. 'The son of his own body is the sole heir to 'his estate, but, that all evil may be removed, let him 'allow a maintenance to the rest;

164. 'And, when the son of the body has taken an 'account of the paternal inheritance, let him give a 'sixth part of it to the son of the wife begotten by a 'kinsman, *before his father's recovery*; or a fifth part, '*if that son be eminently virtuous.*

165. 'The son of the body, and the son of the wife, 'may succeed *immediately* to the paternal estate *in the 'manner just mentioned*; but the ten other sons can 'only succeed in order to the family duties and to their 'share of the inheritance, *those last named being ex-'cluded by any one of the preceeding.*

166. 'Him, whom a man has begotten on his own 'wedded wife, let him know to be the first in rank, as 'the son of his body.

167. 'He, who was begotten, according to law, on 'the wife of a man deceased, or impotent, or disorder-'ed, after due authority given to her, is called the 'lawful son of the wife.

168. 'He, whom his father, or mother *with her hus-'band's assent*, gives to another as his son, provided 'that the donee have no issue, if the boy be of the

'same class and affectionately disposed, is considered 'as a son given, *the gift being confirmed* by *pouring* 'water.

169. 'He is considered as a son made *or adopted,* 'whom a man takes as his own son, the boy being 'equal in class, endued with filial virtues, acquainted 'with *the* merit *of performing obsequies to his adopter,* 'and with *the* sin *of omitting them.*

170. 'In whose mansion soever a male child shall 'be brought forth *by a married woman, whose husband* '*has long been absent,* if the real father cannot be dis- 'covered, *but if it be probable that he was of an equal* '*class,* that child belongs to the lord of the *unfaithful* 'wife, and is called a son of concealed birth in his 'mansion.

171. 'A boy, whom a man receives as his own son, 'after he has been deserted *without just cause* by his 'parents, or by either of them, *if one be dead,* is called 'a son rejected.

172. 'A son, whom the daughter of any man pri- 'vately brings forth in the house of her father, if she '*afterwards* marry her lover, is described as a son 'begotten on an unmarried girl.

173. 'If a pregnant young woman marry, whether 'her pregnancy be known or unknown, the male child 'in her womb belongs to the bridegroom, and is called 'a son received with his bride.

174. 'He is called a son bought, whom a man, for 'the sake of having a son *to perform his obsequies,* 'purchases from his father and mother, whether the 'boy be equal or unequal *to himself in good qualities,* '*for in class all adopted sons must be equal.*

175. 'He, whom a woman, either forsaken by her 'lord or a widow, conceived by a second husband, whom

'she took by her own desire, *though against law,* is called 'the son of a woman twice married :

176. 'If, *on her second marriage,* she be still a virgin, 'or if she left her husband under the age of puberty 'and return to him at his full age, she must again per'form the nuptial ceremony *either* with her second, *or* '*her young and deserted,* husband.

177. 'He, who has lost his parents, or been aban'doned *by them* without just cause, and offers himself 'to a man *as his son,* is called a son self-given.

178. 'A son, begotten through lust on a *Súdrá* by a 'man of the priestly class, is even as a corpse, though 'alive, and is thence called in law a living corpse :

179. 'But a son, begotten by a man of the servile 'class on his female slave, or on the female slave of his 'male slave, may take a share of the heritage, if 'permitted *by the other sons* : thus is the law es'tablished.

180. 'These eleven sons (the son of the wife, and 'the rest as enumerated) are allowed by wise legis'lators to be substitutes *in order* for sons of the 'body, for the sake of preventing a failure of obsequies ;

181. 'Though such, as are called sons for that pur'pose, but were produced from the manhood of others, 'belong in truth to the father, from whose manhood 'they severally sprang, and to no other, *except by a just* '*fiction of law.*

182. 'If, among several brothers of the whole blood, 'one have a son born, MANU pronounces them all 'fathers of a male child by means of that son ; *so that,* '*if such nephew would be the heir, the uncles have no* '*power to adopt sons :*

183. '*Thus* if, among all the wives of the same 'husband, one bring forth a male child, MANU has

'declared them all, by means of that son, to be mothers 'of male issue.

184. 'On failure of the best, *and* of the *next* best '*among those twelve sons*, let the inferior in order take 'the heritage; but, if there be many of equal rank, let 'all be sharers of the estate.

185. 'Not brothers, nor parents, but sons, *if living*, '*or their male issue*, are heirs to the deceased, but of 'him, who leaves no son, *nor a wife, nor a daughter*, 'the father shall take the inheritance; and, *if he leave* '*neither father, nor mother*, the brothers.

186. 'To three *ancestors* must water be given at their 'obsequies; for three (*the father, his father, and the* '*paternal grandfather*) is the funeral cake ordained: 'the fourth *in descent* is the giver *of oblations* '*to them, and their heir, if they die without nearer* '*descendants*; but the fifth has no concern *with the gift* '*of the funeral cake*.

187. 'To the nearest *sapinda, male or female*, after 'him in the third degree, the inheritance *next* belongs; 'then, on failure of *sapindas* and of their issue, the '*samánódaka*, or distant kinsman, shall be the heir; 'or the spiritual preceptor, or the pupil, *or the fellow-* '*student, of the deceased*:

188. 'On failure of all those, the lawful heirs are 'such *Bráhmans*, as have read the three *Vedas*, as are 'pure *in body and mind*, as have subded their passions; '*and they must consequently offer the cake*: thus the 'rites of obsequies cannot fail.

189. 'The property of a *Bráhman* shall never be 'taken *as an escheat* by the king; this is a fixed law: 'but the wealth of the other classes, on failure of all 'heirs, the king may take.

190. 'If the widow of a man, who died without a

'son, raise up a son to him by one of his kinsmen, let 'her deliver to that son, *at his full age,* the collected 'estate of the deceased, whatever it be.

191. 'If two sons, begotten by two *successive husbands, who are both dead,* contend for their property, 'then in the hands of their mother, let each take, exclusive of the other, his own father's estate.

192. 'On the death of the mother, let all the uterine 'brothers and the uterine sisters, *if unmarried,* equally 'divide the maternal estate: *each married sister shall, 'have a fourth part of a brother's allotment.*

193. 'Even to the daughters of those daughters, it 'is fit, that something should be given, from the assets 'of their maternal grandmother, on the score of natural affection.

194. 'What was given before the nuptial fire, what 'was given on the bridal procession, what was given 'in token of love, and what was received from a 'brother, a mother, or a father, are considered as the 'six-fold *separate* property of a *married* woman:

195. 'What she received after marriage from the 'family of her husband, and what her affectionate lord 'may have given her, shall be inherited, even if she 'die in his life-time, by her children.

196. 'It is ordained, that the property of a woman, 'married by the ceremonies called *Bráhma, Daivia, 'A'rsha Gándharva,* or *Prájápatya,* shall go to her 'husband, if she die without issue.

197. 'But her wealth given on the marriage called '*A'sura,* or on either of the *two* others, is ordained, on 'her death without issue, to become the property of her 'father and mother.

198. 'If a widow, *whose husband had other wives of*

'*different classes*, shall have received wealth at any 'time *as a gift* from her father, *and shall die without* '*issue*, it shall go to the daughter of the *Bráhmaní*-'wife, or to the issue of that daughter.

199. 'A woman should never make a hoard from 'the goods of her kindred, *which are* common to *her* '*and* many; or even from the property of her lord, 'without his assent.

200. 'Such ornamental apparel, as women wear 'during the lives of their husbands, the heirs of those 'husbands shall not divide among themselves: they, 'who divide it among themselves, fall deep *into sin*.

201. 'Eunuchs, and outcasts, persons born blind or 'deaf, madmen, idiots, the dumb, and such as have 'lost the use of a limb, are excluded from a share of 'the heritage;

202. 'But it is just, that the heir, who knows his 'duty, should give all of them food and raiment *for* '*life* without stint, according to the best of his power: 'he, who gives them nothing, sinks assuredly *to a region* '*of punishment*.

203. 'If the eunuch and the rest should at any 'time desire to marry, *and if the wife of the eunuch* '*should raise up a son to him by a man legally ap*-'*pointed*, *that son and* the issue of such, as have 'children, shall be capable of inheriting.

204. 'After the death of the father, if the eldest 'brother acquire *wealth by his own efforts before par*-'*tition*, a share of that *acquisition* shall go to the young-'er brothers, if they have made a due progress in 'learning;

205. 'And if all of them, being unlearned, acquire 'property *before partition* by their own labour, there 'shall be an equal division of that property *without*

'*regard to the first-born*; for it was not the wealth of 'their father: this rule is clearly settled.

206. 'Wealth, however, acquired by learning, be- 'longs exclusively to any one *of them, who acquired* '*it*: so does any thing given by a friend, received on 'account of marriage, or presented as a mark of respect 'to a guest.

207. 'If any one of the brethren has a competence 'from his own occupation, and wants not the property '*of his father*, he may debar himself from his own share, 'some trifle being given him as a consideration, *to* '*prevent future strife*.

208. 'What a brother has acquired by labour or 'skill, without using the patrimony, he shall not give 'up without his assent; for it was gained by his own 'exertion:

209. 'And if a son, by his own efforts, recover *a* '*debt or property unjustly detained*, which could not 'be recovered before by his father, he shall not, un- 'less by his free will, put it into parcenary with his 'brethren, since in fact it was acquired by himself.

210. 'If brethren, once divided and living again 'together as parceners, make a second partition, the 'shares must in that case be equal; and the first-born 'shall have no right of deduction.

211. 'Should the eldest or youngest of several bro- 'thers be deprived of his share *by a civil death on his* '*entrance into the fourth order*, or should any one of 'them die, his *vested interest in a* share shall not wholly 'be lost;

212. 'But, *if he leave neither son, nor wife, nor* '*daughter, nor father nor mother*, his uterine brothers 'and sisters, and such brothers as were re-united after a 'separation, shall assemble and divide his share equally.

213. 'Any eldest brother, who from avarice shall 'defraud his younger brother, shall forfeit *the honour* '*of* his primogeniture, be deprived of his own share, 'and pay a fine to the king.

214. 'All those brothers, who are addicted to any 'vice, lose their title to the inheritance: the first-born 'shall not appropriate it to himself, but shall give 'shares to the youngest, *if they be not vicious.*

215. 'If, among undivided brethren *living* with their 'father, there be a common exertion for common gain, 'the father shall never make an unequal division among 'them *when they divide their families.*

216. 'A son, born after a division *in the lifetime of* '*his father*, shall alone inherit the patrimony, or shall 'have a share of it with the divided brethren, if they 'return and unite themselves with him.

217. 'Of a son, dying childless *and leaving no* '*widow*, the *father and* mother shall take the estate; 'and, the mother also being dead, the paternal *grand-* '*father and* grandmother shall take the heritage, *on* '*failure of brothers and nephews.*

218. 'When all the debts and wealth have been 'justly distributed according to law, any property, 'that may afterwards be discovered, shall be subject to 'a similar distribution.

219. 'Apparel, carriages, or riding-horses, and or- 'naments *of ordinary value, which any of the heirs had* '*used by consent before partition*, dressed rice, water *in* '*a well or cistern*, female slaves, family priests, or 'spiritual counsellors, and pasture ground for cattle, 'the wise have declared indivisible, *and still to be used* '*as before.*

220. 'Thus have the laws of inheritance, and the 'rule for the conduct of sons (whether the son of the

'wife or others) been expounded to you in order: 'learn at present the law concerning games of chance.

221. 'Gaming, either with inanimate or with animated things, let the king exclude wholly from his 'realm: both those modes of play cause destruction to 'princes.

222 'Such play with dice *and the like,* or by 'matches *between rams and cocks,* amounts to open 'theft; and the king must ever be vigilant in suppressing both *modes of play:*

223. 'Gaming with lifeless things is known among 'men by the name of *dyûta;* but *samâhwaya* signifies 'a match between living creatures.

224. 'Let the king punish corporally at discretion 'both the gamester and the keeper of a gaming-house, 'whether they play with inanimate or animated things; 'and men of the servile class, who wear the *string and 'other* marks of the twice-born.

225. 'Gamesters, public dancers and singers, revilers 'of scripture, open heretics, men who perform not the 'duties of their several classes, and sellers of spirituous 'liquor, let him instantly banish from the town:

226. 'Those wretches, lurking like unseen thieves in 'the dominion of a prince, continually harass his good 'subjects with their vicious conduct.

227. 'Even in a former creation was this *vice of 'gaming* found a great provoker of enmity: let no 'sensible man, therefore, addict himself to play even 'for his amusement:

228. 'On the man addicted to it, either privately 'or openly, let punishment be inflicted, at the discretion 'of the king.

229. 'A man of the military, commercial, or servile

'class, who cannot pay a fine, shall discharge the debt 'by his labour: a priest shall discharge it by little 'and little.

230. 'For women, children, persons of crazy intel-'lect, the old, the poor, and the infirm, the king shall 'order punishment with a small whip, a twig, or a 'rope.

231. 'Those ministers, who are employed in public 'affairs, and, inflamed by the blaze of wealth, mar the 'business of any person concerned, let the king strip 'of all their property.

232. 'Such, as forge royal edicts, cause dissensions 'among the great ministers, or kill women, priests, 'or children, let the king put to death; and such, as 'adhere to his enemies.

233. 'Whatever business has at any time been 'transacted conformably to law, let him consider as 'finally settled, and refuse to unravel;

234. 'But whatever business has been concluded 'illegally by his ministers or by a judge, let the king 'himself re-examine; and let him fine them each a 'thousand *panas*.

235. 'The slayer of a priest, *a soldier or merchant* 'drinking arak, *or a priest drinking arak*, mead, or rum, 'he, who steals *the gold of a priest*, and he, who violates 'the bed of his *natural or spiritual* father, are all to be 'considered respectively as offenders in the highest 'degree, *except those, whose crimes are not fit to be* '*named*:

236. 'On such of those four, as have not actually 'performed an expiation, let the king legally inflict 'corporal punishment, together with a fine.

237. 'For violating the paternal bed, let *the mark of*

'a female part be impressed *on the forehead with hot* '*iron;* for drinking spirits, a vintner's flag; for stealing 'sacred gold, a dog's foot; for murdering a priest, *the* '*figure of* a headless corpse:

238. 'With none to eat with them, with none to 'sacrifice with them, with none to read with them, with 'none to be allied by marriage to them, abject and 'excluded from all social duties, let them wander over 'this earth:

239. 'Branded with *indelible* marks, they shall be 'deserted by their paternal and maternal relations, 'treated by none with affection, received by none with 'respect: such is the ordinance of MANU.

240. '*Criminals of* all the classes, having performed 'an expiation, as ordained by law, shall not be marked 'on the forehead, but condemned to pay the highest 'fine:

241. 'For crimes by a priest, *who had a good cha-* '*racter before his offence,* the middle fine shall be set 'on him; or, *if his crime was premeditated,* he shall be 'banished from the realm, *taking* with *him* his effects 'and his family;

242. 'But men of the other classes, who have com- 'mitted those crimes, though without premeditation, 'shall be stripped of all their possessions; and, if their 'offence was premeditated, shall be corporally, or even 'capitally, punished, *according to circumstances.*

243. 'Let no virtuous prince appropriate the wealth 'of a criminal in the highest degree; for he, who ap- 'propriates it through covetousness, is contaminated 'with the same guilt:

244. 'Having thrown such a fine into the waters, let 'him offer it to VARUNA; or let him bestow it on 'some priest of eminent learning in the scriptures:

245. 'Varuna is the lord of punishment; he holds a 'rod even over kings; and a priest who has gone 'through the whole *Veda*, is *equal to* a sovereign of all 'the world.

246. 'Where the king abstains from receiving *to his* '*own use* the wealth of such offenders, there children are 'born in due season and enjoy long lives;

247. '*There* the grain of husbandmen rises abund-'antly, as it was respectively sown; there no young-'lings die, nor is one deformed animal born.

248. 'Should a man of the basest class, with pre-'conceived malice, give pain to *Bráhmans*, let the 'prince corporally punish him by various modes, that 'may raise terror.

249. 'A king is pronounced equally unjust in re-'leasing the man who deserves punishment, and in 'punishing the man who deserves it not: he is just, 'who always inflicts the punishment ordained by law.

250. 'These established rules for administering jus-'tice between two litigant parties, have been propound-'ed at length under eighteen heads.

251. 'Thus fully performing all duties required by 'law, let a king seek *with justice* to possess regions yet 'unpossessed, and, when they are in his possession, let 'him govern them well.

252. 'His realm being completely arranged and his 'fortresses amply provided, let him ever apply the 'most diligent care to eradicate *bad men resembling* 'thorny weeds, as the law directs.

253. 'By protecting such as live virtuously, and by 'rooting up such as live wickedly, those kings, whose 'hearts are intent on the security of their people, shall 'rise to heaven.

254. 'Of that prince, who takes a revenue, without 'restraining rogues, the dominions are thrown into 'disorder, and himself shall be precluded from a 'celestial abode;

255. 'But of him, whose realm, by the strength of 'his arm, is defended and free from terror, the domi- 'nions continually flourish, like trees duly watered.

256. 'Let the king, whose emissaries are his eyes, 'discern well the two sorts of rogues, the open and the 'concealed, who deprive other men of their wealth:

257. 'Open rogues are they, who subsist by cheat- 'ing in various marketable commodities; and conceal- 'ed rogues are they, who steal and rob in forests and 'the like secret places.

258. 'Receivers of bribes, extorters of money by 'threats, debasers of metals, gamesters, fortune-tellers, 'imposters, and professors of palmistry;

259. 'Elephant-breakers, and quacks, not performing 'what they engage to perform, pretended artists, and 'subtile harlots;

260. 'These and the like thorny weeds, overspread- 'ing the world, let the king discover with a quick 'sight, and others, who act ill in secret; worthless 'men, yet bearing the outward signs of the worthy.

261. 'Having detected them, by means of trusty 'persons disguised, who *pretend to* have the same oc- 'cupation with them, and of spies placed in several 'stations, let him bring them by artifice into his 'power;

262. 'Then, having fully proclaimed their respective 'criminal acts, let the king inflict punishment legally, 'according to the crimes proved;

263. 'Since, without certain punishment, it is impossible to restrain the delinquency of scoundrels with 'depraved souls, who secretly prowl over this earth.

264. 'Much-frequented places, cisterns of water, 'bake-houses, the lodgings of harlots, taverns and 'victualling-shops, squares where four ways meet, large 'well known trees, assemblies, and public spectacles;

265. 'Old court-yards, thickets, the houses of artists, 'empty mansions, groves, and gardens;

266. 'These and the like places let the king guard, 'for the prevention of robberies, with soldiers, both 'stationary and patroling, as well as with secret 'watchmen.

267. 'By the means of able spies, once thieves, *but* '*reformed,* who, well knowing the various machina'tions of rogues, associate with them and follow them, 'let the king detect and draw them forth.

268. 'On pretexts of dainty food and gratifications, 'or of seeing some wise priest, *who could ensure their* '*success,* or on pretence of *mock battles and the like* 'feats of strength, let the spies procure an assembly of 'those men.

269. 'Such as refuse to go forth on those occasions, 'deterred by *former punishments, which* the king *had* '*inflicted,* let him *seize* by force, *and* put to death, '*on proof of their guilt,* with their friends and kinsmen, 'paternal and maternal, *if proved to be their confede*'*rates.*

270. 'Let not a just prince kill a man convicted of 'simple theft, unless taken with the mainer or with 'implements of robbery; but any thief, taken with 'the mainer, or with such implements, let him destroy 'without hesitation;

271. 'And let them slay all those, who give robbers 'food in towns, or supply them with implements, or 'afford them shelter.

272. 'Should those men, who were appointed to 'guard any districts, or those of the vicinity, who 'were employed for that purpose, be neutral in attacks 'by robbers *and inactive in seizing them*, let him in-'stantly punish them as thieves.

273. 'Him, who lives *apparently* by the rules of his 'class, but *really* departs from those rules, let the king 'severely punish by fine, as a wretch, who violates his 'duty.

274. 'They, who give no assistance on the plundering 'of a town, on the forcible breaking of a dike, or on 'seeing a robbery on the highway, shall be banished 'with their cattle and utensils.

275. 'Men, who rob the king's treasure, or obsti-'nately oppose his commands, let him destroy by various 'modes of just punishment; and those, who encourage 'his enemies.

276. 'Of robbers, who break a wall or partition, and 'commit theft in the night, let the prince order the 'hands to be lopped off, and themselves to be fixed on 'a sharp stake.

277. 'Two fingers of a cutpurse, *the thumb and the 'index*, let him cause to be amputated on his first con-'viction; on the second, one hand and one foot; on 'the third, he shall suffer death.

278. 'Such, as give thieves fire, such as give them 'food, such as give them arms and apartments, and 'such as knowingly receive a thing stolen, let the king 'punish as *he would punish* a thief.

279. 'The breaker of a *dam to secure a* pool, let him

'punish by long immersion under water, or by keen 'corporal suffering; or the offender shall repair it, but 'must pay the highest mulct.

280. 'Those, who break open the treasury, or the 'arsenal, or the temple of a deity, and those, who carry 'off royal elephants, horses, or cars, let him without 'hesitation destroy.

281. 'He, who shall take away the water of an an-'cient pool, or shall obstruct a water-course, must be 'condemned to pay the lowest usual amercement.

282. 'He, who shall drop his ordure on the king's 'highway, except in case of necessity, shall pay two '*panas* and immediately remove the filth;

283. 'But a person in urgent necessity, a very old 'man, a pregnant woman, and a child, only deserve 'reproof, and shall clean the place themselves: that is 'a settled rule.

284. 'All physicians and surgeons acting unskilfully 'in their several professions, must pay for *injury to* 'brute animals the lowest, but for *injury to* human 'creatures the middle, amercement.

285. 'The breaker of a foot-bridge, of a public flag, 'of a palisade, and of idols *made of clay*, shall repair 'what he has broken, and pay a mulct of five hundred '*panas*.

286. 'For mixing impure with pure commodities, for 'piercing fine gems, *as diamonds or rubies,* and for 'boring *pearls or inferior gems* improperly, the fine 'is the lowest of the three; *but damages must always* '*be paid.*

287. 'The man, who shall deal unjustly with pur-'chasers at a fair price *by delivering goods of less value,* 'or shall sell at a high price *goods of ordinary value,*

'shall pay, *according to circumstances*, the lowest or 'the middle amercement.

288. 'Let the king place all prisons near a public 'road, where offenders may be seen wretched or dis-'figured.

289. 'Him, who breaks down a *public* wall, him, 'who fills up a *public* ditch, him, who throws down a '*public* gate, the king shall speedily banish.

290. 'For all sacrifices to destroy innocent men, the 'punishment is a fine of two hundred *panas*; and for 'machinations with *poisonous* roots, and for the various '*charms and* witcheries *intended* to kill, by persons not 'effecting their purpose.

291. 'The seller of bad grain for good, or of good 'seed placed at the top *of the bag, to conceal the bad below*, and the destroyer of known land-marks, must 'suffer such corporal punishment as will disfigure them;

292. 'But the most pernicious of all deceivers is a 'goldsmith, who commits frauds: the king shall order 'him to be cut piecemeal with razors.

293. 'For stealing implements of husbandry, wea-'pons, and prepared medicines, let the king award 'punishment according to the time and according to 'their use.

294. 'The king, and his council, his metropolis, 'his realm, his treasure, and his army, together with 'his ally, are the seven members of his kingdom; '*whence* it is called *Saptânga*:

295. 'Among those seven members of a kingdom, 'let him consider the ruin of the first, and so forth in 'order, as the greatest calamity;

296. 'Yet, in a seven-parted kingdom here below

'there is no supremacy among the several parts, from 'any pre-eminence in useful qualities: but all the parts 'must reciprocally support each other, like the three 'staves of a holy mendicant:

297. 'In these and those acts, *indeed*, this and that 'member may by distinguished; *and* the member by 'which any affair is transacted, has the pre-eminence in 'that particular affair.

298. 'When the king employs emissaries, when he 'exerts power, when he regulates public business, let 'him invariably know both his own strength and that 'of his enemy,

299. 'With all *their several* distresses and vices: 'let him then begin his operations, having maturely 'considered the greater and less importance *of par-'ticular acts:*

300. 'Let him, *though frequently disappointed*, re-'new his operations, how fatigued soever, again and 'again; since fortune always attends the man, who, '*having begun well*, strenuously renews his efforts.

301. 'All the ages, called *Satya*, *Tretá*, *Dwápara*, 'and *Kali*, depend on the conduct of the king; who 'is declared *in turn* to represent each of those ages:

302. 'Sleeping, he is the *Kali* age; waking, the '*Dwápara*; exerting himself in action, the *Tretá*; 'living virtuously, the *Satya*.

303. 'Of INDRA, of SU'RYA, of PAVANA, of YAMA, of 'VARUNA, of CHANDRA, of AGNI, and of PRITHIVI, let 'the king emulate the power and attributes.

304. 'As INDRA sheds plentiful showers during the 'four rainy months, thus let him, acting like the regent 'of clouds, rain just gratifications over his kingdom:

305. 'As SU'RYA with strong rays draws up the

'water during eight months, thus let him, performing 'the function of the sun, gradually draw from his realm 'the legal revenue:

306. 'As PAVANA, when he moves, pervades all 'creatures, thus let him, imitating the regent of wind, 'pervade *all places* by his concealed emissaries:

307. 'As YAMA, at the appointed time, punishes 'friends and foes, *or those who revere, and those who 'contemn him*, thus let the king, resembling the judge 'of departed spirits, punish *offending subjects*:

308. 'As VARUNA most assuredly binds the guilty 'in fatal cords, thus let him, representing the genius of 'water, keep offenders in close confinement:

309. 'When the people are no less delighted on 'seeing the king, than on seeing the full moon, he 'appears in the character of CHANDRA:

310. 'Against criminals let him ever be ardent in 'wrath, let him be splendid in glory, let him consume 'wicked ministers, thus emulating the functions of 'AGNI, regent of fire.

311. 'As PRITHIVÌ supports all creatures equally, 'thus a king, sustaining all subjects, resembles in his 'office the goddess of earth.

312. 'Engaged in these duties and in others, with 'continual activity, let the king, *above all things* re-'strain robbers, both in his own territories and in those 'of other princes, *from which they come, or in which 'they seek refuge*.

313. 'Let him not, although in the greatest distress '*for money*, provoke *Bráhmans* to anger *by taking their 'property*; for they, once enraged, could immediately '*by sacrifices and imprecations* destroy him with his 'troops, elephants, horses and cars.

314. 'Who, without perishing, could provoke those 'holy men, by whom, *that is, by whose ancestors, under* 'BRAHMA', the all-devouring fire was created, the sea 'with waters not drinkable, and the moon with its 'wane and increase?

315. 'What prince could gain wealth by oppressing 'those, who, if angry, could frame other worlds and 'regents of worlds, could give being to new gods and 'mortals?

316. 'What man, desirous of life, would injure 'those, by the aid of whom, *that is, by whose oblations,* 'worlds and gods perpetually subsist; those, who are 'rich in the learning of the *Veda*?

317. 'A *Bráhman*, whether learned or ignorant, is a 'powerful divinity; even as fire is a powerful divinity, 'whether consecrated or popular.

318. 'Even in places for burning the dead, the 'bright fire is undefiled; and, when presented with 'clarified butter at *subsequent* sacrifices, blazes again 'with extreme splendour:

319. 'Thus, although *Bráhmans* employ them-'selves in all sorts of mean occupation, they must 'invariably be honoured; for they are something 'transcendently divine.

320. 'Of a military man, who raises his arm vio-'lently on all occasions against the priestly class, the 'priest himself shall be the chastiser; since the soldier 'originally proceeded from the *Bráhman*.

321. 'From the waters arose fire; from the priests, 'the soldier; from stone, iron: their all-penetrating 'force is ineffectual in the place, whence they res-'pectively sprang.

322. 'The military class cannot prosper without the

'sacerdotal, nor can the sacerdotal be raised without 'the military: both classes, by cordial union, are ex- 'alted in this world and in the next.

323. 'Should the king *be near his end through some 'incurable disease, he* must bestow on the priests all 'his riches accumulated from legal fines; and, having 'duly committed his kingdom to his son, let him seek 'death in battle, *or, if there be no war, by abstaining 'from food.*

324. 'Thus conducting himself, *and* ever firm in 'discharging his royal duties, let the king employ all 'his ministers in acts beneficial to his people.

325. 'These rules for the conduct of a military man 'having been propounded, let mankind next hear the 'rules for the commercial and servile classes in due 'order.

326. 'Let the *Vaisya*, having been girt with his 'proper sacrificial thread, and having married an equal 'wife, be always attentive to his business *of agriculture 'and trade*, and to that of keeping cattle;

327. 'Since the Lord of created beings, having 'formed herds, and flocks, intrusted them to the care 'of the *Vaisya*, while he intrusted the whole human 'species to the *Bráhman* and the *Kshatriya;*

328. 'Never must a *Vaisya*, be disposed to say, '"I keep no cattle;" nor, he being willing to keep 'them, must they by any means be kept by men of 'another class.

329. 'Of gems, pearls, and coral, of iron, of woven 'cloth, of perfumes and of liquids, let him well know 'the prices both high and low:

330. 'Let him be skilled likewise in *the time and 'manner of* sowing seeds, and in the bad or good

'qualities of land; let him also perfectly know the 'correct modes of measuring and weighing,

331. 'The excellence or defects of commodities, the 'advantages and disadvantages of different regions, the 'probable gain or loss on vendible goods, and the 'means of breeding cattle with large augmentation:

332. 'Let him know the just wages of servants, the 'various dialects of men, the best way of keeping goods, 'and *whatever else belongs to* purchase and sale.

333. 'Let him apply the most vigilant care to 'augment his wealth by *performing* his duty; and, 'with great solicitude, let him give nourishment to all 'sentient creatures.

334. 'Servile attendance on *Bráhmans* learned in 'the *Veda*, chiefly on such as keep house and are 'famed for virtue, is of itself the highest duty of a '*Súdra*, and leads him to future beatitude.

335. 'Pure *in body and mind*, humbly serving the 'three higher classes, mild in speech, never arrogant, 'ever seeking refuge in *Bráhmans* principally, he may 'attain the most eminent class *in another transmigra-'tion.*

336. 'This clear system of duties has been pro-'mulgated for the four classes, when they are not in 'distress for subsistence; now learn in order their 'several duties in times of necessity.'

CHAP. X.

On the mixed Classes; and on Times of Distress.

---

1. 'Let the three twice-born classes, remaining firm 'in their several duties, carefully read the *Veda*; but 'a *Bráhman* must explain it to them, not *a man of* the 'other two *classes*: this is an established rule.

2. 'The *Bráhman* must know the means of subsistence 'ordained by law for all the classes, and must declare 'them to the rest: let himself likewise act in con- 'formity *to law*.

3. 'From priority of birth, from superiority of ori- 'gin, from a more exact knowledge of scripture, and 'from a distinction in the sacrificial thread, the *Bráh- 'man* is the lord of all classes.

4. 'The three twice-born classes are sacerdotal, the 'military, and the commercial; but the fourth, or 'servile, is once-born, *that is, has no second birth from 'the* gáyatrí, *and wears no thread*: nor is there a fifth 'pure class.

5. 'In all classes they, and they only, who are 'born, in a direct order, of wives equal in class and 'virgins at the time of marriage, are to be considered 'as the same in class *with their fathers*:

6. 'Sons, begotten by twice-born men, on women 'of the class next immediately below them, wise le- 'gislators call similar, *not the same*, in class *with their 'parents*, because they are degraded, *to a middle rank 'between both*, by the lowness of their mothers: *they*

'*are named in order*, Múrdhábhishikta, Máhishya, *and* 'karana, *or* káyast'ha; *and their several employments* '*are teaching military exercises; music, astronomy, and* '*keeping herds; and attendance on princes.*

7. 'Such is the primeval rule for the sons of women 'one degree lower *than their husbands*: for the sons of 'women two or three degrees lower, let this rule of law 'be known.

8. 'From a *Bráhman*, on a wife of the *Vaisya*-class, 'is born a son called *Ambasht'ha*, or *Vaidya*, on a '*Súdrà*-wife a *Nishádà*, named also *Párasava*:

9. 'From a *Kshatriya*, on a wife of the *Súdrá*-class, 'springs a creature, called *Ugra*, with a nature partly 'warlike and partly servile, ferocious in his manners, 'cruel in his acts.

10. 'The sons of a *Bráhman* by *women of* three *lower* 'classes, of a *Kshatriya* by *women of* two, and of a '*Vaisya* by one *lower* class, are called *Ápasadáh* or 'degraded *below their fathers*.

11. 'From a *Kshatriya* by a *Bráhmaní*-wife, springs 'a *Súta* by birth; from a *Vaisya*, by a military or 'sacerdotal wife, spring a *Màgadha* and a *Vaideha*.

12. 'From a *Súdra*, on women of the commercial, 'military, and priestly classes, are born sons of a mixed 'breed, called *A'yógava*, *Kshattri* and *Chandàla*, the 'lowest of mortals.

13. 'As the *Ambasht'ha* and *Ugra* born in a direct 'order, with one class between *those of their parents*, 'are considered in law, so are the *Kshattri*, and the '*Vaideha*, born in an inverse order *with one intermediate* '*class; and all four may be touched without impurity.*

14. 'Those sons of the twice-born, who are begot-'ten on women without an interval *(Antara)* between

'the classes mentioned in order, the wise call *Anantaras*, giving them a *distinct* name from the lower 'degree of their mother.

15. 'From a *Bráhman*, by a girl of the *Ugra*-tribe, 'is born an *A'vrita*; by one of the *Ambast'ha*-tribe, an '*A'bhíra*; by one of the *A'yógava*-tribe, a *Dhigvana*.

16. 'The *Ayógava* the *Kshattri*, and the *Chandala*, 'the lowest of men, spring from a *Súdrà* in an inverse 'order *of the classes*, and are *therefore*, all three excluded '*from the performance of obsequies to their ancestors*:

17. 'From a *Vaisya* the *Mágadha* and *Vaidéha*, from 'a *Kshatriya* the *Súta* only, are born in an inverse 'order; and they are three other sons excluded *from* '*funeral rites to their fathers*.

18. 'The son of a *Nis'háda* by a woman of the '*Súdra*-class, is by tribe a *Pukkasa*; but the son of a '*Súdra* by a *Nis'hádi*-woman, is named *Kukkutaka*.

19. 'One, born of a *Kshattri* by an *Ugrá*, is called '*Swapáca*; and one, begotten by a *Vaidéha* on an '*Ambashtai*-wife, is called *Véna*.

20. 'Those, whom the twice-born beget on women, 'of equal classes, but who perform not the proper cere-'monies *of assuming the thread, and the like*, people de-'nominate *Vrátyas*, or excluded from the *gáyatrì*.

21. 'From such an outcast *Bráhman* springs a son 'of a sinful nature, *who in different countries is* named 'a *Bhúrjakantaka*, an *Avantya*, a *Vátadhána*, a *Push-'padha* and a *Saic'ha*:

22. 'From such an outcast *Kshatrya* comes a son 'called a *Jhalla*, a *Malla*, a *Nichhivi*, a *Nata*, a '*Karana*, a *Khasa*, and a *Dravira*:

23. 'From such an outcast *Vaisya* is born a son

'called *Sudhanwan*, *Charya*, *Kárusha*, *Vijanman*, *Maitra*, and *Sátwata*.

24. 'By intermixtures of the classes, by their marriages with women who ought not to be married, and by their omission of prescribed duties, impure classes have been formed.

25. 'Those men of mingled births, who were born in the inverse order of classes, and who intermarry among themselves, I will now compendiously describe.

26. 'The *Súta*, the *Vaideha*, and the *Chandála*, that lowest of mortals, the *Mágadha*, the *Kshattri* by tribe, and the *A'yógava*.

27. 'These six beget similar sons on women of their own classes, or on women of the same class with their mothers; and they produce the like from women of the two highest classes, *and of the lowest*:

28. 'As a twice-born son may spring from a *Bráhman* by women of two classes out of three, *a similar son*, when there is no interval, and *an equal son* from a woman of his own class, it is thus in the case of the low tribes in order.

29. 'Those six beget, on women of their own tribes, reciprocally, very many despicable and abject races even more foul than their begetters.

30. 'Even as a *Súdra* begets, on a *Bráhmaní*,-woman, a son more vile than himself, thus any other low man begets, on *women of* the four classes, a son yet lower.

31. 'The six low classes, marrying inversely, beget fifteen yet lower tribes, the base producing still baser; *and in a direct order they produce fifteen more*.

32. 'A *Dasyu*, or outcast of any pure class, begets

'on an *A'yógavì*-woman a *Sairindhra*, who should 'know how to attend and to dress his master; though 'not a slave, he must live by slavish work, and 'may also gain subsistence by catching wild beasts in 'toils:

33. 'A *Vaidéha* begets on her a sweet-voiced *Maitréyaka*, who, ringing a bell at the appearance of 'dawn, continually praises great men:

34. 'A *Nisháda* begets on her a *Márgava*, or *Dàsa*, 'who subsists by his labour in boats, and is named '*Kaiverta* by those, who dwell in *A'ryávata, or the land 'of the venerable.*

35. 'Those three of a base tribe are severally begotten on *A'yógavì*-women, who wear the clothes of the 'deceased and eat reprehensible food.

36. 'From a *Nisháda* springs *by a woman of the* 'Vaidéha-*tribe*, a *Kárávara*, who cuts leather, and 'from a *Vaidéha* spring *by women of* the Kárávara *and* 'Nisháda-*casts*, an *Andhr*, and a *Méda*, who must live 'without the town.

37. 'From a *Chandála* by a *Vaidéhì*-woman, comes 'a *Pánduśópáka*, who works with cane and reeds; and 'from a *Nisháda*, an *Ahindiska, who acts as a jailor.*

38. 'From a *Chandála*, by a *Pukkasì*-woman, is born 'a *Sópáka*, who lives by punishing criminals *condemned 'by the king*, a sinful wretch ever despised by the 'virtuous.

39. 'A *Nishádì*-woman, by a *Chandála*, produces a 'son called *Antyávasáyin*, employed in places for burn'ing the dead, contemned even by the contemptible.

40. 'These, among various mixed classes, have been 'described by their several fathers and mothers; and, 'whether concealed or open, they may be known by 'their occupations.

41. 'Six sons, *three* begotten on women of the same 'class, and *three* on women of lower classes, must per-'form the duties of twice-born men; but those, who 'are *born in an inverse order, and* called low-born, are 'equal, in respect of duty, to mere *Súdras.*

42. 'By the force of extreme devotion and of exalted 'fathers, all of them may rise *in time* to high birth, as '*by the reverse* they may sink to a lower state, in every 'age among mortals in this inferior world.

43. 'The following races of *Kshatriyas,* by their omis-'sion of holy rites and by seeing no *Bráhmans,* have 'gradually sunk among men, to the lowest of the four 'classes:

44. '*Paund'rakas, Odras,* and *Draviras; Kàmbójas,* '*Yavanas,* and *Sakas; Páradas, Pahlavas, Chínas, Ki-*'*rátas, Deradas,* and *C'hasas;*

45. 'All those tribes of men, who sprang from the 'mouth, the arm, the thigh, and the foot of BRAH-'MA', *but* who became outcasts *by having neglected their* '*duties,* are called *Dasyus,* or *plunderers,* whether they 'speak the language of *Mlechch'has,* or that of *A'ryas.*

46. 'Those sons of the twice-born, who are said to 'be degraded, and who are considered as low-born, shall 'subsist only by such employments, as the twice-born 'despise.

47. '*Sútas* must live by managing horses and by 'driving cars; *Ambasht'has,* by curing disorders; *Vai-*'*dehas,* by waiting on women; *Mágadhas,* by travel-'ling with merchandize;

48. '*Nishádas,* by catching fish; an *A'yógava,* by 'the work of a carpenter; a *Meda,* an *Andhra,* and '(the sons of a *Bráhman* by wives of the *Vaidéha* and '*Ugra* classes, respectively called) a *Chunchu* and a '*Madgu,* by slaying beasts of the forest;

49. 'A *Kshattri*, an *Ugra*, and a *Pukkasa*, by killing 'or confining such animals as live in holes: *Bhigvanas*, 'by selling leather; *Vénas*, by striking musical in-'struments:

50. 'Near large public trees, in places for burning 'the dead, on mountains, and in groves, let those 'tribes dwell, generally known, and engaged in their 'several works.

51. 'The abode of a *Chandála* and a *Swapáka* must 'be out of the town; they must not have the use 'of entire vessels; their sole wealth must be dogs and 'asses:

52. 'Their clothes must be the mantles of the de-'ceased; their dishes for food, broken pots; their 'ornaments, rusty iron; continually must they roam 'from place to place:

53. 'Let no man, who regards his duty religious 'and civil, hold any intercourse with them; let their 'transactions be confined to themselves, and their 'marriages only between equals:

54. 'Let food be given to them in potsherds, *but not 'by the hands of the giver;* and let them not walk by 'night in cities or towns:

55. 'By day they may walk about for the purpose 'of work, distinguished by the king's badges; and they 'shall carry out the corpse of every one, who dies with-'out kindred: such is the fixed rule.

56. 'They shall always kill those, who are to be 'slain by the sentence of the law, and by the royal 'warrant; and let them take the clothes of the slain, 'their beds, and their ornaments.

57. 'Him, who was born of a sinful mother, *and 'consequently* in a low class, but is not openly known

' who, though worthless in truth, bears the semblance ' of a worthy man, let people discover by his acts:

58. ' Want of virtuous dignity, harshness of speech, ' cruelty, and habitual neglect of prescribed duties, ' betray in this world the son of a criminal mother.

59. ' Whether a man of debased birth assume the ' character of his father, or of his mother, he can at ' no time conceal his origin:

60. ' He, whose family had been exalted, but whose ' parents were criminal in marrying, has a base nature, ' according as the offence *of his mother* was great or ' small.

61. ' In whatever country such men are born, as ' destroy the purity of the four classes, that country ' soon perishes, together with the natives of it.

62. ' Desertion of life, without reward, for the sake ' of preserving a priest or a cow, a woman or a child, ' may cause the beatitude of those base-born tribes.

63. ' Avoiding all injury *to animated beings*, veracity, ' abstaining from theft, *and from unjust seizure of* ' *property*, cleanliness, and command over the bodily ' organs, form the compendious system of duty, which ' MANU has ordained for the four classes.

64. ' Should the tribe sprung from a *Bráhman*, by ' a *Súdrá*-woman, produce *a succession of children* by ' the marriages of its women with other *Bráhmans*, ' the low tribe shall be raised to the highest in the ' seventh generation.

65. ' As *the son of a Súdra* may *thus* attain the rank ' of a *Bráhman*, and *as the son of* a *Bráhman* may sink ' to a level with *Súdras*, even so must it be with him, ' who springs from a *Kshatriya*; even so with him, ' who was born of a *Vaisya*.

66. 'If there be a doubt, as to the preference 'between him, who was begotten by a *Bráhman* for 'his pleasure, *but not in wedlock*, on a *Súdra*-woman, 'and him who was begotten by a *Súdra* on a *Bráhmaní*.

67. '*Thus is it removed:* he, who was begotten by 'an exalted man on a base woman, may by his good 'acts become respectable; but he, who was begotten 'on an exalted woman by a base man, must himself 'continue base:

68. 'Neither of the two (as the law is fixed) shall be 'girt with a sacred string; not the former, because 'his mother was low; nor the second, because the 'order of the classes was inverted.

69. 'As good grain, springing from good soil, is 'in all respects excellent, thus a man, springing from 'a respectable father by a respectable mother, has a 'claim to the whole institution of the twice-born.

70. 'Some sages give a preference to the grain; 'others to the field; and others consider both field and 'grain; on this point the decision follows:

71. 'Grain, cast into bad ground, wholly perishes, 'and a good field, with no grain sown in it, is a mere 'heap of clods;

72. 'But since, by the virtue of eminent fathers, 'even the sons of wild animals, *as* Rishyasringa, *and 'others*, have been transformed into holy men revered 'and extolled, the paternal side, therefore, prevails.

73. 'BRAHMA' himself, having compared a *Súdra*, 'who performs the duties of the twice-born, with a 'twice-born man, who does the acts of a *Súdra*, said: '"Those two are neither equal nor unequal," *that is, 'they are neither equal in rank, nor unequal in bad 'conduct*.

74. 'Let such *Bráhmans*, as are intent on the means 'of attaining the supreme godhead, and firm in their 'own duties, completely perform, in order, the six fol- 'lowing acts :

75. 'Reading the *Vedas*, and teaching *others* to 'read them, sacrificing, and assisting *others* to sacrifice, 'giving *to the poor, if themselves have enough*, and ac- 'cepting *gifts from the virtuous if themselves are poor*, 'are the six prescribed acts of the first-born class ;

76. 'But, among those six acts of *Bráhman*, three 'are his *means of* subsistence ; assisting to sacrifice, 'teaching the *Vedas*, and receiving gifts from a pure- 'handed giver.

77. 'Three acts of duty cease with the *Bráhman*, 'and belong not to the *Kshatriya* ; teaching the *Vedas*, 'officiating at a sacrifice, and, thirdly, receiving pre- 'sents :

78. Those *three* are also (by the fixed rule of law) 'forbidden to the *Vaisya* ; since MANU, the lord of 'all men, prescribed not those acts to the two *classes*, '*military and commercial*.

79. 'The means of subsistence, peculiar to the '*Kshatriya*, are bearing arms, either held for striking 'or missile, to the *Vaisya*, merchandize, attending on 'cattle, and agriculture : but, *with a view to the next* '*life*, the duties of both are almsgiving, reading, sacri- 'ficing.

80. 'Among the several occupations *for gaining a* '*livelihood* the most commendable respectively for the 'sacerdotal, military, and mercantile classes, are teach- 'ing the *Veda*, defending the people, and commerce or 'keeping herds and flocks.

81. 'Yet a *Bráhman*, unable to subsist by his duties

'just mentioned, may live by the duty of a soldier; for 'that is the next in rank.

82. 'If it be asked, how he must live, should he 'be unable to get a subsistence by either of those 'employments; *the answer is*, he may subsist as a 'mercantile man, applying himself *in person* to tillage 'and attendance on cattle:

83. 'But a *Bráhman* and a *Kshatriya*, obliged to 'subsist by the acts of a *Vaisya*, must avoid with care, '*if they can live by keeping herds*, the buisness of tillage, 'which gives great pain *to sentient creatures*, and is de'pendant on *the labour of* others, *as bulls and so forth*.

84. 'Some are of opinion, that agriculture is excel'lent; but it is a mode of subsistence which the 'benevolent greatly blame; for the iron mouthed 'pieces of wood not only wound the earth, but the 'creatures dwelling in it.

85. If, through want of a virtuous livelihood, they 'cannot follow laudable occupations, they may then 'gain a competence of wealth by selling commodities 'usually sold by merchants, avoiding what ought to be 'avoided:

86. 'They must avoid selling liquids of all sorts, 'dressed grain, seeds of *tila*, stones, salt, cattle, and 'human creatures;

87. 'All woven cloth dyed red, cloth made of *sana*, 'of *cshumá*-bark, and of wool, even though not red; 'fruit, roots, and medicinal plants;

88. 'Water, iron, poison, flesh-meat, the moonplant, 'and perfumes of any sort; milk, honey, buttermilk, 'clarified butter, oil of *tila*, wax, sugar, and blades of '*kusa*-grass;

89. 'All beasts of the forest, *as deer and the like*

'ravenous beasts, birds, *and fish*; spirituous liquors, '*níli*, or indigo, and *lákshá*, or lac; and all beasts with 'uncloven hoofs.

90. 'But the *Bráhman*-husbandman may at pleasure 'sell pure *tila*-seeds for the purpose of holy rites, if 'he keep them not long *with a hope of more gain*, and 'shall have produced them by his own culture:

91. 'If he apply seeds of *tila* to any purpose but 'food, anointing, and sacred oblations, he shall be 'plunged in the shape of a worm, together with his 'parents, into the ordure of dogs.

92. 'By selling flesh-meat, *lákshá*, or salt, a *Bráhman* immediately sinks low; by selling milk three 'days, he falls to a level with a *Súdra*;

93. 'And by selling the other forbidden commodi'ties with his own free will, he assumes in this world, 'after seven nights, the nature of a mere *Vaisya*.

94. 'Fluid things may, however, be bartered for 'other fluids, but not salt for any thing liquid; so may 'dressed grain for grain undressed, and *tila*-seeds for 'grain in the husk, equal weights or measures being 'given and taken.

95. 'A Military man, in distress, may subsist by all 'these means, but at no time must he have recourse 'to the highest, *or sacerdotal*, function.

96. 'A man of the lowest class, who, through 'covetousness, lives by the acts of the highest, let the 'king strip of all his wealth and instantly banish:

97. 'His own office, though defectively performed, 'is preferable to that of another, though performed 'completely; for he, who *without necessity* discharges 'the duties of another class, immediately forfeits his 'own.

98. 'A mercantile man, unable to subsist by his 'own duties, may descend even to the servile acts 'of a *Súdra*, taking care never to do what ought never 'to be done; but, when he has gained a competence, 'let him depart from service.

99. 'A man, of the fourth class, not finding employ- 'ment by waiting on the twice-born, while his wife and 'son are tormented with hunger, may subsist by 'handicrafts:

100. 'Let him principally follow those mechanical 'occupations, *as joinery and masonry*, or those various 'practical arts, *as painting and writing*, by following 'which, he may serve the twice-born.

101. 'Should a *Bráhman*, afflicted and pining 'through want of food, choose rather to remain fixed 'in the path of his own duty, than to adopt the prac- 'tice of *Vaisyas*, let him act in this manner:

102. 'The *Bráhman*, having fallen into distress, may 'receive gifts from any person whatever; for by no 'sacred rule can it be shown, that absolute purity can 'be sullied.

103. 'From interpreting the *Veda*, from officiating 'at sacrifices, or from taking presents, though in modes 'generally disapproved, no sin is committed by priests '*in distress*; for they are as pure as fire or water.

104. 'He, who receives food, when his life could 'not otherwise be sustained, from any man whatever, 'is no more tainted by sin, than the subtile ether by 'mud:

105. 'AJI'GARTA, dying with hunger, was going to 'destroy his own son (*named* SU'NAH-S'EPHA) *by selling* '*him for some cattle*; yet he was guilty of no crime, 'since he only sought a remedy against famishing

106. 'VA'MADEVA, who well knew right and wrong, 'was by no means rendered impure, though desirous, 'when oppressed *with hunger*, of eating the flesh of 'dogs for the preservation of his life :

107. 'BHARADWA'JA, eminent in devotion, when he 'and his son were almost starved in a dreary forest, 'accepted several cows from the carpenter VRIDHU :

108. 'VISWA'MITRA, too, than whom none better 'knew the distinctions between virtue and vice, re-'solved, when he was perishing with hunger, to eat the 'haunch of a dog, which he had received from a *Chan-'dála*.

109. 'Among *the* acts *generally disapproved, namely*, 'accepting presents *from low men*, assisting *them* to 'sacrifice, and explaining the scripture *to them*, the 'receipts of presents is the meanest *in this world*, and 'the most blamed in a *Bráhman* after his present life ;

110. 'Because assisting to sacrifice and explaining 'the scripture are two acts always performed for those, 'whose minds have been improved *by the sacred initia-'tion* ; but gifts are also received from a servile man of 'the lowest class.

111. 'The guilt, incurred by assisting *low men* to 'sacrifice and by teaching *them* the scripture, is re-'moved by repetitions of the *gáyatrí* and oblations to 'fire ; but that, incurred by accepting gifts *from them*, 'is expiated only by abandoning the gifts and by 'rigorous devotion.

112. 'It were better for a *Bráhman*, who could not 'maintain himself, to glean ears and grains after har-'vest from *the field of* any person whatever : gleaning 'whole ears would be better than accepting a present, 'and picking up single grains would be still more 'laudable.

113. '*Bráhmans*, who keep house, and are in want 'of any metals *except gold and silver*, or of other arti- 'cles *for good uses*, may ask the king for them, if he 'be of the military class; but a king, *known to be ava- 'ricious and* unwilling to give, must not be solicited.

114. 'The foremost, *in order*, of these things may 'be received more innocently than that, which follows 'it: a field untilled, a tilled field, cows, goats, sheep, 'precious metals or gems, new grain, dressed grain.

115. 'There are seven virtuous means of acquiring 'property; succession, occupancy or donation, and 'purchase or exchange, *which are allowed to all 'classes*; conquest, *which is peculiar to the military 'class*; lending at interest, husbandry or commerce, '*which belong to the mercantile class*; and acceptance 'of presents, *by the sacerdotal class*, from respectable 'men.

116. 'Learning, *except that contained in the scrip- 'tures*, art, *as mixing perfumes and the like*, work for 'wages, menial service, attendance on cattle, traffic, 'agriculture, content with little, alms, and receiving 'high interest on money, are ten modes of subsistence '*in times of distress*.

117. 'Neither a priest nor a military man, *though 'distressed*, must receive interest on loans, but each 'of them, if he please, may pay *the* small interest *per- 'mitted by law, on borrowing* for some pious use, to the 'sinful man, *who demands it*.

118. 'A military king, who takes even a fourth 'part *of the crops of his realm* at a time of urgent 'necessity, *as of war or invasion*, and protects his 'people to the utmost of his power, commits no sin:

119. 'His peculiar duty is conquest, and he must 'not recede from battle; so that, while he defends by

'his arms the merchant and husbandman, he may levy 'the legal tax *as the price of protection.*

120. 'The tax on the mercantile class, *which in 'times of prosperity must be only a twelfth part of 'their crops, and a fiftieth of their personal profits,* 'may be an eighth of their crops *in a time of dis-'tress, or a sixth, which is the medium, or even a fourth 'in great public adversity;* but a twentieth of their '*gains on* money, and other moveables, is the highest '*tax:* serving men, artisans, and mechanics must assist 'by their labour, *but at no time pay taxes.*

121. 'If a *Súdra* want a subsistence *and cannot 'attend a priest,* he may serve a *Kshatriya;* or, *if he 'cannot wait on a soldier by birth,* he may gain his 'livelihood by serving an opulent *Vaisya.*

122. 'To him, who serves *Bráhmans* with a view to 'a heavenly reward, or even with a view to both *this 'life and the next,* the union of the word *Bráhman* 'with his *name of servant* will assuredly bring success.

123. 'Attendance on *Bráhmans* is pronounced the 'best work of a *Súdra:* whatever else he may perform 'will comparatively avail him nothing.

124. 'They must allot him a fit maintenance accord-'ing to their own circumstances, after considering his 'ability, his exertions, and the number of those, whom 'he must provide with nourishment.

125. 'What remains of their dressed rice must be 'given to him; and apparel which they have worn, 'and the refuse of their grain, and their old household 'furniture.

126. 'There is no guilt in a man of the servile class '*who eats leeks and other forbidden vegetables:* he must 'not have the sacred investiture: he has no business 'with *the* duty *of making oblations to fire and the like;*

'but there is no prohibition against *his offering dressed* '*grain as a sacrifice, by way of discharging* his own duty.

127. 'Even *Súdras*, who are anxious to perform 'their entire duty, and, knowing what they should per- 'form, imitate the practice of good men *in the household* '*sacraments*, but without any holy text, *except those* '*containing praise and salutation*, are so far from sin- 'ning, that they acquire just applause :

128. 'As a *Súdra*, without injuring another man, 'performs the *lawful* acts of the twice-born, even thus, 'without being censured, he gains exaltation in this 'world and in the next.

129. 'No *superfluous* collection of wealth must be 'made by a *Súdra*, even though he has power *to make* '*it*, since a servile man, who has amassed riches, *be*- '*comes proud, and, by his insolence or neglect*, gives pain 'even to *Bráhmans*.

130. 'Such, as have been fully declared, are the 'several duties of the four classes in distress for sub- 'sistence; and, if they perform them exactly, they 'shall attain the highest beatitude.

131. 'Thus has been propounded the system of duties, 'religious and civil; ordained for all classes: I next 'will declare the pure law of expiation for sin.'

CHAPTER XI.

On Penance and Expiation.

1. 'Him, who intends to marry for the sake of 'having issue; him, who wishes to make a sacrifice; 'him, who travels; him, who has given all his wealth 'at a sacred rite; him, who desires to maintain his 'preceptor, his father, or his mother; him, who needs 'a maintenance for himself, when he first reads the '*Vedas*; and him, who is afflicted with illness;

2. 'These nine *Bráhmans* let mankind consider as 'virtuous mendicants, called *snátakas*; and, to relieve 'their wants, let gifts *of cattle or gold* be presented to 'them in proportion to their learning:

3. 'To these most excellent *Bráhmans* must rice 'also be given, with holy presents *at oblations to fire 'and within the consecrated circle*; but the dressed rice, 'which others are to receive, must be delivered on the 'outside of the sacred hearth: *gold and the like may be 'given any where.*

4. 'On such *Bráhmans* as well know the *Veda*, let 'the king bestow, as it becomes him, jewels of all 'sorts, and the solemn reward for officiating at the 'sacrifice.

5. 'He, who has a wife, and, having begged money '*to defray his nuptial expences*, marries another woman, 'shall have no advantage but sensual enjoyment: the 'offspring belongs to the bestower of the gift.

6. 'Let every man, according to his ability, give 'wealth to *Bráhmans* detached from the world and 'learned in scripture: such a giver shall attain heaven 'after this life.

7. 'He alone is worthy to drink the juice of the 'moon-plant, who keeps a provision of grain sufficient, 'to supply those, whom the law commands him to 'nourish, for the term of three years or more;

8. 'But a twice-born man, who keeps a less provi-'sion of grain, yet presumes to taste the juice of the 'moon-plant, shall gather no fruit from that sacrament, 'even though he taste it at the first, *or solemn, much 'less at any occasional*, ceremony.

9. 'He, who bestows gifts on strangers, *with a view 'to worldly fame*, while he suffers his family to live in 'distress, though he has power *to support them*, touches 'his lips with honey, but swallows poison; such virtue 'is counterfeit:

10. 'Even what he does for the sake of his future 'spiritual body, to the injury of those, whom he is 'bound to maintain, shall bring him ultimate misery 'both in this life and in the next.

11. 'Should a sacrifice, performed by any twice-'born sacrificer, and by a *Bráhman*, especially, be im-'perfect from the want of some ingredient, during the 'reign of a prince, who knows the law.

12. 'Let him take that article, for the completion of 'the sacrifice, from the house of any *Vaisya*, who pos-'sesses considerable herds, but neither sacrifices, nor 'drinks the juice of the moon-plant:

13. 'If such a *Vaisya* be not near, he may take two 'or three such necessary articles at pleasure from the 'house of a *Súdra;* since a *Súdra* has no business with 'solemn rites.

14. 'Even from the house of a *Bráhman* or a *Ksha-'triya*, who possesses a hundred cows, but has no con-'secrated fire, or a thousand cows, but performs no

'sacrifice *w.th the moon-plant*, let a priest without scru-
'ple take *the articles wanted*.

15. 'From another *Bráhman*, who continually receives presents but never gives, let him take such ingredients of the sacrifice, if not bestowed *on request*: 'so shall his fame be spread abroad, and his habits 'of virtue increase.

16. 'Thus, likewise, may a *Bráhman*, who has not 'eaten at the time of six meals, *or has fasted three 'whole days*, take at the time of the seventh meal, *or on 'the fourth morning*, from the man, who behaves basely '*by not offering him food*, enough to supply him till the 'morrow:

17. 'He may take it from the floor, where the grain 'is trodden out of the husk, or from the field, or from 'the house, or from any place whatever; but, if the 'owner ask *why he takes it*, the cause of the taking 'must be declared.

18. 'The wealth of a virtuous *Bráhman* must at no 'time be seized by a *Kshatriya*; but having no other 'means *to complete a sacrifice*, he may take the goods 'of any men, who acts wickedly, and of any who per'forms not his religious duties:

19. 'He who takes property from the bad *for the 'purpose before-mentioned*, and bestows it on the good, 'transforms himself into a boat, and carries both *the 'good and the bad* over *a sea of calamities*.

20. 'Wealth, possessed by men for the performance 'of sacrifices, the wise call the property of the gods; 'but the wealth of men, who perform no sacrifice, they 'consider as the property of demons.

21. 'Let no pious king fine the man *who takes by 'stealth or by force what he wants to make a sacrifice per-*

'*fect*; since it is the king's folly, that causes the hunger or wants of a *Bráhman*:

22. 'Having reckoned up the persons, whom the *Bráhman* is obliged to support, having ascertained his divine knowledge and moral conduct, let the king allow him a suitable maintenance from his own household;

23. 'And, having appointed him a maintenance, let the king protect him on all sides; for he gains from the *Bráhman* whom he protects, a sixth part of *the reward for* his virtue.

24. 'Let no *Bráhman* ever beg a gift from a *Súdra*; for if he perform a sacrifice after such begging, he shall, in the next life, be born a *Chandála*.

25. 'The *Bráhman* who begs any articles for a sacrifice, and disposes not of them all for that purpose, shall become a kite or a crow for a hundred years.

26. 'Any evil-hearted wretch, who, through covetousness, shall seize the property of the gods or of *Bráhmans*, shall feed in another world on the orts of vultures.

27. 'The sacrifice *Vaiswánarí* must be constantly performed on the first day of the new year, or on the new moon of *Chaitra*, as an expiation for having omitted, *through mere forgetfulness*, the appointed sacrifices of cattle and the rites of the moon-plant:

28. 'But a twice-born man, who, without necessity, does an act allowed only in a case of necessity, does an act allowed only in a case of necessity, reaps no fruit from it hereafter: thus has it been decided.

29. 'By the *Viswédévas*, by the *Sadhyas*, and by eminent *Rishis* of the sacerdotal class, the substitute

'was adopted for the principal act, when they were 'apprehensive of dying in times of imminent peril;

30. 'But no reward is prepared in a future state for 'that ill-minded man, who, when able to perform the 'principal sacrifice, has recourse to the substitute.

31. 'A priest, who well knows the law, needs not 'complain to the king of any grievous injury; since, 'even by his own power, he may chastise those, who 'injure him:

32. 'His own power, *which depends on himself alone*, 'is mightier than the royal power, *which depends on* '*other men:* by his own might, therefore, may a '*Bráhman* coerce his foes.

33. 'He may use, without hesitation, the powerful 'charms revealed to AT'HARVAN, and *by him* to 'ANGIRAS; for speech is the weapon of a *Bráhman* 'with that he may destroy his oppressors.

34. 'A soldier may avert danger from himself by 'the strength of his arm; a merchant and a mechanic, 'by their property; but the chief of the twice-born, by 'holy texts and oblations to fire.

35. 'A priest, who performs his duties, who justly 'corrects *his children and pupils,* who advises expiations 'for sin, and who loves all animated creatures, is truly 'called a *Bráhman:* to him let no man say any thing 'unpropitious, nor use any offensive language.

36. 'Let not a girl, nor a young woman *married* '*or unmarried,* nor a man with little learning, nor a 'dunce, perform an oblation to fire; nor a man dis-'eased, nor one uninvested *with the sacrificial string;*

37. 'Since any of those persons, who make such an 'oblation, shall fall into a region of torture, together 'with him, who suffers his hearth to be used: he alone,

'who perfectly knows the sacred ordinances, and has 'read all the *Vedás*, must officiate at an oblation to 'holy fire.

38. 'A *Bráhman* with abundant wealth, who presents 'not the priest, that hallows his fire, with a horse con-'secrated to PRAJA'PATI, becomes equal to one who has 'no fire hallowed.

39. 'Let him, who believes the scripture, and keeps 'his organs in subjection, perform all other pious acts; 'but never in this world let him offer a sacrifice with 'trifling gifts to the officiating priest:

40. 'The organs of sense and action, reputation *in 'this life*, a heavenly mansion *in the next*, life *itself*, 'a great name *after death*, children *and* cattle, are all 'destroyed by a sacrifice offered with trifling present: 'let no man, therefore, sacrifice without liberal gifts.

41. 'The priest, who keeps a sacred hearth, but 'voluntarily neglects *the morning and evening oblations 'to* his fires, must perform, *in the manner to be describ-'ed*, the penance *chándráyana* for one month; since 'that *neglect* is equally sinful with the slaughter of a 'son.

42. 'They, who receive property from a *Súdra* for 'the performance of rites to consecrated fire, are con-'temned, as ministers of the base, by all such as pro-'nounce texts of the *Veda*:

43. 'Of those ignorant priests, who serve the holy 'fire for the wealth of a *Súdra*, the giver shall always, 'tread on the foreheads, and thus pass over miseries *in 'the gloom of death*.

44. 'Every man, who does not an act prescribed, or 'does an act forbidden, or is guilty of excess, *even* in '*legal* gratifications of the senses, must perform an 'expiatory penance.

45. 'Some of the learned consider an expiation as 'confined to involuntary sin; but others, from the 'evidence of the *Veda*, hold it effectual even in the case 'of a voluntary offence:

46. 'A sin, involuntarily committed, is removed by 'repeating certain texts of the scripture; but a sin 'committed intentionally, through strange infatuation, 'by harsh penances of different sorts.

47. 'If a twice-born man, by the will of God in 'this world, or from his natural birth, have any cor- 'poreal mark of an expiable sin committed in this or 'a former state, he must hold no intercourse with the 'virtuous, while his penance remains unperformed.

48. 'Some evil-minded persons, for sins committed 'in this life, and some for bad actions in a preceding 'state, suffer a morbid change in their bodies:

49. 'A stealer of gold *from a Bráhman* has whit- 'lows on his nails; a drinker of spirits, black teeth; 'the slayer of a *Brahman*, a marasmus; the violator 'of his *guru's* bed, a deformity in the generative 'organs;

50. 'A malignant informer, fetid ulcers in his nos- 'trils; a false detractor, stinking breath; a stealer of 'grain, the defect of some limb; a mixer *of bad words 'with good*, some redundant member;

51. 'A stealer of dressed grain, dyspepsia; a stealer 'of holy words, *or an unauthorized reader of the scrip- 'tures*, dumbness; a stealer of clothes, leprosy; a 'horse-stealer, lameness;

52. 'The stealer of a lamp, total blindness; the 'mischievous extinguisher of it, blindness in one eye; 'a delighter in hurting sentient creatures, perpetual 'illness; an adulterer, windy swellings in his limbs;

53. 'Thus, according to the diversity of actions, 'are born men despised by the good, stupid, dumb, 'blind, deaf, and deformed.

54. 'Penance, therefore, must invariably be per-'formed for the sake of expiation; since they, who 'have not expiated their sins, will again spring to 'birth with disgraceful marks.

55. 'Killing a *Brahman*, drinking forbidden liquor, 'stealing *gold from a priest*, adultery with the wife of a 'father, *natural or spiritual*, and associating with such 'as commit those offences, wise legislators must declare 'to be crimes in the highest degree, *in respect of those 'after mentioned, but less than incest in a direct line, 'and some others.*

56. 'False boasting of a high tribe, malignant in-'formation, before the king, *of a criminal who must 'suffer death*, and falsely accusing a spiritual preceptor, 'are crimes *in the second degree, and nearly* equal to 'killing a *Brahman*.

57. 'Forgetting the texts of scripture, showing con-'tempt of the *Veda*, giving false evidence *without a bad 'motive*, killing a friend *without malice*, eating things 'prohibited, or, *from their manifest impurity*, unfit to be 'tasted, are six crimes nearly equal to drinking spirits; '*but perjury and homicide require in atrocious cases the 'harshest expiation*.

58. 'To appropriate a thing deposited *or lent for a 'time*, a human creature, a horse, precious metals, a 'field, a diamond, or any other gem, is nearly equal to 'stealing *the* gold *of a* Bráhman.

59. 'Carnal commerce with sisters by the same 'mother, with little girls, with women of the lowest 'mixed class, or with the wives of a friend or of a son, 'the wise must consider as nearly equal to a violation 'of the paternal bed.

60. 'Slaying a bull or cow, sacrificing what ought 'not to be sacrificed, adultery, selling oneself, deserting 'a preceptor, a mother, a father, or a son, omitting to 'read the scripture, and neglect of the fires *prescribed* '*by the* Dharma'ṣástra *only*.

61. 'The marriage of a younger brother before the 'elder, and that elder's omission to marry before the 'younger, giving a daughter to either of them, and 'officiating at their nuptial sacrifice,

62. 'Defiling a damsel, usury, want of perfect 'chastity in a student, selling a holy pool or garden, a 'wife, or a child,

63. 'Omitting the sacred investiture, abandoning a 'kinsman, teaching the *Vedà* for hire, learning it from 'a hired teacher, selling commodities, that ought not 'to be sold,

64. 'Working in mines of any sort, engaging in '*dykes, bridges, or other* great mechanical works, spoil-'ing medicinal plants *repeatedly*, subsisting by *the* '*harlotry of* a wife, offering sacrifices and preparing 'charms to destroy *the innocent*.

65. 'Cutting down green trees for firewood, per-'forming holy rites with a selfish view merely, and 'eating prohibited food *once without a previous design*.

66. 'Neglecting to keep up the consecrated fire, 'stealing *any valuable thing besides gold*, non-payment 'of *the three* debts, application to the books of a false 'religion, and excessive attention to music or dancing,

67. 'Stealing grain, base metals, or cattle, famili-'arity *by the twice-born* with women who have drunk 'inebriating liquor, killing *without malice* a woman, *a* '*Sùdra, a Vaisya*, or a *Kshatriya*, and denying a future 'state of rewards and punishments, are all crimes in the 'third degree, *but higher or lower according to cir-* '*cumstances*.

68. 'Giving pain to a *Bráhman*, smelling at any 'spirituous liquor or any thing *extremely fetid and* 'unfit to be smelt, cheating, and unnatural practices 'with a male, are considered as causing a loss of 'class.

69. 'To kill an ass, a horse, a camel, a deer, an 'elephant, a goat, a sheep, a fish, a snake, or a buffalo, 'is declared an offence, which degrades the killer to a 'mixed tribe.

70. 'Accepting presents from despicable men, ille'gal traffic, attendance on a *Súdra*-master, and speak'ing falsehood, must be considered as causes of exclu'sion from social repasts.

71. 'Killing an insect, small or large, a worm, or 'a bird, eating what has been brought *in the same* '*basket* with spirituous liquor, stealing fruit, wood, or 'flowers, and great perturbation of mind *on trifling* '*occasions*, are offences which cause defilement.

72. 'You shall now be completely instructed in 'those penances, by which all the sins just mentioned 'are expiable.

73. 'If a *Bráhman* have killed a man of the sa'cerdotal class, *without malice prepense, the slayer* '*being far superior to the slain in good qualities*, he 'must himself make a hut in a forest and dwell in 'it twelve whole years, subsisting on alms for the 'purification of his soul, placing near him, as a token '*of his crime*, the skull of the slain, *if he can procure* '*it, or, if not, any human skull. The time of penance* '*for the three lower classes must be twenty-four, thirty-six,* '*and forty-eight, years.*

74. 'Or, *if the slayer be of the military class*, he may 'voluntarily expose himself as a mark to archers, who 'know *his intention*; or, *according to circumstances*,

'may cast himself headlong thrice, *or even till he die,* 'into blazing fire.

75. 'Or, *if he be a king, and slew a priest without* '*malice or knowledge of his class,* he may perform, '*with presents of great wealth,* one of the following 'sacrifices; an *Aswamedha,* or a *Swerjit,* or a *Gósava,* 'or an *Abhijit,* or a *Viswajit,* or a *Trivrit,* or an '*Agnishtut.*

76. Or, to expiate the guilt of killing a priest '*without knowing him and without design,* the killer may 'walk *on a pilgrimage* a hundred *yójanas,* repeating 'any one of the *Vedas,* eating barely enough to sustain 'life, and keeping his organs in perfect subjection;

77. 'Or, *if in that case the slayer be unlearned but* '*rich,* he may give all his property to some *Bráhman* 'learned in the *Veda,* or a sufficiency of wealth for his 'life, or a house and furniture *to hold while he lives.*

78. 'Or, eating only such wild grains as are offered 'to the gods, he may walk to *the head of* the river '*Saraswati* against the course of the stream; or, 'subsisting on very little food, he may thrice repeat 'the whole collection of *Vedas,* or the *Rig, Yajur,* 'and *Sáman.*

79. 'Or, his hair being shorn, he may dwell near 'a town, or on pasture-ground for cows, or in some 'holy place, or at the root of a sacred tree, taking 'pleasure in doing good to cows and to *Bráhmans:*

80. 'There, for the preservation of a cow or a '*Bráhman,* let him instantly abandon life; since the 'preserver of a cow or a *Bráhman,* atones for the crime 'of killing a priest:

81. 'Or, by attempting at least three times forcibly 'to recover *from robbers* the property of a *Bráhman,* 'or by recovering it in one of his attacks, or even by 'losing his life in the attempt, he atones for his crime.

82. 'Thus, continually firm in religious austerity 'chaste as a student in the first order, with his mind 'intent on virtue, he may expiate the guilt of *unde-'signedly* killing a *Bráhman*, after the twelfth year 'has expired.

83. 'Or, *if a virtuous* Bráhman *unintentionally kill 'another, who had no good quality*, he may atone for 'his guilt by proclaiming it in an assembly of priests 'and military men, at the sacrifice of a horse, and 'by bathing with other *Bráhmans* at the close of the 'sacrifice :

84. '*Bráhmans* are declared to be the basis, and '*Kshatriyas* the summit, of the legal system : he, there-'fore, expiates his offence by fully proclaiming it in 'such an assembly.

85. 'From his high birth alone, a *Bráhman* is an 'object of veneration even to deities ; his declarations 'to mankind are decisive evidence ; and the *Veda* itself 'confers on him that character.

86. 'Three at least, who are learned in the *Veda*, 'should be assembled to declare the proper expiation 'for the sin *of a priest, but for the three other classes, 'the number must be doubled, tripled, and quadrupled :* 'what they declare shall be an atonement for sinners ; 'since the words of the learned give purity.

87. 'Thus a *Bráhman*, who has performed one of 'the preceding expiations, *according to the circum-'stances of the homicide and the characters of the persons 'killed and killing*, with his whole mind fixed on God, 'purifies his soul, and removes the guilt of slaying a 'man of his own class :

88. 'He must perform the same penance for killing 'an embryo, *the sex of which was* unknown, *but whose 'parents were sacerdotal*, or a military or a commercial

'man employed in a sacrifice, or a *Bráhmaní*-woman, 'who has bathed after temporary uncleanness;

89. 'And *the same* for giving false evidence *in a 'cause concerning land or gold, or precious commo- 'dities*, and for accusing his preceptor unjustly, and 'for appropriating a deposit, and for killing the wife of 'a priest, *who keeps a consecrated fire*, or for slaying a 'friend.

90. 'Such is the atonement ordained for killing a 'priest *without malice*; but for killing a *Bráhman* with 'malice prepense, this is no expiation: *the term of 'twelve years must be doubled, or if the case was atrocious, 'the murderer must actually die in flames or in battle.*

91. 'Any twice-born man, who has *intentionally* drunk 'spirit of rice, through perverse delusion of mind, 'may drink more spirit in flame, and atone for his of- 'fence by severely burning his body;

92. 'Or he may drink boiling hot, until he die, the 'urine of a cow, or pure water, or milk, or clarified 'butter, or juice expressed from cow-dung:

93. 'Or *if he tasted it unknowingly*, he may expiate 'the sin of drinking spirituous liquor, by eating only 'some broken rice or grains of *tila*, from which oil has 'been extracted, once every night for a whole year, 'wrapped in coarse vesture of hairs from a cow's tail, '*or sitting unclothed in his house*, wearing his locks 'and beard uncut, and putting out the flag of a 'tavern-keeper.

94. 'Since the spirit of rice is *distilled from the* 'Mala, *or* filthy refuse, of the grain, and since *Mala* 'is also a name for sin, let no *Bráhman*, *Kshatriya*, or '*Vaisya* drink that spirit.

95. 'Inebriating liquor may be considered as of 'three *principal* sorts: that extracted from dregs of

'sugar, that extracted from bruised rice, and that 'extracted from the flowers of the *Madhúka:* as one, 'so *are* all; they shall not be tasted by the chief of the 'twice-born.

96. 'Those liquors, and *eight* other sorts, with the 'flesh of animals, and *A'sava, the most pernicious be-'verage, prepared with narcotic drugs,* are swallowed 'at the juncates of *Yakshas, Rakshases,* and *Pisáchas:* 'they shall not, therefore, be tasted by a *Bráhman,* who 'feeds on clarified butter offered to gods.

97. 'A *Bráhman,* stupefied by drunkenness, might 'fall on something very impure, or might even, when 'intoxicated, pronounce a *secret* phrase of the *Veda,* 'or might do some other act, which ought not to be 'done.

98. 'When the divine spirit, *or the light of holy 'knowledge,* which has been infused into his body, has 'once been sprinkled with any intoxicating liquor, even 'his priestly character leaves him, and he sinks to the 'low degree of a *Súdra.*

99. 'Thus have been promulgated the various modes 'of expiation for drinking spirits: I will next pro-'pound the atonement for stealing *the* gold *of a priest 'to the amount of a* savarna.

100. 'He, who has purloined the gold of a *Bráhman,* 'must hasten to the king, and proclaim his offence 'adding, "Inflict on me the punishment due to my 'crime."

101. 'Then shall the king himself, taking *from him* 'an iron mace, *which the criminal must bear on his 'shoulder,* strike him with it once; and by that stroke, '*whether he die or be only left as dead,* the thief is re-'leased from sin: a *Bráhman,* by rigid penance alone '*can expiate that offence; another twice-born man may 'also perform such penance at his election.*

102. 'The twice-born man, who desires to remove 'by austere devotion the taint caused by stealing gold, 'must perform in a forest, covered with a mantle of 'rough bark, the penance *before ordained* for him, 'who *without malice prepense* has killed a *Bráhman*.

103. 'By these expiations may the twice-born atone 'for the guilt of stealing *gold from a priest*; but the sin 'of adultery with the wife of a father, *natural or* '*spiritual*, they must expiate by the following penances.

104. 'He, who *knowingly and actually* has defiled 'the wife of his father, *she being of the same class*, 'must extend himself on a heated iron bed, loudly 'proclaiming his guilt; and, there embracing the red 'hot iron image of a woman, he shall atone for his 'crime by death:

105. 'Or, having himself amputated his penis and 'scrotum, and holding them in his fingers, he may 'walk in a direct path toward the south-west, or the 'region of NIRRITI, until he fall dead on the ground:

106. 'Or, *if he had mistaken her for another woman*, 'he may perform for a whole year, with intense ap- 'plication of mind, the penance *prájápatya*, with part 'of a bed, *or a human bone*, in his hand, wrapped in 'vesture of coarse bark, letting his hair and beard 'grow, and living in a deserted forest:

107. 'Or, *if she was of a lower class and a corrupt* '*woman*, he may expiate the sin of violating the bed 'of his father, by continuing the penance *chandráyana* 'for three months, always mortifying his body by 'eating only forest herbs, or wild grains boiled in 'water.

108. 'By the preceding penances may sinners of the '*two* higher degrees atone for their guilt; and the 'less offenders may expiate theirs by the following 'austerities.

109. 'He, who has committed the smaller offence of 'killing a cow *without malice*, must drink for the first 'month barley-corns *boiled soft in water; his head 'must be* shaved *entirely;* and, covered with the hide '*of the slain cow*, he must fix his abode on *her late* 'pasture guard:

110. 'He may eat a moderate quantity *of wild 'grains*, but without any factitious salt, for the next 'two months at the time of each fourth repast, *on the 'evening of every second day*; regularly bathing in 'the urine of cows, and keeping his members under 'control:

111. 'All day he must wait on the herd, and stand 'quaffing the dust raised *by their hoofs;* at night, 'having servilely attended *and stroked* and saluted 'them, *he must surround them with a fence*, and sit near '*to guard* them:

112. 'Pure and free from passion, he must stand, 'while they stand; follow them, when they move together; and lie down by them, when they lie down:

113. 'Should a cow be sick or terrified by tigers or 'thieves, or fall, or stick in mud, he must relieve her 'by all possible means:

114. 'In heat, in rain, or in cold, or while the blast 'furiously rages, let him not seek his own shelter, 'without first sheltering the cows to the utmost of his 'power:

115. 'Neither in his own house, or field, or floor 'for treading out grain, nor in those of any other 'person, let him say a word of a cow, who eats *corn or 'grass*, or of a calf, who drinks *milk:*

116. 'By waiting on a herd, according to these 'rules, for three months, the slayer of a cow atones for 'his guilt;

117. '*But*, his penance being performed, he must 'give ten cows and a bull, or, his stock not being so 'large, must deliver all he possesses, to such as best 'know the *Veda*.

118. 'The preceding penances, or that called *chándráyana*, must be performed for the absolution of all 'twice-born men, who have committed sins of the 'lower *or third* degree; except those, who have in'curred the guilt of an *avakírna*;

119. 'But he, who has become *Avakírna*, must sa'crifice *a black or* a one-eyed ass, by way of a meat'offering to NIRRITI, *patroness of the south-west*, by 'night, in a place where four ways meet:

120. 'Let him daily offer to her in fire the fat of 'that ass, and, at the close *of the ceremony*, let him 'offer clarified butter, with the holy text *Sem* and so 'forth, to PAVANA, to INDRA, to VRIHASPATI, and to 'AGNI, *regents of wind, clouds, a planet, and fire*.

121. 'A voluntary effusion, *naturally or otherwise*, 'of that which may produce a man, by a twice-born 'youth during the time of his studentship, *or before 'marriage*, has been pronounced *avakírna*, or a vio'lation *of the rule prescribed for the first order*, by sages, 'who knew the whole system of duty, and uttered the 'words of the *Veda*.

122. 'To the four *deities of purification*, MA'RUTA, 'INDRA, VRIHASPATI, AGNI, goes all the divine light, 'which the *Veda* had imparted, from the student, who 'commits the foul sin *avakírna*;

123. 'But, this crime having actually been commit'ted, he must go begging to seven houses, clothed only 'with the hide of the *sacrificed* ass, and openly 'proclaiming his act:

124. 'Eating a single meal begged from them, at the

'regular time of the day, *that is in the morning or evening*, and bathing *each day* at the three *savanas*, he 'shall be absolved from his guilt at the end of one 'year.

125. 'He, who has voluntarily committed any sin, 'which causes a loss of class, must perform the *tormenting* penance, *thence* called *sántapana*; or the '*prájapatya*, if he offended involuntarily.

126. 'For sins, which degrade to a mixed class, or 'exclude from society, the sinner must have recourse to 'the lunar expiation *chándráyana* for one month: to 'atone for acts which occasion defilement, he must 'swallow nothing for three days but hot barley-gruel.

127. 'For killing *intentionally* a *virtuous* man of the 'military class, the penance must be a fourth part of 'that ordained for killing a priest; for killing a '*Vaisya*, only an eighth; for killing a *Súdra* who 'had been constant in *discharging* his duties, a six-'teenth part:

128. 'But, if a *Brahman* kill a *Kshatriya* without 'malice, he must, after a full performance of his re-'ligious rites, give *the priests* one bull together with a 'thousand cows;

129. 'Or he may perform for three years the pe-'nance for slaying a *Brahman*, mortifying his organs, of 'sensation and action, letting his hair grow long, and 'living remote from the town, with the root of a tree 'for his mansion.

130. 'If he kill *without malice* a *Vaisya*, who had a 'good moral character, he may perform the same pe-'nance for one year, or give *the priests* a hundred cows 'and a bull:

131. 'For six months must he perform this whole

'penance, if *without intention* he kill a *Súdra*; or he 'may give ten white cows and a bull to the priests.

132. 'If he kill *by design* a cat, or an ichneumon, 'the bird *chásha*, or a frog, a dog, a lizard, an owl, or 'a crow, he must perform the *ordinary* penance requir- 'ed for the death of a *Súdra, that is the chándráyana*:

133. 'Or, *if he kill one of them undesignedly*, he may 'drink nothing but milk for three *days and* nights, or '*each night* walk a *yójan*, or *thrice* bathe in a river, or 'silently repeat the text on the divinity of water; *that 'is, if he be disabled by real infirmity from performing 'the first mentioned penances, he may have recourse to 'the next in order.*

134. 'A *Bráhman*, if he kill a snake, must give *to 'some priest* a hoe, *or iron-head stick*; if an eunuch, a 'load of rice-straw, and a *másha* of lead;

135. 'If a boar, a pot of clarified butter; if the 'bird *tittiri*, a *dróna* of *tila*-seeds; if a parrot, a steer 'two years old; if the water-bird *craunchа*, a steer 'aged three years:

136. 'If he kill *a goose, or* a phenicopteros, a '*heron, or* cormorant, a bittern, a peacock, an ape, a 'hawk, or a kite, he must give a cow to some *Bráh- 'man*:

137. 'If he kill a horse, he must give a mantle; if 'an elephant, five black bulls; if a goat or a sheep, 'one bull; if an ass, a calf one year old:

138. 'If he kill a carnivorous wild beast, he must 'give a cow with abundance of milk; if a wild beast 'not carnivorous, a fine heifer; and a *ractica* of gold, 'if he slay a camel:

139. 'If he kill a woman *of any class* caught in ad- 'ultery, he must give as an expiation, in the direct

'order of the four classes, a leathern pouch, a bow, a 'goat, and a sheep.

140. 'Should a *Bráhman* be unable to expiate by 'gifts the sin of killing a snake and the rest, he must 'atone for his guilt by performing, on each occasion, 'the penance *prájápatya*.

141. 'For the slaughter of a thousand small animals 'which have bones, or for that of boneless animals 'enough to fill a cart, he must perform the *chándráyana*, '*or common penance for killing a Súdra*;'

142. 'But, for killing boned animals, he must also 'give some trifle, *as a* pana *of copper*, to a *Bráhman*: 'for killing those without bones, *he may be absolved* 'by holding his breath, *at the close of his penance, while* '*he thrice repeats the gáyatrí* with its *head*, the *pranava*, '*and the vyáhritis*.

143. 'For cutting *once without malice* trees yielding 'fruit, shrubs with many crowded stems, creeping or 'climbing plants, or such as grow again when cut, 'if they were in blossom *when he hurt them*, he must 'repeat a hundred texts of the *Veda*.

144. 'For killing insects of any sort bread in rice 'or other grains, or those bred *in honey or other* fluids, 'or those bread in fruit or flowers, eating clarified 'butter is a full expiation.

145. 'If a man cut, *wantonly and* for no good pur-'pose, such grasses as are cultivated, or such as rise 'in the forest spontaneously, he must wait on a cow 'for one day, nourished by milk alone.

146. 'By these penances may mankind atone for 'the sin of injuring sentient creatures, whether com-'mitted by design or through inadvertence: hear now 'what penances are ordained for eating or drinking 'what ought not to be tasted.

147. 'He, who drinks undesignedly any spirit *but that of rice,* may be absolved by a new investiture 'with the sacrificial string: even for drinking intentionally *the weaker sorts of spirit,* a penance extending 'to death must not (as the law is now fixed) be 'prescribed.

148. 'For drinking water which has stood in a 'vessel, where spirit of rice or any other spirituous 'liquor had been kept, he must swallow *nothing,* for 'five *days and* nights, but the plant *sanc'hapushpi* 'boiled in milk:

149. 'If he touch any spirituous liquor, or give 'any away, or accept any in due form, *or with thanks,* 'or drink water left by a *Súdra,* he must swallow 'nothing for three *days and* nights, but *kusá*-grass 'boiled in water.

150. 'Should a *Bráhman,* who has once tasted the 'holy juice of the moon-plant, even smell the breath 'of a man who has been drinking spirits, he must 'remove the taint by thrice repeating the *gáyatrí,* while 'he suppresses his breath in water, and by eating 'clarified butter *after that ceremony.*

151. 'If any of the three twice-born classes have 'tasted unknowingly human ordure or urine, or any 'thing that has touched spirituous liquor, they must, '*after a penance,* be girt anew with the sacrificial 'thread;

152. 'But, in such new investiture of the twice-'born, the partial tonsure, the zone, the staff, the 'petition of alms, and the strict rules of abstinence, 'need not be renewed.

153. 'Should one of them eat the food of those 'persons, with whom he ought never to eat, or food 'left by a woman or a *Súdra,* or any prohibited flesh,

'he must drink barley-gruel only for seven *days and* 'nights.

154. 'If a *Bráhman* drink sweet liquors turned acid, 'or astringent juices from impure fruits, he becomes 'unclean, as long as those fluids remain undigested.

155. 'Any twice-born man, who *by accident* has 'tasted the dung or urine of a tame boar, an ass, a 'camel, a shakal, an ape, or a crow, must perform the 'penance *chándráyana.*

156. 'If he taste dried flesh-meat, or mushrooms 'rising from the ground, or any thing brought from a 'slaughter-house, though he knew not whence it came, 'he must perform the same penance.

157. 'For *knowingly* eating the flesh of carnivorous 'beasts, of town-boars, of camels, of gallinaceous birds, of 'human creatures, of crows, or of asses, the penance *tap-* '*takrich'hra,* or *burning and severe,* is the *only* atonement.

158. 'A *Bráhman,* who, before he has completed his 'theological studies, eats food at monthly obsequies *to* '*one ancestor,* must fast three days *and nights,* and sit 'in water a day :

159. 'But a student in theology, who at any time '*unknowingly* tastes honey or fish, must perform the 'lowest penance, or the *prájápatya,* and proceed to 'finish his studentship.

160. 'Having eaten what has been left by a cat, 'a crow, a mouse, a dog, or an ichneumon, or what 'has even been touched by a louse, he must drink, '*boiled in water,* the plant *brahmasuverchalá.*

161. 'By the man, who seeks purity of soul, no 'forbidden food must be tasted : what he has unde- 'signedly swallowed he must instantly vomit up, or 'must purify himself with speed by legal expiations.

162. 'Such, as have been declared, are the various 'penances for eating prohibited food: hear now the 'law of penance for an expiation of theft.

163. 'The chief of the twice-born, having voluntarily stolen such property, as grain, raw or dressed, 'from the house of another *Bráhman,* shall be absolved 'on performing the penance *prájápatya* for a whole 'year;

164. 'But the penance *chándráyana* must be performed for stealing a man, woman, or child, for 'seizing a field, or a house, or for taking the waters of 'an enclosed pool or well.

165. 'Having taken goods of little value from the 'house of another man, he must procure absolution 'by performing the penance *sántapana;* having first 'restored, *as the penitent thief always must,* the goods 'that he stole.

166. 'For taking what may be eaten, or what may 'be sipped, a carriage, a bed, or a seat, roots, flowers, 'or fruit, an atonement may be made by swallowing 'the five *pure* things produced by a cow, *or milk, curds,* '*butter, urine, dung:*

167. 'For stealing grass, wood, or trees, rice in the 'husk, molasses, cloth or leather, *fish, or other* 'animal food, a strict fast must be kept three *days* '*and three* nights.

168. 'For stealing gems, pearls, coral, copper, silver, 'iron, brass, or stone, nothing but broken rice must be 'swallowed for twelve days;

169. 'And *nothing but* milk for three days, if cotton 'or silk, or wool had been stolen, or a beast either with 'cloven or uncloven hoofs, or a bird, or perfumes, or 'medicinal herbs, or cordage.

170. 'By these penances may a twice-born man 'atone for the guilt of theft; but the following aus- 'terities only can remove the sin of carnally approaching 'those, who must not be carnally approached.

171. 'He, who has wasted his manly strength with 'sisters by the same womb, with the wives of his friend, 'or of his son, with girls under the age of puberty, 'or with women of the lowest classes, must perform the 'penance ordained for defiling the bed of a preceptor:

172. 'He, who has carnally known the daughter of 'his paternal aunt, *who is almost equal to* a sister, or 'the daughter of his maternal aunt, or the daughter of 'his maternal uncle, *who is* a near kinsman, must per- 'form the *chándráyana*, or *lunar penance;*

173. 'No man of sense would take one of those 'three as his wife: they shall not be taken in marriage 'by reason of their consanguinity; and he, who mar- 'ries any one of them, falls deep *into sin.*

174. 'He, who has wasted, what might have pro- 'duced a man, with female brute animals, with a 'woman during her courses, or in any but the natural 'part, or in water, must perform the penance *sán- 'tapana: for a bestial act with a cow the penance must be 'far more severe.*

175. 'A twice-born man, dallying lasciviously with 'a male *in any place or at any time,* or with a fe- 'male in a carriage drawn by bullocks, or in water, or 'by day, *shall be degraded, and* must bathe himself '*publicly* with his apparel.

176. 'Should a *Bráhman* carnally know a woman 'of the *Chandála* or *Mlechha*-tribes, or taste their food, 'or accept a gift from them, he loses his own class, if he 'acted unknowingly, or, if knowingly, sinks to a level '*with them.*

177. 'A wife, excessively corrupt, let her husband 'confine to one apartment, and compel her to per- 'form the penance ordained for a man, who has com- 'mitted adultery:

178. 'If, having been solicited by a man of her own 'class, she again be defiled, her expiation must be the 'penance *prájápatya* added to the *chánndráyana*.

179. 'The guilt of a *Bráhman*, who has dallied a 'whole night with a *Chandála*-woman, he may remove 'in three years by subsisting on alms, and incessantly 'repeating the *gáyatri* with other mysterious texts.

180. 'These penances have been declared for sinners 'of four sorts, *those who hurt sentient creatures, those who 'eat prohibited food, those who commit theft, and those who 'are guilty of lasciviousness*: hear now the prescribed 'expiation for such, as hold any intercourse with 'degraded offenders.

181. 'He, who associates himself for one year with 'a fallen sinner, falls like him; not by sacrificing, 'reading the *Veda*, or contracting affinity with him, '*since by those acts he loses his class immediately*, but 'even by using the same carriage or seat, or by taking 'his food at the same board:

182. 'That man who holds an intercourse with any 'one of those degraded offenders, must perform, as an 'atonement for such intercourse, the penance ordained 'for that sinner himself.

183. 'The *sapindas* and *samánódakas* of a man de- 'graded, *for a crime in the first degree*, must offer a 'libation of water *to his manes, as if he were naturally 'dead*, out of the town, in the evening of some in- 'auspicious day, *as the ninth of the moon*, his paternal 'kinsmen, his officiating priest, and his spritual guide 'being present.

184. 'A female slave must kick down with her foot 'an *old* pot filled with water, *which had for that purpose 'been placed before the south*, as if it were an oblation 'for the dead; and all the kinsmen, in the nearer and 'remoter degrees, must remain impure for a day and 'a night:

185. 'They must thenceforth desist from speaking 'to him, from sitting in his company, from delivering 'to him any inherited or other property, and from 'every civil or usual attention, *as inviting him on the 'first day of the year, and the like.*

186. 'His right of primogeniture, *if he was an elder 'brother*, must be withholden from him, and whatever 'perquisites arise from priority of birth: a younger 'brother, excelling him in virtue, must appropriate the 'share of the first-born.

187. 'But, when he has performed his due penance, 'his kinsmen and he must throw down a new vessel 'full of water, after having bathed together in a pure 'pool:

188. 'Then must he cast that vessel into the water; 'and, having entered his house, he may perform, as 'before, all the acts incident to his relation by blood.

189. 'The same cermony must be performed by the 'kindred even of women degraded, for whom clothes, 'dressed rice, and water must be provided; and they 'must dwell *in huts* near the family house.

190. 'With sinners, whose expiations are unperform-'ed, let not a man transact business of any kind; but 'those, who have performed their expiations, let him 'at no time reproach:

191. 'Let him not, however, live with those, who 'have slain children, or injured their benefactors, or 'killed suppliants for protection, or put women to death,

'even though such offenders have been legally purified.

192. 'Those men of the twice-born classes, to whom the *gáyatrì* has not been repeated and explained, according to law, the assembly must cause to perform three *prájápatya* penances, and *afterwards* to be girt with the sacrificial string;

193. 'And the same penance they must prescribe to such twice-born men, as are anxious to atone for some illegal act, or a neglect of the *Veda*.

194. 'If priests have accepted any property from base hands, they may be absolved by relinquishing the presents, by repeating mysterious texts, and by acts of devotion:

195. 'By three thousand repetitions of the *gáyatrì* with intense application of mind, and by subsisting on milk only for a whole month on the pasture of cows, a *Bráhman*, who has received any gift from a bad man, *or a bad gift from any man*, may be cleared from sin.

196. 'When he has been mortified by abstinence, and has returned from the pasturage, let him bend low to the other *Bráhmans*, who must thus interrogate him: "Art thou really desirous, good man, of re-admission to an equality with us?"

197. 'If he answer in the affirmative, let him give some grass to the cows, and in the place, made pure by their having eaten on it, let the men of his class give their assent to his re-admission.

198. 'He, who has officiated at a sacrifice for outcasts, or burned the corpse of a stranger, or performed rites to destroy the innocent, or made the impure sacrifice, called *Ahína*, may expiate his guilt by three *prájápatya* penances.

199. 'A twice-born man, who has rejected a suppliant for his protection, or taught the *Veda* on a 'forbidden day, may atone for his offence by subsisting 'a whole year on barley alone.

200. 'He, who has been bitten by a dog, a shakal, 'or an ass, by any carnivorous animal frequenting a 'town, by a man, a horse, a camel, or a boar, may be 'purified by stopping his breath during one repetition 'of the *gáyatri*.

201. 'To eat only at the time of the sixth meal, '*or on the evening of every third day*, for a month, 'to repeat a *Sanhitá* of the *Vedas*, and to make *eight* 'oblations to fire, accompanied with *eight* holy texts, 'are always an expiation for those, who are excluded 'from society at repasts.

202. 'Should a *Bráhman* voluntarily ascend a carriage borne by camels or drawn by asses, or designedly bathe quite naked, he may be absolved by one 'suppression of breath, *while he repeats in his mind the* '*most holy text*.

203. 'He, who has made any excretion, being greatly pressed, either without water *near him*, or in water, 'may be purified by bathing in his clothes out of town, 'and by touching a cow.

204. 'For an omission of the acts, which the *Veda* 'commands to be constantly performed, and for a violation of the duties prescribed to a housekeeper, the 'atonement is fasting *one day*.

205. 'He, who says hush or pish to a *Bráhman*, or 'thou *to a superior*, must *immediately* bathe, eat nothing 'for the rest of the day, and appease him by clasping 'his feet with respectful salutation.

206. 'For striking a *Bráhman* even with a blade of 'grass, or tying him by the neck with a cloth, or over-

'powering him in argument, and adding contemptuous 'words, the offender must soothe him by falling 'prostrate.

207. 'An assaulter of a *Bráhman*, with intent to kill, 'shall remain in hell a hundred years; for actually 'striking him *with the like intent*, a thousand:

208. 'As many small pellets of dust as the blood of 'a *Bráhman* collects on the ground, for so many 'thousand years must the shedder of that blood be 'tormented in hell.

209. 'For a simple assault, the first *or common* pe-'nance must be performed; for a battery, the *third or* 'very severe penance; but for shedding blood, *without* '*killing*, both of those penances.

210. 'To remove the sins, for which no particular 'penance has been ordained, the assembly must award 'a fit expiation, considering the ability of the sinner *to* '*perform it*, and the *nature of the* sin.

211. 'Those penances, by which a man may atone 'for his crimes, I now will describe to you; penances, 'which have been performed by deities, by holy sages, 'and by forefathers *of the human race*.

212. 'When a twice-born man performs the *common* 'penance, *or that* of PRAJA'PATI, he must for three days 'eat only in the morning; for three days, only in the 'evening; for three days, food unasked *but presented to* '*him*; and for three more days, nothing.

213. 'Eating *for a whole day* the dung and urine 'of cows mixed with curds, milk, clarified butter, 'and water boiled with *kusa*-grass, and then fasting 'entirely for a *day and a* night, is the penance 'called *Sántapana*, (either from the devout man SAN-'TAPANA, or from *tormenting*).

214. 'A twice-born man performing the penance, 'called very severe, *in respect of the common,* must eat, 'as before, a single mouthful, *or a ball of rice as* '*large as a hen's egg,* for three times three days; and 'for the last three days, must wholly abstain from 'food.

215. 'A *Bráhman,* performing the ardent penance, 'must swallow nothing but hot water, hot milk, hot 'clarified butter, and hot steam, each of them for 'three days successively, performing an ablution and 'mortifying all his members.

216. 'A total fast for twelve days *and nights,* by 'a penitent with his organs controlled and his mind 'attentive, is the penance named *paráka,* which ex-'piates all *degrees of* guilt.

217. 'If he diminish his food by one mouthful *each* '*day,* during the dark fortnight, *eating fifteen mouthfuls* '*on the day of the opposition,* and increase it, *in the* '*same proportion,* during the bright fortnight, *fasting* '*entirely on the day of the conjunction,* and perform an 'ablution regularly at sunrise, noon, and sunset, this 'is the *chándráyana,* or the lunar penance:

218. 'Such is the *penance* called ant-shaped *or nar-*'*row in the middle;* but, if he perform the barley-'shaped, *or broad in the middle,* he must observe the 'same rule, beginning with the bright half-month, and 'keeping under command his organs of action and 'sense.

219. 'To perform the lunar penance of an anchoret, 'he must eat only eight mouthfuls of forest grains at 'noon *for a whole month,* taking care to subdue his mind.

220. 'If a *Bráhman* eat only four mouthfuls at sun-'rise, and four at sunset, *for a month,* keeping his 'organs controlled, he performs the lunar penance of 'children.

221. 'He, who, for a whole month, eats no more 'than thrice eighty mouthfuls of wild grains, *as he 'happens* by any means *to meet with them*, keeping his 'organs in subjection, shall attain the same abode with 'the regent of the moon:

222. 'The *eleven Rudras*, the *twelve A'dityas*, the '*eight Vasus*, the *Maruts*, or genii of the winds, and 'the *seven* great *Rishis*, have performed this lunar 'penance as a security from all evil.

223. 'The oblation *of clarified butter* to fire must every 'day be made by *the penitent* himself, accompanied 'with the mighty words, *earth, sky, heaven*; he must 'perfectly abstain from injury to sentient creatures, 'from falsehood, from wrath, and from crooked 'ways.

224. 'Or, thrice each day, and thrice each night 'for a month, the penitent may plunge into water 'clothed in his mantle, and at no time conversing with 'a woman, a *Súdra*, or an outcaste.

225. 'Let him be always in motion, sitting and 'rising alternately; or, if unable *to be thus restless*, let 'him sleep low *on the bare ground*; chaste as a student 'of the *Veda, bearing the sacred zone and staff*, showing 'reverence to his preceptor, to the gods, and to priests;

226. 'Perpetually must he repeat the *gáyatrí*, and 'other pure texts to the best of his knowledge: thus 'in all penances for absolution from sin, must he 'vigilantly employ himself.

227. 'By these expiations are twice-born men ab'solved whose offences are publicly known, *and are 'mischievous by their example*; but for sins not public, 'the assembly of priests must award them penances, 'with holy texts and oblations to fire.

228. 'By open confession, by repentance, by devo-

'tion, and by reading the scripture, a sinner may be released from his guilt; or by alms-giving, in case of his inability *to perform the other acts of religion.*

229. 'In proportion as a man, who has committed a sin, shall truly and voluntarily confess it, so far he is disengaged from that offence, like a snake from his slough;

230. 'And, in proportion as his heart sincerely loathes his evil deed, so far shall his vital spirit be freed from the taint of it.

231. 'If he commit sin, and actually repent, that sin shall be removed from him; but if he merely say, "I will sin thus no more," he can only be released by an actual abstinence from guilt.

232. 'Thus revolving in his mind the certainty of retribution in a future state, let him be constantly good in thoughts, words, and action.

233. 'If he desire complete remission of any foul act which he has committed, either ignorantly or knowingly, let him beware of committing it again; *for the second fault his penance must be doubled.*

234. 'If, having performed any expiation, he feel not a perfect satisfaction of conscience, let him repeat the same devout act, until his conscience be perfectly satisfied.

235. 'All the bliss of deities and of men is declared by sages, who discern the sense of the *Veda*, to have in devotion its cause, in devotion its continuance, in devotion its fulness.

236. 'Devotion is *equal to the performance of all duties; it is* divine knowledge in a *Bráhman*; it is defence of the people in a *Kshatriya*; devotion is *the* business *of trade and agriculture* in a *Vaisya*; devotion is dutiful service in a *Súdra*.

237. 'Holy sages, with subdued passions, feeding 'only on fruit, roots, and air, by devotion alone are 'enabled to survey the three worlds, *terrestrial, ethereal, 'and celestial*, peopled with animal creatures, locomo- 'tive and fixed.

238. 'Perfect health, or unfailing medicines, divine 'learning, and the various mansions of deities, are 'acquired by devotion alone: their efficient cause is 'devotion.

239. 'Whatever is hard to be traversed, whatever 'is hard to be visited, whatever is hard to be performed, 'all this may be accomplished by true devotion; for 'the difficulty of devotion is the greatest of all.

240. 'Even sinners in the highest degree, and of 'course the other offenders, are absolved from guilt 'by austere devotion well practised.

241. '*Souls, that animate* worms, and insects, ser- 'pents, moths, beasts, birds, and vegetables, attain 'heaven by the power of devotion.

242. 'Whatever sin has been conceived in the hearts 'of men, uttered in their speech, or committed in 'their bodily acts, they speedily burn it all away 'by devotion, if they preserve devotion as their best 'wealth.

243. 'Of a priest, whom devotion has purified the 'divine spirits accept the sacrifices, and grant the 'desires with ample increase.

244. 'Even BRAHMA', lord of creatures, by devotion 'enacted this code of laws; and the sages by devotion 'acquired a knowledge of the *Veda*.

245. 'Thus the gods themselves, observing in this 'universe the incomparable power of devotion, have

'proclaimed aloud the transcendent excellence of pious 'austerity,

246. 'By reading each day as much as possible of 'the *Veda*, by performing the *five* great sacraments, 'and by forgiving all injuries, even sins of the highest 'degree shall be soon effaced:

247. 'As fire consumes in an instant with his 'bright flame the wood, that has been placed on it, 'thus, with the flame of knowledge, a *Bráhman*, who 'understands the *Veda*, consumes all sin.

248. 'Thus has been declared, according to law, the 'mode of atoning for open sins: now learn the mode 'of obtaining absolution for secret offences.

249. 'SIXTEEN suppressions of the breath, *while the 'holiest of texts is repeated* with the three mighty words, 'and the triliteral syllable, continued each day for a 'month, absolve even the slayer of a *Bráhman* from 'his hidden faults.

250. 'Even a drinker of spirituous liquors is ab-'solved by repeating each day the text *apa* used by 'the sage KAUTSA, or that beginning with *preti* used 'by VASISHTHA, or that called *máhitra*, or that, of 'which the first word is *suddhavatyah*.

251. 'By repeating *each day for a month* the text '*ásyavámiya*, or the hymn *Sivasankalpa*, the stealer of 'gold *from a priest* becomes instantly pure.

252. 'He who has violated the bed of his preceptor, 'is cleared *from secret faults* by repeating *sixteen times 'a day* the text *havishyantíya*, or that beginning with '*na tamanhah*, or by revolving in his mind the *sixteen* 'holy verses, called *Paurusha*.

253. 'The man, who desires to expiate *his hidden*

'sins great and small, must repeat *once a day* for a year 'the text *ava,* or the text *yatcinchida.*

254. 'He, who has accepted an illegal present, or 'eaten prohibited food, may be cleansed in three days 'by repeating the text *taratsamandíya.*

255. 'Though he have committed many secret sins, 'he shall be purified by repeating for a month the text '*sómáraudra,* or the three texts *áryamna,* while he 'bathes in a sacred stream.

256. 'A grievous offender must repeat the seven 'verses, beginning with INDRA, for half a year; and he, 'who has defiled water with any impurity, must sit a 'whole year subsisting by alms.

257. 'A twice-born man, who shall offer clarified 'butter for a year, with *eight* texts appropriated to *eight* 'several oblations, or with the texts *na me,* shall efface 'a sin even of an extremely high degree.

258. 'He, who had committed a crime of the first 'degree, shall be absolved, if he attend a herd of kine 'for a year, mortify his organs, and continually repeat 'the texts beginning with *pávamání,* living solely on 'food given in charity.

259. 'Or, if he thrice repeat a *Sanhitá* of the *Vedas,* or '*a large portion of them with all the* mantras *and* bráhme-'nas, dwelling in a forest with subdued organs, and 'purified by three *parákas,* he shall be set free from 'all sins how heinous soever.

260. 'Or he shall be released from all deadly sins, if 'he fast three days, with his members mortified, and 'twice a day plunge into water, thrice repeating the 'text *aghamarshana*:

261. 'As the sacrifice of a horse, the king of sa-

'crifices, removes all sin, thus the text *aghamarshana* 'destroys all offences.

262. 'A priest, who should retain in his memory the 'whole *Rigveda*, would be absolved from guilt, even if 'he had slain the inhabitants of the three worlds, and 'had eaten food from the foulest hands.

263. 'By thrice repeating the *mantras* and *bráhmanas* 'of the *Rig*, or those of the *Yajur*, or those of the '*Sáman*, with the *upanishads*, he shall perfectly be 'cleansed from every possible taint:

264. 'As a clod of earth, cast into a great lake, sinks 'in it, thus is every sinful act submerged in the triple '*Veda*.

265. 'The divisions of the *Rig*, the several branches 'of the *Yajur*, and the manifold strains of the *Sáman* 'must be considered as forming the triple *Veda*: he 'knows the *Veda*, who knows them collectively.

266. 'The primary triliteral syllable, in which the 'three *Vedás* themselves are comprised, must be kept 'secret, as another triple *Veda*: he knows the *Veda*, 'who *distinctly* knows *the mystic sense of* that word.'

CHAPTER XII.

On Transmigration and Final Beatitude.

---

1. 'O thou, who art free from sin,' *said the devout sages*, 'thou hast declared the whole system of duties 'ordained for the four classes of men: explain to us 'now, from the first principles, the ultimate retribution 'for their deeds.'

2. Bhrigu, whose heart was the pure essence of 'virtue, who proceeded from MANU himself, thus addressed the great sages: 'Hear the infallible rules for '*the fruit of* deeds in this universe.

3. 'Action, either mental, verbal, or corporeal, bears 'good or evil fruit, *as itself is good or evil*; and from 'the actions of men proceed their various transmigrations in the highest, the mean, and the lowest degree:

4. 'Of that three-fold action, connected with bodily 'functions, disposed in three classes, and consisting of 'ten orders, be it known in this world, that the heart 'is the instigator.

5. 'Devising means to appropriate the wealth of 'other men, resolving on any forbidden deed, and conceiving notions of atheism or materialism, are the 'three bad acts of mind:

6. 'Scurrilous language, falsehood, indiscriminate 'backbiting, and useless tattle, are the four bad acts of 'the tongue:

7. 'Taking effects not given, hurting sentient creatures without the sanction of law, and criminal intercourse with the wife of another, are the three bad 'acts of the body; *and all the ten have their opposites, 'which are good in an equal degree.*

8. 'A rational creature has a reward or a punishment for mental acts, in his mind; for verbal acts, in 'his organs of speech; for corporeal acts, in his bodily 'frame.

9. 'For sinful acts *mostly* corporeal, a man shall 'assume *after death* a vegetable or mineral form; for 'such acts *mostly* verbal, the form of a bird or a beast; 'for acts *mostly* mental, the lowest of human conditions:

10. 'He, whose firm understanding obtains a command over his words, a command over his thoughts, 'and a command over his whole body, may justly be 'called a *tridandi*, or *triple commander: not a mere 'anchoret, who bears three visible staves.*

11. 'The man, who exerts this triple self-command 'with respect to all animated creatures, wholly subduing both lust and wrath, shall by those means attain 'beatitude.

12. 'That substance, which gives a power of motion 'to the body, the wise call *Kshetrajnya*, or *jívátman*, 'the vital spirit; and that body, which thence derives 'active functions, they name *bhútátman*, or *composed of 'elements:*

13. 'Another internal spirit, *called* mahat, or *the 'great soul*, attends the birth of all creatures imbodied, 'and thence in all mortal forms is conveyed a perception 'either pleasing or painful.

14. 'Those two, the vital spirit and reasonable soul, 'are closely united with *five* elements, but connected 'with the supreme spirit, or divine essence, which 'pervades all beings high and low:

15. 'From the substance of that *supreme spirit* are 'diffused, *like sparks from fire*, innumerable vital spirits, which perpetually give motion to creatures exalted and base.

16. 'By the vital souls of those men, who have committed sins *in the body reduced to ashes*, another body, 'composed of *nerves with* five sensations, in order to be 'susceptible of torment, shall certainly be assumed 'after death;

17. 'And, being intimately united with those minute 'nervous particles, according to their distribution, they

'shall feel, in that new body, the pangs inflicted in 'each case by the sentence of YAMA.

18. 'When the vital soul has gathered the fruit of 'sins, which arise from a love of sensual pleasure, 'but must produce misery, and, when its taint has 'thus been removed, it approaches again those two 'most effulgent essences, *the intellectual soul and the 'divine spirit:*

19 'They two, closely conjoined, examine without 'remission the virtues and vices of that sensitive soul, 'according to its union with which it acquires plea-'sure or pain in the present and future worlds.

20. 'If the vital spirit had practised virtue for the 'most part, and vice in a small degree, it enjoys delight 'in celestial abodes, clothed with a body formed of 'pure elementary particles;

21. 'But, if it had generally been addicted to vice, 'and seldom attended to virtue, then shall it be de-'serted by those pure elements, and, *having a coarser 'body of sensible nerves*, it feels the pains to which 'YAMA shall doom it:

22. 'Having endured those torments according to 'the sentence of YAMA, and its taint being almost 'removed, it again reaches those five pure elements in 'the order of their natural distribution.

23. 'Let each man, considering with his intellectual 'powers these migrations of the soul according to its 'virtue or vice, *into a region of bliss or pain*, continually 'fix his heart on virtue.

24. 'Be it known, that the three qualities of the 'rational soul are a tendency to goodness, to passion, 'and to darkness; and, endued with one or more of 'them, it remains incessantly attached to all these 'created substances:

25. 'When any one of the *three* qualities predominates in a mortal frame, it renders the imbodied spirit 'eminently distinguished for that quality.

26. 'Goodness is declared to be true knowledge; 'darkness, gross ignorance; passion, an emotion of 'desire or aversion: such is the compendious description of those qualities, which attend all souls.

27. 'When a man perceives in the reasonable soul 'a disposition tending to virtuous love, unclouded with 'any malignant passion, clear as the purest light, let 'him recognise it as the quality of goodness:

28. 'A temper of mind, which gives uneasiness and 'produces disaffection, let him consider as the adverse quality of passion, ever agitating imbodied spirits:

29. 'That indistinct, inconceivable, unaccountable 'disposition of a mind naturally sensual, and clouded 'with infatuation, let him know to be the quality of 'darkness.

30. 'Now will I declare at large the various acts, in 'the highest, middle, and lowest degrees, which proceed 'from those three dispositions of mind.

31. 'Study of scripture, austere devotion, sacred 'knowledge, corporeal purity, command over the organs, performances of duties, and meditation on the 'divine spirit, accompany the good quality of the soul:

32. 'Interested motives for acts *of religion or morality*, perturbation of mind *on slight occasions*, commission of acts forbidden by law, and habitual indulgence in selfish gratifications, are attendant on the 'quality of passion:

33. 'Covetousness, indolence, avarice, detraction, 'atheism, omission of prescribed acts, a habit of solicit-

'ing favours, and inattention to necessary business, be-'long to the dark quality.

34. 'Of those three qualities, as they appear in the 'three times, *past, present, and future,* the following in 'order *from the lowest* may be considered as a short *but* '*certain* criterion.

35. 'Let the wise consider, as belonging to the qua-'lity of darkness, every act, which a man is ashamed of 'having done, of doing, or of going to do:

36. 'Let them consider, as proceeding from the qua-'lity of passion, every act, by which a man seeks ex-'altation and celebrity in this world, though he may 'not be much afflicted, if he fail of attaining his 'object:

37. 'To the quality of goodness belongs every act, 'by which he hopes to acquire divine knowledge, which 'he is never ashamed of doing, and which brings placid 'joy to his conscience.

38. 'Of the dark quality, as described, the principal 'object is pleasure; of the passionate, worldly prosperi-'ty; but of the good quality, the chief object is virtue: 'the last mentioned *objects* are superior in dignity.

39. 'Such transmigrations, as the soul procures in 'this universe by each of those qualities, I now will de-'clare in order succinctly.

40. 'Souls, endued with goodness, attain always the 'state of deities; those filled with ambitious passions, 'the condition of men; and those immersed in dark-'ness, the nature of beasts: this is the triple order of 'transmigration.

41. 'Each of those three transmigrations, caused by 'the several qualities, must also be considered as 'three-fold, the lowest, the mean, and the highest,

'according to as many distinctions of acts and of know-'ledge.

42. 'Vegetable and mineral substances, worms, in-'sects, and reptiles, *some very minute, some rather 'larger,* fish, snakes, tortoises, cattle, shakals, are the 'lowest forms, to which the dark quality leads :

43. 'Elephants, horses, men of the servile class, and 'contemptible *Mlech'has,* or *barbarians,* lions, tigers, 'and boars, are the mean states procured by the quali-'ty of darkness :

44. 'Dancers and singers, birds, and deceitful men, 'giants and blood-thirsty savages, are the highest con-'ditions, to which the dark quality can ascend.

45. '*J'hallas,* or cudgel-players, *Mallas,* or boxers 'and wrestlers, *Natas,* or actors, those who teach the 'use of weapons, and those who are addicted to gaming 'or drinking, are the lowest forms occasioned by the 'passionate quality :

46. 'Kings, men of the fighting class, domestic 'priests of kings, and men skilled in the war of con-'troversy, are the middle states caused by the quality 'of passion :

47. '*Gandharvas,* or aerial musicians, *Guhyakas* and '*Yakshas,* or servants and companions of KUVERA, 'genii attending superior gods, as the *Vidyádharas* 'and others, together with various companies of *Apsa-'rases* or nymphs, are the highest of those forms, which 'the quality of passion attains.

48. 'Hermits, religious mendicants, other *Bráhmans,* 'such orders of demi gods as are wafted in airy cars, 'genii of the signs and lunar mansions, and *Daityas,* '*or the offspring of* Diti, are the lowest of states procur-'ed by the quality of goodness :

49. 'Sacrificers, holy sages, deities of the lower 'heaven, genii of the *Vedas*, regents of stars *not in the paths of the sun and moon*, divinities of years, *Pitris* 'or progenitors of mankind, and the demigods named '*Sádhyas*, are the middle forms, to which the good 'quality conveys *all spirits moderately endued with it:*

50. 'Brahma' with four faces, creators of worlds '*under him, as* Mari'chi *and others,* the genius of 'virtue, the divinities presiding over *(two principles of nature in the philosophy of* Kapila) *mahat*, or the '*mighty*, and *avyakta*, or *unperceived*, are the highest 'conditions, to which, by the good quality, souls are 'exalted.

51. 'This triple system of transmigrations, in which 'each class has three orders, according to actions of 'three kinds, and which comprises all animated beings, 'has been revealed in its full extent:

52. 'Thus, by indulging the sensual appetites, and 'by neglecting the performance of duties, the basest of 'men, ignorant of sacred expiations, assume the basest 'forms.

53. 'What particular bodies the vital spirit enters 'in this world, and in consequence of what sins here 'committed, now hear at large and in order.

54. 'Sinners in the first degree, having passed 'through terrible regions of torture for a great num'ber of years, are condemned to the following births 'at the close of that period, *to efface all remains of their sin.*

55. 'The slayer of a *Bráhman* must enter *accord'ing to the circumstances of his crime* the body of 'a dog, a boar, an ass, a camel, a bull, a goat, a sheep, 'a stag, a bird, a *Chandála*, or a *Pukkasa*.

56. 'A priest, who has drunk spirituous liquor, shall

'migrate into the form of a smaller or larger worm or 'insect, of a moth, of a fly feeding on ordure, or of 'some ravenous animal.

57. 'He, who steals *the* gold *of a priest*, shall pass 'a thousand times into the bodies of spiders, of snakes 'and cameleons, of *crocodiles and other* aquatic mon- 'sters, or of mischievous blood-sucking demons.

58. 'He, who violates the bed of his *natural or* '*spiritual* father, migrates a hundred times into the 'forms of grasses, of shrubs with crowded stems, or of 'creeping and twining plants, of *vultures and other* 'carnivorous animals, of *lions and other* beasts with 'sharp teeth, or of *tigers and other* cruel brutes.

59. 'They, who hurt any sentient beings, are born '*cats and other* eaters of raw flesh; they who taste 'what ought not to be tasted, maggots or small flies; 'they, who steal *ordinary things*, devourers of each 'other: they, who embrace very low women, become 'restless ghosts.

60. 'He, who has held intercourse with degraded 'men, or been criminally connected with the wife of 'another, or stolen *common things* from a priest, shall 'be changed into a spirit called *Bráhmarákshasa*.

61. 'The wretch, who through covetousness has 'stolen *rubies or other* gems, pearls, or coral, or pre- 'cious things of which there are many sorts, shall be 'born *in the tribe of goldsmiths, or* among *birds called* 'hemakáras, *or gold-makers*.

62. 'If a man steal grain in the husk, he shall be 'born a rat; if a yellow mixed metal, a gander; if 'water, a *plava*, or diver; if honey, a great stinging 'gnat; if milk, a crow; if expressed juice, a dog; if 'clarified butter, an ichneumon-weasel;

63. 'If he steal flesh-meat, a vulture; if any sort of

'fat, the water-bird *madgu*; if oil, a blatta, or oil-'drinking beetle; if salt, a kikaṭa or cricket; if curds, 'the bird *valáka*;

64. 'If silken clothes, the bird *tittiri*; if woven 'flax, a frog; if cotton cloth, the water-bird *crauncha*; 'if a cow, the lizard *gódhá*; if molasses, the bird '*vágguda*;

65. 'If exquisite perfumes, a musk-rat; if potherbs, 'a peacock; if dressed grain in any of its various forms, 'a porcupine; if raw grain, a hedge-hog;

66. 'If he steal fire, the bird *vaka*; if a household 'utensil, an ichneumon-fly; if dyed cloth, the bird '*chakóra*;

67. 'If a deer or an elephant, he shall be born a 'wolf; if a horse, a tiger; if roots or fruit, an 'ape; if a woman, a bear; if water *from a jar*, the 'bird *chátaka*; if carriages, a camel; if small cattle, a 'goat.

68. 'That man, who designedly takes away the pro-'perty of another, or eats any holy cakes not first 'presented *to the deity* at a solemn rite, shall inevitably 'sink to the condition of a brute.

69. 'Women, who have committed similar thefts, 'incur a similar taint, and shall be paired with those 'male beasts in the form of their females.

70. 'If any of the four classes omit, without urgent 'necessity, the performance of their several duties, they 'shall migrate into sinful bodies, and become slaves 'to their foes.

71. 'Should a *Bráhman* omit his peculiar duty, he 'shall be changed into a demon called *Ulcámuc'ha* or '*with a mouth like a firebrand*, who devours what has

'been vomited; a *Kshatriya,* into a demon called '*Katapútana, who feeds on ordure and carrion.*

72. 'A *Vaisya,* into an evil being called *Maitráksha*-'*jyótika,* who eats purulent carcasses; and a *Súdra,* 'who neglects his occupations, becomes a foul imbodi-'ed spirit called *Chailásaka, who feeds on lice.*

73. 'As far as vital souls, addicted to sensuality, 'indulge themselves in forbidden pleasures, even to 'the same degree shall the acuteness of their senses 'be raised *in their future bodies, that they may endure* '*analogous pains;*

74. 'And, in consequence of their folly, they shall 'be doomed as often as they repeat their criminal acts, 'to pains more and more intense in despicable forms 'on this earth.

75. 'They shall first have a sensation of agony in '*Támisra* or *utter darkness,* and in other seats of 'horror; in *Asipatravana,* or *the sword-leaved forest,* 'and in different places of binding fast and of rend-'ing:

76. 'Multifarious tortures await them: they shall be 'mangled by ravens and owls, shall swallow cakes 'boiling hot; shall walk over inflamed sands; and 'shall feel the pangs of being baked like the vessels of 'a potter:

77. 'They shall assume the forms of beasts con-'tinually miserable, and suffer alternate afflictions from 'extremities of cold and of heat, surrounded with 'terrors of various kinds:

78. 'More than once shall they lie in different 'wombs; and, after agonizing births, be condemned 'to severe captivity, and to servile attendance on 'creatures like themselves:

79. 'Then shall follow separations from kindred and 'friends, forced residence with the wicked, painful 'gains and ruinous losses of wealth ; friendships hardly 'acquired and at length changed into enmities,

80. 'Old age without resource, diseases attended 'with anguish, pangs of innumerable sorts, and, lastly, 'unconquerable death.

81. 'With whatever disposition of mind a man shall 'perform in this life any act *religious or moral,* in a 'future body endued with the same quality, shall he 'receive his retribution.

82. 'Thus has been revealed to you the system of 'punishments for evil deeds : next learn those acts of 'a *Bráhman,* which lead to eternal bliss.

83. 'Studying and comprehending the *Veda,* practis-'ing pious austerities, acquiring divine knowledge *of* '*law and philosophy,* command over the organs of sense 'and action, avoiding all injury to sentient creatures, 'and showing reverence to a *natural and spiritual* 'father, are the chief branches of duty which ensure 'final happiness.'

84. 'Among all those good acts performed in this 'world, *said the sages,* is no single act held more power-'ful than the rest in leading men to beatitude ?'

85. 'Of all those duties, *answered* BHRIGU, the 'principal is to acquire from the *Upanishads* a true 'knowledge of one supreme GOD ; that is the most 'exalted of all sciences, because it ensures immor-'tality :

86. 'In this life, indeed, as well as the next, the 'study of the *Veda, to acquire a knowledge of GOD,* 'is held the most efficacious of those six duties in 'procuring felicity to man ;

87. 'For in the knowledge *and adoration of one* 'GOD, which the *Veda* teaches, all the rules of good 'conduct, *before-mentioned* in order, are fully com-'prised.

88. 'The ceremonial duty, prescribed by the *Veda*, 'is of two kinds; *one* connected with this world, and 'causing prosperity on earth; *the other* abstracted from 'it, and procuring bliss in heaven.

89. 'A religious act, proceeding from selfish views 'in this world, *as a sacrifice for rain*, or in the next, *as* '*a pious oblation in hope of a future reward*, is declared 'to be concrete and interested; but an act performed 'with a knowledge of GOD, and without self-love, is 'called abstract and disinterested.

90. 'He, who *frequently* performs interested rites, 'attains an equal station with the regents of the lower 'heaven; but he, who *frequently* performs disinterested 'acts of religion, becomes for ever exempt from *a body* '*composed of* the five elements:

91. 'Equally perceiving the supreme soul in all be-'ings and all beings in the supreme soul, he sacrifices 'his own spirit *by fixing it on the spirit of GOD*, and 'approaches the nature of that sole divinity *who shines* '*by his own effulgence*.

92. 'Thus must the chief of the twice-born, though 'he neglect the ceremonial rites mentioned in the '*Sástras*, be diligent alike in attaining a knowledge of 'GOD and in repeating the *Veda*:

93. 'Such is the advantageous privilege of those, 'who have a double birth *from their natural mothers* '*and from the* gáyatrì *their spiritual mother*, especially 'of a *Bráhman*; since the twice-born man, by perform-'ing this duty but not otherwise, may soon acquire 'endless felicity.

94. 'To patriarchs, to deities, and to mankind, the 'scripture is an eye giving constant light; nor could 'the *Veda-Sástra* have been made by human faculties; 'nor can it be measured by human reason *unassisted* '*by revealed glosses and comments:* this is a sure 'proposition.

95. 'Such codes of law as are not grounded on the '*Veda*, and the various heterodox theories of men, 'produce no good fruit after death; for they all are de-'clared to have their basis on darkness.

96. 'All systems, which are repugnant to the *Veda*, 'must have been composed by mortals, and shall soon 'perish: their modern date proves them vain and false.

97. 'The three worlds, the four classes of men, and 'their four distinct orders, with all that has been, 'all that is, and all that will be, are made known by 'the *Veda:*

98. 'The nature of sound, of *tangible and visible* 'shape, of taste, and of odour, the fifth *object of* '*sense,* is clearly explained in the *Veda* alone, together 'with the three qualities of mind, the births attended 'with them, and the acts which they occasion.

99. 'All creatures are sustained by the primeval '*Veda-Sástra*, which the wise therefore hold supreme, 'because it is the supreme source of prosperity to this 'creature, man.

100. 'Command of armies, royal authority, power 'of inflicting punishment, and sovereign dominion over 'all nations, he only well deserves, who perfectly un-'derstands the *Veda-Sástra*.

101. 'As fire with augmented force burns up even 'humid trees, thus he, who well knows the *Veda*, burns 'out the taint of sin, which has infected his soul.

102. 'He, who completely knows the sense of the '*Veda-Sástra,* while he remains in any one of the four 'orders, approaches the divine nature, even though he 'sojourn in this low world.

103. 'They who have read many books, are more 'exalted than such as have seldom studied; they who 'retain what they have read, than forgetful readers; 'they who fully understand, than such as only remem-'ber; and they who perform their known duty, than 'such men as barely know it.

104. 'Devotion and sacred knowledge are the best 'means by which a *Bráhman* can arrive at beatitude; 'by devotion he may destroy guilt; by sacred know-'ledge he may acquire immortal glory.

105. 'Three modes of proof, ocular demonstration, 'logical inference, and the authority of those various 'books, which are deduced from the *Veda,* must be well 'understood by that man, who seeks a distinct know-'ledge of all his duties.

106. 'He alone comprehends the system of duties, 'religious and civil, who can reason, by rules of logic 'agreeable to the *Veda,* on the general heads of that 'system as revealed by the holy sages.

107. 'These rules of conduct, which lead to supreme 'bliss, have been exactly and comprehensively declar-'ed: the more secret learning of this *Mánava Ṣástra* 'shall now be disclosed.

108. 'If it be asked, how the law shall be ascertain-'ed, when particular cases are not comprised *under any 'of the general rules, the answer is this:* "That, which 'well-instructed *Bráhmans* propound, shall be held in-'contestible law."

109. 'Well instructed *Bráhmans* are they, who can 'adduce ocular proof from the scripture itself, having

'studied, as the law ordains, the *Vedas* and their extended branches, or *Védángas, Mimánsá, Nyáya, Dharma-ṣástra, Puránas:*

110. 'A point of law, *before not expressly revealed,* 'which shall be decided by an assembly of ten such 'virtuous *Bráhmans* under one chief, or, *if ten be not 'procurable,* of three such under one president, let no 'man controvert.

111. 'The assembly of ten under a chief, *either the 'king himself or a judge appointed by him,* must 'consist of three, each of them peculiarly conversant 'with one of the three *Vedas, of a fourth skilled 'in the Nyáya, and a fifth in the Mimánsá philosophy;* of a sixth, who has particularly studied the '*Nirukta;* a seventh, who has applied himself most 'assiduously to the *Dharma-sástra;* and of three *universal scholars,* who are in the three first orders.

112. 'One, who has chiefly studied the *Rig Veda,* a 'second, who principally knows the *Yajush,* and a third 'best acquainted with the *Sáman,* are the assembly of 'three under a head, who may remove all doubts both 'in law and casuistry.

113. 'Even the decision of one priest, *if more cannot be assembled,* who perfectly knows the principles 'of the *Vedas,* must be considered as law of the highest 'authority; not the opinion of myriads, who have no 'sacred knowledge.

114. 'Many thousands of *Bráhmans* cannot form a 'legal assembly for the decision of contests, if they 'have not performed the duties of a regular studentship, are unacquainted with scriptural texts, and subsist only by *the name of* their sacerdotal class.

115. 'The sin of that man, to whom dunces, pervaded by the quality of darkness, propound the law, 'of which they are themselves ignorant, shall pass,

'increased a hundred-fold, to the wretches who pro'pound it.

116. 'This comprehensive system of duties, the chief 'cause of ultimate felicity, has been declared to you; 'and the *Bráhman*, who never departs from it, shall 'attain a superior state above.

117. 'Thus did the all-wise MANU, who possesses 'extensive dominion, and blazes with heavenly splen'dour, disclose to me, from his benevolence to man'kind, this transcendent system of law, which must 'be kept devoutly concealed *from persons unfit to* '*receive it.*

118. 'Let every *Bráhman* with fixed attention con'sider all nature, both visible and invisible, as existing 'in the divine spirit; for, when he contemplates the 'boundless universe existing in the divine spirit, he 'cannot give his heart to iniquity:

119. 'The divine spirit alone is the whole assem'blage of gods; all worlds are seated in the divine 'spirit; and the divine spirit no doubt produces, *by a* '*chain of causes and effects consistent with freewill*, 'the connected series of acts performed by imbodied 'souls.

120. 'He may contemplate the subtile ether in the 'cavities of his body; the air in his muscular motion 'and sensitive nerves; the supreme *solar and igneous* 'light, in his digestive heat and his visual organs; in 'his corporeal fluids, water; in the terrene parts of his 'fabric, earth;

121. 'In his heart, the moon; in his auditory 'nerves, the guardians of eight regions; in his pro'gressive motion, VISHNU; in his muscular force, 'HARA; in his organs of speech, AGNI; in excretion, 'MITRA; in procreation, BRAHMÁ':

122. 'But he must consider the supreme omnipresent intelligence as the sovereign lord of them all, *by whose energy alone they exist*; a spirit, *by no means the object of any sense*, which can only be conceived by a mind *wholly abstracted from matter, and as it were* slumbering; but which, *for the purpose of assisting his meditation*, he may imagine more subtile than the finest conceivable essence, and more bright than the purest gold.

123. 'Him some adore as transcendently present in elementary fire; others, in MANU, lord of creatures, *or an immediate agent in the creation*; some, as more distinctly present in INDRA, *regent of the clouds and the atmosphere*; others, in pure air; others, as the most High Eternal Spirit.

124. 'It is He, who, pervading all beings in five elemental forms, causes them by the gradations of birth, growth, and dissolution, to revolve in this world, *until they deserve beatitude*, like the wheels of a car.

125. 'Thus the man, who perceives in his own soul the supreme soul present in all creatures, acquires equanimity toward them all, and shall be absorbed at last in the highest essence, even that of the Almighty himself.'

126. Here ended the sacred instructor; and every twice-born man, who, attentively reading this *Mánava Śástra*, promulgated by BHRIGU, shall become habitually virtuous, will attain the beatitude which he seeks.

GENERAL NOTE.

The learned *Hindus* are unanimously of opinion, that many laws enacted by MANU, their oldest reputed legislator, were confined to the three first ages of the world, and have no force in the present age, in which a few of them are certainly obsolete; and they ground their opinion on the following texts, which are collected in a work entitled, *Madana-ratna-pradipa*.

I. KRATU: In the *Kali*-age a son must not be begotten *on a widow* by the brother *of the deceased husband;* nor must a damsel, *once* given away *in marriage*, be given a *second time;* nor must a bull be offered in a sacrifice; nor must a water-pot be carried *by a student in theology*.

II. VRIHASPATI: 1. Appointments *of kinsmen to beget children on widows, or married women, when the husbands are deceased or impotent,* are mentioned by the sage MANU, but forbidden by himself with a view to the order of the four ages: no such act can be legally done in this age by any others *than the husband.*

2. In the first and second ages men were endued with true piety and sound knowledge; so *they were* in the third age; but in the fourth, a diminution of their *moral and intellectual* powers was ordained *by their Creator:*

3. Thus were sons of many different sorts made by ancient sages, but such cannot now be adopted by men destitute of those eminent powers.

III. PARA'SARA: 1. A man, *who has held intercourse with a deadly sinner*, must abandon his country in the first age; he must leave his town, in the second; his family, in the third age; but in the fourth he needs only desert the offender.

2. In the first age, he is degraded by mere conversation with a degraded man; in the second, by touching him; in the third, by receiving food from him; but in the fourth, the sinner alone bears his guilt.

IV. NA'RADA: The procreation of a son by a brother *of the deceased,* the slaughter of cattle in the entertainment of a guest, the repast on flesh-meat at funeral obsequies, and the order of a hermit, *are forbidden or obsolete in the fourth age.*

V. *A'ditya purána:* 1. What was a duty in the first age, must not, *in all cases,* be done in the fourth; since, in the *Kali-yuga,* both men and women are addicted to sin:

2. Such are a studentship continued for a very long time, and the necessity of carrying a water-pot, marriage with a paternal kinswoman, or with a near maternal relation, and the sacrifice of a bull,

3. Or of a man, or of a horse: and all spirituous liquor, must, in the *Kali*-age, be avoided by twice-born men; so must a second gift of a married young woman, *whose husband has died before consummation,* and the larger portion of an eldest brother, and procreation on a brother's widow or wife.

VI. *Smrüti:* 1. The appointment of a man to beget a son on the widow of his brother; the gift of a young married woman to another bridegroom, *if her husband should die* while she remains a virgin;

2. The marriage of twice-born men with damsels not of the same class; the slaughter, in a religious war, of *Bráhmans,* who are assailants with intent to kill;

3. Any intercourse with a twice-born man, who has passed the sea in a ship, even though he have performed an expiation; performances of sacrifices for all sorts of men; and *the necessity of* carrying a water-pot;

4. Walking on a pilgrimage till the pilgrim die; and the slaughter of a bull at a sacrifice; the acceptance of spirituous liquor, even at the ceremony called *Sautrámani*;

5. Receiving what has been licked off, at an oblation to fire, from the pot of clarified butter; entrance into the third order, or that of a hermit, though ordained *for the first ages*;

6. The diminution of crimes in proportion to the religious acts and sacred knowledge *of the offenders*; the rule of expiation for a *Bráhman* extending to death;

7. The sin of holding any intercourse with sinners; the secret expiation of any great crimes except theft; the slaughter of cattle in honour of eminent guests or of ancestors;

8. The filiation of any but a son legally begotten or given in adoption *by his parents*; the desertion of a lawful wife for any offence less than actual adultery:

9. 'These *parts of ancient law* were abrogated by wise legislators, as the cases arose at the beginning of the *Kali*-age, with an intent of securing mankind from evil.

On the preceding texts it must be remarked, that none of them, except that of VRIHASPATI, are cited by KULLU'KA, who never seems to have considered any other laws of MANU as restrained to the three first ages; that of the *Smrĭti*, or sacred code, is quoted without the name of the legislator; and that the prohibition, in any age, of *self-defence*, even against *Bráhmans*, is repugnant to a text of SUMANTU, to the precept and example of KRISHNA himself, according to the *Mahábhárat*, and even to a sentence in the *Veda*, by which every man is commanded *to defend his own life from all* violent aggressors.

NOTES.

CHAP. I.

Verse 15. In Hindu metaphysics, 'the five perceptions of sense' imply the sight as referable to the eyes, the hearing to the ears, the scent to the nose, the taste to the tongue, and the touch to the skin. By 'the five organs of sensation' (sense?), are intended the hand, the foot, the voice, the organ of generation, and that of excretion. The commentator identifies what is mentioned here with what is said Chap. II. verses 90 and 91, but the difference in the denominations would lead to a doubt whether the same objects are intended in the two places; for in the latter verses the first class are termed 'organ of sense,' and the second 'organs of action.' Were it not for this interpretation of the passage, Chap. I. verse 15, by the Hindu commentators, I should be inclined to translate the hemistich thus: 'and the five organs of sense, and the five senses gradually.'

In the twelfth chapter and the fiftieth verse, Sir William Jones has mentioned the agreement of the system of theogony and cosmogony of MANU with that of KAPILA, the reputed founder of the S'ANK'HYA, or sceptical school of philosophy. The essay given by Mr. Colebrooke on this branch of Hindu metaphysics, in the first volume of the Transactions of the Royal Asiatic Society, is a real favour to all who take an interest in so important a link between ancient and modern opinions. The notices on the same subject, to be found at the end of Dr. Taylor's translation of the *Prabód'ha-chandródaya*, were too scanty to do more than excite a wish that some one competently versed in the philosophical opinions of Europe and Asia would undertake the task. While that given by the late Mr. Ward in his account of the Hindus, is evidently too hastily prepared to give any, but a general impression of the very curious and interesting documents of ancient Hindu civilization and refined speculation. Neglected as these matters have heretofore been, it must prove highly satisfactory to every Sanskrit scholar that the philosophy of the Hindus has found so able an expositor as Mr. Colebrooke. It is to be hoped, that he will complete what he has so well begun, by affording the world the means of judging of the other schools in which are contained the philosophical speculations of a portion of the human race so anciently civilized as the Hindus; and whose literature is impressed with characteristic features, that are ample pledges of its antiquity and originality.

CHAP. II.

Verse 25. The word 'universe,' has, by an error of the press, been printed in Italic instead of Roman letters, as it originally stood in Sir W. Jones's works. It may not be uninteresting to observe, that the word *sarva*, employed here to signify the universe, in its original and primary sense implies *all*, or *the whole*. Hence it is employed as an epithet of SIVA, as well as of VISHNU, by the worshippers of those Gods, agreeably to the Hindu doctrine, that contemplates the *universal whole* through any one of its multiform parts. In the account given in Enfield's History of Philosophy*, it will be seen that ZARVA was the chief of all the Gods among the Persians, and produced the good and evil principles, or HORMISDA and SATANA. I think, from the evident connexion between the religious systems of the Persians and the Hindus, the identity of the god ZARVA and the SARVA of India must be incontestible; and we are thus enabled to take a new and most accurate view of the real nature of the Magian religion. In it we find the same prevailing idea common in all the theogonies of the ancients, namely, the finite nature of their gods, and

* Vol I. p. 64.

their subordinate rank, as the personifications or the powers of the *boundless whole*, that is of *nature*. Moses Chorenensis speaks of the same mythological character under the name of ZEROVAN. Anquetil du Perron in his Zend Avesta,* likewise mentions ZERVAN, whom he considers as time personified ; but the sense of the word *Sarva* or *Sarvam* enables us at once to find a clue to the real nature of 'the chief of all the Gods.' Good and evil were, under this point of view, the inevitable results or offspring of material existence ; and the pantheism which saw *God in all*, by the language of personification, made *Sarva*, or *the whole*, the parent of the two principles, which were named HORMISDA and SATANA.

41. *Sana* is both hemp (Cannabis sativa), and Bengal *san*, a plant from which a kind of hemp is prepared, *viz*: crotolaria juncea, and other kinds.

Kshumà, is the linum usitatissimum.

42. *Munja* is a sort of grass (saccharum munja).

Múrvá is a sort of creeper, from the fibres of which bowstrings are made. (Sanseviera zeylanica).

43. *Kusa* is a species of grass used in many solemn and religious observances, hence called sacrificial grass (Poa cynosuroides).

The *Asmántaka* does not occur in the dictionaries.

The *Valvaja* is a sort of grass (saccharum cylindricum).

45. The *Vilva* is a fruit-tree, commonly named *Bél* (Ægle marmelos).

The *Palása* is the Butea frondosa.

The *Vata* is the Ficus Indica.

C'handira is a tree, the resin of which is used in medicine, *khayar* or catechu (Mimosa catechu).

The *Venu* is the bamboo, but the text says the *Pílu*, which is either the Careya arborea or the Salvadora Persica. It likewise implies the stem of the palm-tree.

* Tom. II. 90. *n.* 2.

The *Udumbara* is the glomerous fig-tree (Ficus glomerata).

87. The learned translator has, in conformity with the view of his commentator, varied in translating the sentence *maitra bráhmena uchyaté,* which occurs again in Chap. XI. v. 35.

99. 'As water flows through one hole of a bottle.' The original is more expressive, and alludes to the custom of carrying water in goat-skins in India. The skin is sewed together again, just as taken off the animal, and one of the feet is left open for the purpose of filling and emptying the skin, which is carried on a man's back; the foot for use being firmly grasped by the hand of the carrier, who thus distributes the water at his pleasure. Hence the passage would be more exactly rendered 'as water from one foot of a skin.'

113. The expression 'should rather die with his learning,' would be more exactly rendered 'should rather willingly die with his learning.'

142. Instead of 'father' the text reads 'brahman,' but the comment favours Sir W. Jones's translation; yet v. 144 inclines to the latter interpretation.

156. The word *viduh,* which the translator has rendered in the past, is most commonly employed in a present sense, which is required in this verse. See Mr. Wilkins' grammar, page 174, Rule 196.

CHAP. III.

Verse 24. In the original we have *kavayó viduh,* 'poets, *i. e.,* legislators consider' and not 'some consider.'

34. 'That sinful marriage' should have been 'that most sinful marriage.'

44. The word *pratóda* rather implies a goad used to compel oxen, than a whip.

It may be remarked, that there seems to be some difficulty in reconciling the allusion in this verse of a *Súdrá* marrying a priest, when we find the prohibition so strong in verses 13, 14, 15, and 16 of this chapter. The text clearly intends a marriage with a *Bráhman* by the expression *utkrishté vêde* 'in the highest marriages.'

76. I have been particular in marking the words of this verse in Italic letters, as the translation is very paraphrastical. Indeed the original verse, which will be found exactly in the Roman letters, conveys in the latter part the exact germ of the doctrine which has been so ably handled of late by an eminent writer, namely, the dependence of population upon sustenance.

123. The words 'of the *Pitris*,' should follow 'the monthly *ṣráddha*.'

133. 'Spears' should be included with 'iron balls' as among the number of things to be swallowed in the next world, by the giver of the *ṣráddha*.

158. It is not the mountain-rue, but the swallow-wort (the Asclepias acida).

261. The word *purastát*, which I find in the MSS. as well as in the Calcutta edition, implies 'before,' therefore we should read 'before the repast,' and not 'after the repast.'

270. Though the learned translator has rendered the word *sasa* by 'rabbits or hares,' yet I think there is a reasonable doubt whether the rabbit came within the contemplation of the law-giver, as such an interpretation is not given even by the commentator. As far as my experience goes, it is decidedly against the supposition that the rabbit is indigenous in India. The opinion of the natives is clear from their designating them '*wiláyatì khargósh*,' 'Foreign or English hares.' But I have the

authority of the two most eminent oriental scholars in this country for the same opinion, and one of them suggests, with great justice, that it may perhaps be found in the mountain districts to the north of India, though it be unknown to the inhabitants of the plains.

272. The potherb *kálasáka* is not found in the dictionaries. The *mahásalka* is the shrimp or prawn.

CHAP IV.

6. The meaning of '*satyánrita*,' is 'truth and falsehood,' by which commercial dealings are not unaptly designated; there being necessarily a mixture of both in such transactions.

47. The passage 'on the bank of a river,' would be more exact if rendered 'on reaching the bank of a river.'

49. I have ventured to alter the word 'potherb' into 'potsherd,' which I think must have been the word intended by the translator. The selection of potherbs, for the purpose noticed, carries with it something ridiculous, the sole intention of the injunction being to preserve the earth from contamination. The original passage is '*kásht'ha-lóshta-patra-trin'ádina*,' 'with wood, clods, leaves, grass, and the like.'

52. The words 'in water,' should be inserted, and then the passage will read 'in water or against a twice-born man.'

68. Here, as in v. 44 of Chap. III. the word *pratóda* should be rendered 'goad,' and not 'whip.'

69. 'The sun in the sign *kanyà*.' *Kanyà*, in its general sense, means a virgin, and here designates the sign VIRGO.

74. We should here read, 'let him not himself put off his sandals with his hand.'

82. The verb '*na candúyêt*' implies (as coming from the root *kandú*, 'itch') 'let him not scratch his head with both hands,' instead of 'let him not stroke.'

90. Among the list of places of future punishment here enumerated, I have in the Sanskrit text adopted, on the authority of other MSS. that of '*Lóhadárika*' or 'iron-pincers,' instead of '*Lóhángárika*' or 'the pit of red hot charcoal.' By 'iron-pincers' I suppose a place of torment where the damned are continually tortured by being torn with iron-pincers.

129. The word 'repeatedly' should be here added, and the passage will then stand 'nor repeatedly with many clothes.'

156. The passage 'such practice gives desirable offspring' has been omitted by the translator, and should immediately follow the first sentence.

168. The same idea that is found in this couplet, will be seen in Chap. XI. v. 208.

230. 'A giver of silver, exquisite beauty.' Beauty has been assigned as the reward for a gift of silver, apparently because it made a sort of pun; *rúpya* implying both silver and beautiful. Similar cases occur throughout the work, in which a play upon words has been allowed, when no solid reason could be assigned for any other allotment of rewards or punishments. In the twelfth chapter many such are to be observed.

243. This verse has not been translated with the same felicity and exactness which distinguish the rest: perhaps it might be rendered more in consonance with the general spirit of the version thus (See v. 167. Chap. II.):

"Yes, verily! Sovereign virtue instantly conducts the man whose sins have been expiated by penance, to the higher world, with a radiant and ethereal body."

CHAP. V.

6. The *sélu* is the cordia myxa.

11. The *tittibha* is the Parra jacana or goensis.

12. The *plava*, is both the diver and a sort of duck, (*Wilson*); and Mr. Wilkins considers it the same as the plover.

The *chakraváka* is the ruddy goose, familiarly known in India by the name of Brahmany duck or goose (Anas kasarka).

The *sárasa* is the Indian crane.

The *rajjuvála* is not found in the dictionaries.

The *dátyúha* which Sir William Jones has translated 'woodpecker,' is rendered 'a gallinule' by Mr. Colebrooke in the Amera Cósha, to which Mr. Wilson adds in his Dictionary, 'the *chátaka*, a sort of cuckoo.' The *chátaka* is specified by Mr. Colebrooke to be the cuculus melano-leucus.

It is worthy of remark, that the *sáriká*, which Sir William Jones renders female parrot, is actually a species of jay (gracula religiosa). By a similar connexion, the *sáriká* is fixed upon as a suitable mate for the parrot in the Bengálí 'Tales of a Parrot.' Are we here to suppose, for the purpose of reconciling this apparent inconsistency, that the word *sáriká* is familiarly applied to the female parrot, though unnoticed in such a sense by the dictionaries?

13. The *kóyashti* is the lapwing.

14. Sir William Jones has omitted to render the *baláka*, which should have been inserted between 'the heron, the raven,' and which Mr. Wilson renders 'a sort of crane.'

The word which Sir William Jones writes *c'hanjana*, as it is given in the comment, is spelt *c'hanjarítaka* in the text. Neither the one or the other is found in the dictionaries.

16. The *pát'hína* is the sheat-fish (Silurus pelorius. Buchannon MSS.).

The *róhita* is familiarly known as the róhi-fish (cyprinus denticulatus).

The *rájíva* is a largo fish (cyprinus niloticus. *Buchannon.*)

The *sinhatunda* (lion-faced) is not noticed in the dictionarics.

The *sasalká* is likewise unmentioned in the dictionaries; but KULL'UKA in his comment on the *Mahásalka*, Chap. III. v. 272, identifies these fish with one another: it is therefore the shrimp or prawn.

18. I am happy to be able to quote the words of an eminent orientalist, as explanatory of the proper import of the passage 'the lizard *gódhá*, the *gandaka*.' The first of which, namely, 'the *gódhá*, not being the lizard or iguana.'

"With deference I wish to correct the translation of a verse of MANU relating to this subject. In his interlineary version, Sir William Jones has translated *chadga* rhinoceros, which is the undoubted meaning of the word? I can assign no reason for his substituting the Sanskrit word *gandaka*, which is another name for the rhinoceros. In the same version, Sir William Jones translated *gódhá*, iguana; I am led to understand by that term the *gódhika*, or lacerta gangetica, named *góhí* and *gariál* in the vulgar dialects of Bengal; the iguana is in Sanskrit called *gaud'hera*, *gaud'heya*, *gaud'hara*, and *gód'hikátmaja*, which literally signifies offspring of the lacerta gangetica. May I add, that this species of alligator has been ill-described by Europen naturalists; and through a strange mistake, has been called the open-bellied crocodile." *A Digest of Hindu Law, translated by H. T. Colebrooke, Esq.* Vol. III. p. 345, *note.*

The interlineary version alluded to by Mr. Colebrooke, was made by Sir William Jones in his own copy of the original text. The reason why Sir William Jones substituted *gandaka* for the original word *chadga*, arose, probably, from that word being adopted by KULLU'KA in his comment upon the text: a practice repeatedly followed by Sir William Jones; as the commentator has generally given those terms which are most sanctioned by familiar usage. It must be likewise borne in mind, that at the period when the translation was made, many of the commonest objects of natural history had not been identified with their Sanskrit designations.

The '*rabbit* and hare:' see note on Chap. III. v. 270.

20. The nature of the penance *sántapana* may be seen in v. 213, Chap. XI.

An explanation of the *chandráyana* penance will be found in v. 217 and 218, Chap. XI.

21. The penance *prájápatya* is given in v. 212 of the eleventh chapter.

25. The term *chirastit'ham* 'stale,' which qualifies every article enumerated, has not been rendered by the translator.

63. The translator has followed the comment rather than the text, in translating the last hemistich of this verse, 'but after begetting a child on a *parapúrvá*, he must meditate three days on his impure state.' The text is more general, being 'after any seminal connexion, &c.' For, an explanation of *parapúrvá*, see v. 103 of this chapter.

66. The translator, in rendering the word *rajas* by 'blood,' has made the legislator adopt a vulgar prejudice to which he was superior. That word does not mean blood, but, according to the Hindus, the fructifying medium: they apply it equally to the pollen

of a flower, or the monthly secretion of a female ; both being indispensable to precede production, the one in all vegetable, and the other in the human and in some animal bodies. One of the terms by which this appearance is known in Sanskrit, *viz. pushpa* a flower, will strikingly support the idea of an ancient connexion between the popular opinions of the Gothic and Hindu nations.

71. Every manuscript I have been enabled to consult reads ' one,' and not ' three days of impurity.'

83. The evident order of progression would be sufficient to point out an error in the number five. The MSS. all say fifteen, agreeably to which the text has been restored, as there is no doubt the error is the effect of a mere oversight, perhaps of the printer. This is likewise the opinion of Mr. Colebrooke, *Hindu Digest*, Vol. II. p. 457.

134. The injunction does not apply to *vessels* contaminated, as here mentioned, but to *persons* after performing any of the natural wants. Indeed, the latter part of the injunction clearly shews that *personal* purity was the object of the notice.

CHAP. VI.

Verse 14. The *b'hústrina* is a fragant grass [andropogon schœnanthus].

The *sigruka* is a potherb not yet specified, and is not in the dictionaries. It is different from the *sigru*, a tree [morunga guilandina and hyperanthera].

The *sleshmátaka* appears to be the same mentioned by Mr. Wilson under the form *sleshmáta*, a small tree [cordia myxa].

67. The *kataka* is the clearing-nut plant [strychnos potatorum]. One of the seeds of the plant being rubbed on the inside of the water-jars used in Bengal, occasions

a precipitation of the earthy particles diffused through the water. *Wilson.*

77. Instead of 'the quality of darkness,' we should read 'the quality of passion,' as the original word is *rajaswalam*, 'possessing the quality of passion.'

CHAP. VII.

Verse 3. The learned translator seems to have understood the word *vidrute* as in the present tense of the middle voice, instead of being the prefect participle employed in the ablative absolute to agree with *lóke*, 'on [this] world.' Perhaps the following will be a more literal interpretation of the verse, which is curious, as shewing the ancient opinion of the Hindus as to the origin of sovereignty :

"Since this world, on being destitute of a king, quaked on all sides, therefore the Lord created a king, for the maintenance of this system [*locomotive and stationary*]."

111. The words 'ere long' should be read before 'deprived,' and the passage will then stand '[will] be ere long deprived both of his kingdom and life.'

118. Wherever wood is mentioned here, it is always for the purpose of fuel. The original word, *indhana*, means fuel : *i. e.*, wood, grass, &c. used for that purpose.

119. There appears to be an error here ; for the text states that the 'lord of twenty' is to have five *kula*, each *kula* consisting of two ploughed lands ; therefore, as the lord of ten villages is to enjoy the produce of two ploughed lands, the lord of twenty villages should have that of *ten* and not five ploughed lands.

126. Though the error of the legislator, in assigning a specific sum of money as a remuneration of service, is similar to what our own institutions afford many examples, yet it could not have been attended with so many disadvantages in India as with us, even had the specification been for other servants besides those of a king; firstly, because even for a long course of ages there seems to have been but little variation in the value of exchangeable produce; and secondly, because the wages were to be accompanied with a certain quantity of grain, apparently sufficient for the servant's maintenance.

One *pana* of copper is at present the equivalent of eighty *cowries*, and appears to be the original of the *fanam* now in current use at Madras. In Chap. VIII. v. 136, it is laid down that a *kárshápana* weighs eighty *raktikás*. The *raktiká* is the seed of the abrus precatorius, and weighs one grain five-sixteenths. The commentator considers the *kárshápana* and the *pana* as equal or equivalent to one another.

A *dróna* implies two different measures at the present day: its capacity is either one or four *ád'haka*. Now to determine which of these is meant we must be guided by the quantity. An *ád'haka* is a measure of grain, weighing seven pounds, eleven ounces avoirdupois. This would be clearly insufficient to sustain a man and his family during a month; and we must therefore suppose, if either of the present assignable quantities were those contemplated by the legislator, that it must be the larger one, containing thirty pounds, twelve ounces avoirdupois. As rice is mentioned in the text, it would support more persons than could be effected by any other grain; yet still it seems, if we have the right capacity of the *dróna*, but very poor pay to allow even the lowest servant of a king but little better than one pound of rice each day. I cannot help thinking, therefore, that the *dróna* must have been larger in ancient times than either of the two measures already specified. It is likewise to be remembered, that the *pana* which was to accompany it, would hardly have been sufficient to have purchased the necessary condiments that must be eaten with the rice, to make it either wholesome or nutritious.

Since writing the foregoing remarks, I find that Mr. Carey in his *Bengáli* Dictionary, states that the *ád'haka* varies in capacity, but is considered to be equal to two *mans* in the neighbourhood of Calcutta. The bazar *man* being equal to eighty pounds, the *dróna* would consequently contain six hundred and forty pounds, if it consisted of four such *ád'haka*; and would be equivalent to about twenty-one pounds of rice per diem. In the Indian Algebra, translated by Mr. Colebrooke (page 3), it is stated that a *c'hárí* of *Magad'ha*, contains a solid cubic foot, and that a *dróna* is the fourth part of a *c'hárí*. All that can be learnt from these clashing authorities, is the uncertainty of the real capacity of the *dróna* in ancient times.

195. By wood is meant fuel. See note on v. 118 of this chapter.

202. The words 'and his nobles' should have followed 'the new prince;' we must therefore read, 'and let him gratify the new prince and his nobles with gems, and other precious gifts.'

CHAP. VIII.

Verse 77. The words 'even' and 'pure' are omitted here; and the passage will accordingly read, 'and will have more weight than even many pure women.'

156. Considerable difficulty attends the interpretation of this verse. Sir William Jones renders *chakravrid-d'hi* 'safe carriage.' The word has been before used in these Institutes in the sense of compound interest, which is its usual import. Mr. Colebrooke, in his translation of the DIGEST, gives a gloss of CHANDESWARA as well as that of KULLU'KA: both are here subjoined.

"'Who has agreed on the place and time,' is thus expounded on the authority of CHANDESWARA: the debtor says, 'I will pay the debt at such a place, and at such a time;' and the creditor assents to that proposal. Such a creditor is a lender at wheel-interest (compound interest), having bargained for interest of that description. If he pass that place and time, if he do not go to that place at that time, the creditor shall not receive such interest, namely, wheel-interest: of course he must receive back the sum lent without interest. Hence, even should interest prescribed by the law be stipulated for a certain time and place, it shall not be received by the creditor if he do not attend at that place and time: for that small omission annuls legal interest.

But KULLU'KA BHATTA expounds the text otherwise: the term 'wheel' denotes the use of a wheel-carriage, or the like. A lender who has accepted that by way of interest, and has agreed on the place and time; for instance, *he has agreed*, that 'a journey to *Váránasi*, or the use of a carriage for the year, shall be the only interest:' in such a case, if the debtor fail in time and place, if he do not carry *goods* to *Váránasi*, or do not carry *goods* during the year, he shall receive the benefit, that is, the whole hire of the carriage: consequently, the whole interest is undischarged."* *Hindu Digest*, Vol. I. p. 361.

193. The word 'publicly' should be inserted in the last clause of this verse, and the passage will then read, 'be publicly punished by various degrees of *whipping or mutilation, or even by death*.

234. The word *róchaná*, which the translator interprets 'the liquor exuding from their foreheads may be equally rendered 'the concrete bile of the cow,' which is used as a yellow pigment.

246. Instead of the names which occur in the text,

* Note on the above by Mr. Colebrooke. "The translation (of the text) which I quote unaltered, varies from both comments."

the translator has substituted in some instances the more familiar Sanskrit terms by which they are generally known. Thus, for *nyagród'ha*, he has given *vata*: both imply the ficus Indica. And for *aswatt'ha*, he writes *pippala*: they are the same tree, *viz.* ficus religiosa. The *palása* is likewise substituted for the *cinsuka*, a tree bearing beautiful red blossoms, and hence often alluded to by the poets: they are both known as butea frondosa.

The *sálmali* is the silk-cotton tree (bambu heptaphyllium).

The *sála* is the shorea robusta.

By the *tála* is most probable meant the palmyra-tree, or fan-palm (borassus flabelliformis). It likewise implies a species of the mountain palm (corypha taliera).

Of the two names brought in from the comment as abounding in milk, the first or *udumbara* is the glomerous fig-tree (ficus glomerata), and the second or *vajradru* implies the various species of euphorbia.

247. By *vénu* are intended all the varieties of the bamboo.

Sami is the name for two plants; *viz:* the sami-tree or mimosa suma, and a shrub (serratula anthelmintica).

The *sara* is a sort of reed or grass (saccharum sara).

In Mr. Wilson's Dictionary the *kubjaka* is mentioned as an aquatic plant (trapa bispinosa), this is not therefore likely to be the one alluded to in this version and we may therefore suppose it is the same as the *kubja* (achyranthes aspera). The attributive affix *ka* being often subjoined at pleasure.

268. There is a mistake in the number 'five hundred,' which is out of all proportion when compared with the other fines: all the MSS. state 'fifty.' The mistake is easily accounted for, by remembering how very similar the word *panchasat* is to *panchásat*, there being but the difference of a long and short vowel between them.

289. The words 'flowers, roots, and fruits,' have

been omitted in the translation, and should have followed the words 'wood or clay.'

299. In opposition to the *dictum* of the lawgiver, I feel happy in borrowing a note of Mr. Colebrooke's on this very verse. "May I quote a maxim of no less authority? *Setáparádhair anitám pushpénápi ne tád'yét*; strike not, even with a blossom, a wife guilty of a hundred faults." *Hindu Digest*, Vol. II. p. 209.

359. Instead of 'a man of the servile class,' the text reads '(a man) not a brahman.' The translator has followed KULLU'KA's comment.

375—377. I think the employment of the word 'priestess, hardly admissible, as nothing more is intended by the word *bráhmani* than a female *brahman*, or the wife of a *bráhman*. By the word priestess I am led to understand a female constituted to direct or perform the offices of religion. By a reference to v. 18, Chap. IX. it will be seen that women can have nothing to do with the offices of religion. See likewise v. 155, Chap. V.

CHAP IX.

Verse 108. I am supported by Mr. Colebrook's authority in reading the first hemistich of this verse, 'As a father should support his sons, so let the first-born *support* his younger brothers,' &c. Mr. Colebrooke thinks that Sir William Jones must have read *pitaiva* instead of *pitéva*.

242. The translator has followed the commentator, in reading 'shall be corporally or even capitally punished, *according to circumstances*.' The original simply decrees banishment as the punishment of the crime specified in the preceding verses.

CHAP. XI.

Verse 25. The *bhása* is explained to be a vulture, and not a kite, by Mr. Wilson.

49. The colour *syáva* has been before rendered 'black-yellow' by the translator in v. 153, Chap. III.: here he simply translates it 'black.' It is a matter of little or no consequence, but the colour is generally interpreted brown. In MANU it is only employed to describe the teeth.

90. Instead of 'this is no expiation,' the original reads 'no expiation is decreed,' &c.

136. It has just been remarked in the note on v. 25, that *bhása* is rendered vulture by Mr. Wilson.

Instead of 'if priests have accepted any property from base hands,' we should read 'if priests have acquired any property by infamous actions.'

260. The MSS. state that the sinner should plunge 'thrice a day,' and not 'twice a day,' as perhaps was in Sir William Jones's copy, which he seems to have followed.

CHAP. XII.

The variations from the text in this chapter of the translator's version consist more in amplification, owing to the translator having followed the comment, and not so much in any verbal differences. It will be evident, therefore, that no notice could be given of them that would not have swelled these remarks beyond the space they were intended to occupy. It will be sufficient for the mere English reader to know, that the general sense of the original has been faithfully rendered by the translator.

NOTE.

SINCE the appearance of the Third Edition of the Institutes of Manu it has been suggested that it needs only the addition of an Index to make it complete. The Publisher hopes that the present compilation will be found to furnish all that is required. The Analytical Index will guide the reader to the locality of the chief matters of the Work, whilst in the General Index he will find these again subjected to detailed analysis and reference, together with many articles of subordinate interest. The Work has not before been published with an Index; yet the references in this case having been made not to the pages but to the chapters and verses, the Index may be used either with the present Edition or the quarto of 1825. The Publisher desires to acknowledge his obligation to the Rev. W. O. Simpson, who having compiled the Index for his own use, subsequently placed it at the Publisher's service.

ANALYTICAL INDEX.

CHAPTER I.

ON THE CREATION WITH A SUMMARY OF THE CONTENTS.

CHAPTER II.

ON EDUCATION; OR ON THE SACERDOTAL CLASS, AND THE FIRST ORDER.

CHAPTER III.

ON MARRIAGE OR THE SECOND ORDER.

CHAPTER IV.

ON ECONOMICS: AND PRIVATE MORALS.

Verses.

CHAPTER V.

ON DIET, PURIFICATION AND WOMEM.

CHAPTER VI.

ON DEVOTION, OR ON THE THIRD AND FOURTH ORDERS.

CHAPTER VII.

ON GOVERNMENT AND PUBLIC LAW OR ON THE MILITARY CLASS.

CHAPTER VIII.

ON JUDICATURE; AND ON LAW, PRIVATE AND CRIMINAL.

Verses.

CHAPTER IX.

ON THE SAME; AND ON THE COMMERCIAL AND SERVILE CLASSES.

CHAPTER X.

ON THE MIXED CLASSES AND TIMES OF DISTRESS.

CHAPTER XI.

ON PENANCE AND EXPIATION.

CHAPTER XII.

ON TRANSMIGRATIN AND FINAL BEATITUDE.

GENERAL INDEX.

Int: Introduction.

Roman numerals refer to the chapters and Arabic numerals to the verses.

pp. refers to the page in the notes

D.

E.

F.

N.

O.

P.

R.

S.

T.

U.

V.

W.